"The goal is not necessarily to reach the top, ~~but~~ continually ascend and descend, exploring the ~~rungs of~~ the ladder.... Our epiphany bursts forth when ~~there is~~ no single privileged position from which to ob~~serve.... All~~ the ladder must be honored, must be inhab~~ited, must be~~ invited patiently to tell their story."

—FROM PART SIX

In this unique volume, some of Judaism's most insightful contemporary thinkers bring the words of sages past to bear on the present. They explore how we can become closer to God through our relationships with others, our observance at home and our actions in the world, asking:

- What do *mitzvot* have to do with mysticism?
- Is spirituality selfish?
- Can mysticism enhance community?

Organized thematically, each section focuses on how mysticism engages and complements the dimensions of religious life, including studying Torah, performing *mitzvot* and observing *halakhah*.

"An orchard of spiritual pomegranates, tended by some of today's most gifted Jewish scholars. A delight to read."
–**Jay Michaelson**, author, *Everything Is God: The Radical Path of Nondual Judaism* and *God in Your Body: Kabbalah, Mindfulness and Embodied Spiritual Practice*

"Readable and vital.... Noteworthy.... A wonderful overview of how an eclectic group of teachers find[s] contemporary meaning."
–*Jewish Daily Forward*

"A masterpiece that could itself become a classic text of Jewish spiritual thinking.... A must for anyone serious about Jewish spiritual thought."
–*Tikkun*

ALSO AVAILABLE

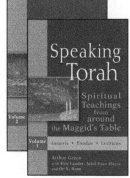

Speaking Torah
Spiritual Teachings from around the Maggid's Table
**By Arthur Green,
with Ebn Leader, Ariel Evan Mayse and Or N. Rose**
The most powerful Hasidic teachings made accessible—from some of the world's preeminent authorities on Jewish thought and spirituality. In two volumes.
6 x 9, Hardcover
Volume 1: 512 pp, 978-1-58023-668-3
Volume 2: 448 pp, 978-1-58023-694-2

Lawrence Fine, Irene Kaplan Leiwant Professor of Jewish Studies at Mount Holyoke College, is author of *Physician of the Soul, Healer of the Cosmos: Isaac Luria and His Kabbalistic Fellowship*, and other books.

Eitan Fishbane, associate professor of Jewish thought at The Jewish Theological Seminary in New York, is author of *The Sabbath Soul: Mystical Reflections on the Transformative Power of Holy Time* (Jewish Lights).

Or N. Rose, director of the Center for Global Judaism at Hebrew College, is coeditor of *God in All Moments: Mystical & Practical Spiritual Wisdom from Hasidic Masters* (Jewish Lights).

"Illuminates and probes deeply in multiple fields while speaking to engaged spiritual seekers and scholars. Studded with gems, often overflowing with learning and insights. All who want to grow spiritually, live more deeply, to both connect to tradition and renew it will find something to nurture their souls in this book."
    –**Rabbi Irving Greenberg**, founding president, Jewish Life Network; founding president, Clal: The National Jewish Center for Learning and Leadership

Also Available by Arthur Green

Ehyeh
A Kabbalah for Tomorrow
Explains how the ancient language of Kabbalah addresses the needs of our generation.
6 x 9, 224 pp, Quality PB, 978-1-58023-213-5

These Are the Words, 2nd Edition
A Vocabulary of Jewish Spiritual Life
With humor, insight and relevance, explores the meaning, history and origin of over 150 core Hebrew words.
6 x 9, 320 pp, Quality PB Original, 978-1-58023-494-8

Seek My Face
A Jewish Mystical Theology
A profound, deeply personal statement of the lasting truths of Jewish mysticism and the basic faith claims of Judaism.
6 x 9, 304 pp, Quality PB, 978-1-58023-130-5

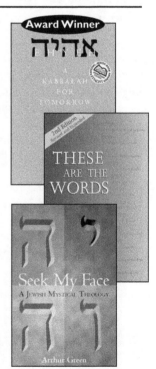

JEWISH LIGHTS Publishing

www.jewishlights.com

Find us on Facebook®
Facebook is a registered trademark of Facebook, Inc.

Jewish
Mysticism
and
the Spiritual
Life

Jewish Mysticism and the Spiritual Life

Classical Texts, Contemporary Reflections

Edited by

Lawrence Fine, Eitan Fishbane,
and Or N. Rose

JEWISH LIGHTS Publishing

Jewish Mysticism and the Spiritual Life:
Classical Texts, Contemporary Reflections

2011 Hardcover Edition, First Printing
© 2011 by Lawrence Fine, Eitan Fishbane, and Or N. Rose

All rights reserved. No part of this book may be reproduced or transmitted in any form or by any means, electronic or mechanical, including photocopying, recording, or by any information storage and retrieval system, without permission in writing from the publisher.

For information regarding permission to reprint material from this book, please mail or fax your request in writing to Jewish Lights Publishing, Permissions Department, at the address / fax number listed below, or e-mail your request to permissions@jewishlights.com.

Grateful acknowledgment is given for permission to use material from the following sources: "The Heart's Counting Knows Only One" from *The Lives of the Heart* by Jane Hirshfield, copyright © 1997 by Jane Hirshfield. Reprinted by permission of HarperCollins Publishers. Excerpt from *The Language of Truth: The Torah Commentary of the Sefat Emet*, © 1998, translated by Arthur Green, published by The Jewish Publication Society. Reprinted by permission of the publisher. Excerpts from *Menahem Nahum of Chernobyl: Upright Practices, The Light of the Eyes*, translation and introduction by Arthur Green, copyright © 1982 by Arthur Green. Paulist Press, Inc., New York / Mahwah, N.J. Reprinted by permission of Paulist Press, Inc. www.paulistpress.com. Excerpt from *Your Word Is Fire: The Hasidic Masters on Contemplative Prayer* © 1993 Arthur Green and Barry W. Holtz (Woodstock, Vt.: Jewish Lights Publishing). Permission granted by Jewish Lights Publishing, P.O. Box 237, Woodstock, VT 05091, www.jewishlights.com. Excerpt from *The Zohar: Pritzker Edition*, volume 4, translated by Daniel Matt, copyright © 2007 by Zohar Educational Project, Inc. All rights reserved. Used with the permission of Stanford University Press, www.sup.org.

Library of Congress Cataloging-in-Publication Data
Jewish mysticism and the spiritual life : classical texts, contemporary reflections / edited by Lawrence Fine, Eitan Fishbane, and Or N. Rose. — 2011 hardcover ed.
    p. cm.
Includes bibliographical references.
ISBN 978-1-58023-434-4 (hardcover)
    1. Mysticism—Judaism. 2. Spiritual life—Judaism. I. Fine, Lawrence. II. Fishbane, Eitan P., 1975– III. Rose, Or N.
BM723.J4854 2011
296.7'12—dc22

2010029713

Manufactured in the United States of America

Jacket Design: Tim Holtz
Jacket Photo: © iStockphoto.com/Burwell and Burwell Photography, modified by Tim Holtz
Interior Design: Kristi Menter

Published by Jewish Lights Publishing
www.jewishlights.com

ISBN 978-1-58023-719-2 (pbk.)

For Arthur Green, our teacher, our rabbi, our friend

With the deepest admiration for all
that you have taught us and so many others.

זכאה חולקנא דזכינא בהאי ארחא
למשמע מלי דעתיק יומין מפומך,
מה דלא זכינן למשמע עד השתא

Happy is our portion that on this path we have
been privileged to hear words of the Ancient of
Days from your mouth, that which we had not
been honored to hear until now.

ZOHAR 2:168A

Contents

Part Six   Torah, *Halakhah, Mitzvot*

Acknowledgments

It is our pleasure to express our deep thanks to Stuart M. Matlins, the publisher of Jewish Lights, for the strong interest he took in this project from the start. We very much appreciate the wise counsel that we received from Stuart as the idea for this volume began to take shape. Our gratitude also goes to Lauren Hill and Emily Wichland at Jewish Lights for all of their excellent work in helping to bring this book to fruition. We greatly appreciate the assistance in the preparation of the final manuscript from the generous and skilled library and instructional technology staff of Mount Holyoke College. Special thanks for the wonderful work of Leigh Mantle and Susan LeDuc, as well as student assistant Sefakor Mote.

This book is the result of the collective efforts of our contributors. As editors, we were most fortunate that so many distinguished and gifted teachers and scholars agreed with joyful enthusiasm to honor our friend and teacher Arthur Green. We thank each of them for contributions that we believe are of the highest order. Many of the contributors to this volume have been in dialogue with one another over the course of decades. We could not be more delighted to be able to share some of this rich conversation with a wider audience.

Finally, for all their loving friendship and support—without which few of our efforts would result in any success—we want to express our deepest gratitude to Deb, Julia, and Judith.

LAWRENCE FINE
EITAN FISHBANE
OR N. ROSE

Introduction

Contemporary Jewish Spirituality

We live in a time of great spiritual renaissance in American religion in general, and within the Jewish community in particular. People of diverse cultural backgrounds are searching for an authentic language to express their quest for meaning—for substance and depth in a society that can so often fall prey to the allure of materialism and vanity, to the seductions of greed and hedonism. Where are the anchors of value, truth, and beauty amid such a vast sea of superficiality and self-satisfaction? The turn to the spiritual may be seen as a reaction to the often mundane concerns of our society, a yearning to connect to something more enduring, more profound. And yet the spiritual quest is not simply reactive. Human beings have always actively sought deeper meaning and purpose in life.

Our age is also marked by a tension between that spiritual quest and the organized structures of traditional religion. "I'm spiritual, not religious," we hear from so many seekers. And by this they imply that the existing models of religion do not resonate with their spiritual path. For many Jews, the synagogue in contemporary America is not necessarily a spiritually satisfying experience. As a result, many have become alienated from the traditional forms, assuming that traditional Judaism has little to say to them about their spiritual yearning. Many may feel that Judaism is all about rote observance and uninspired devotion. With such experiences and perceptions, these individuals have sought spiritual nourishment from other sources, whether they be Jewish alternatives or the vibrant models of Eastern religions.

And how may we define this elusive phenomenon of spirituality? It is, first and foremost, a yearning to connect to the deep essence of things, a sense that there is a layer of existence that lies concealed beneath the surface of perception. It is this same quality that is reflected in the mystical sensibility—one of the reasons why the language of mysticism speaks to so many in our day. It is, however, important to emphasize that the mystical dimensions of Judaism do not separate easily, if at all, from the traditional structures of the religion. For while there are certain core ideas that may be extracted from the ritual and textual web of Judaism (divinity as the all-encompassing Oneness of being; God as a force of metaphysical light; the human quest to ascend and merge into divine Oneness), Jewish mystical spirituality is fundamentally inextricable from the ritual framework of Judaism.

For the kabbalists and the Hasidim, from the twelfth century to the present day, what we characterize as mysticism has been a particular way of approaching the Torah and the life of the *mitzvot*. To these mystics, the path of Torah contains hidden jewels of meaning. The deep mysteries of divinity, the dynamics of God's inner life are secretly alluded to through the symbolic words of the Torah and the commandments. All of the religious life leads the mystic to a transformed consciousness of God; the *mitzvot* are a ladder of ascent to divinity and to the individual's deep connection to the Source of all being.

For some contemporary Jews the turn to mysticism—to Kabbalah and to modern Hasidism—reflects a quest to infuse the life of *mitzvot* with spiritual vitality and purpose. How can the commandments serve both as the fulfillment of a covenantal obligation and as a guided path to illumination and spiritual transformation? How may those *mitzvot* be recaptured as spiritual exercises of renewal and growth? The kabbalists and Hasidim, each in different ways, understood the *mitzvot* to be pathways to the Divine, means by which the human being may access the transcendent from within the earthly and the everyday framework of life.

In addition to *ta'amei ha-mitzvot* (reasons for the commandments), the mystical tradition has provided fertile ground for the recovery of theological language in our day. This endeavor has been powerfully advanced by Arthur Green, our teacher to whom this volume is dedicated. To spiritual seekers for whom the classical language of biblical and Rabbinic theology may be inaccessible or unsatisfying—involving a portrait of God in which the deity is often described in paternal and regal imagery—the mystical vision offers a more expansive and complex web of associations. For the kabbalist, divinity is an always-flowing force of light and energy that can be imagined in a nearly infinite variety of ways. Hasidic mysticism, with its emphasis on the immanent presence of God in the here and now, has spoken even more directly to the theological sensibilities of contemporary spiritual seekers. In this view, God is located not only in the heavens above, but also in every dimension of this world.

The Contributions to This Book

It is these insights that have shaped a mystical revival of Jewish theology and spiritual practice in our day, and the manifold dimensions of these themes are reflected in the texts and commentaries presented by the contributors to this volume. Jewish mysticism has come to serve as a source of intellectual, theological, and spiritual nourishment in our time. In this collection of texts, and the reflections and commentaries upon those texts by leading teachers and scholars from both North America and Israel, we encounter vivid and diverse examples of how centuries-old kabbalistic and Hasidic traditions are being brought to life in the twenty-first century. It is interesting to note that all but four of the textual selections derive from Hasidic tradition, representing spiritual masters from the beginnings of Hasidism in southeastern Poland in the eighteenth century, through the twentieth. This, of course, attests to the particular attraction that Hasidism holds for contemporary Jewish spiritual seekers. At the same time, many of the chapters whose point of departure is Hasidism also draw upon texts and traditions from earlier kabbalistic literature in significant ways.

The six sections into which our collection is divided attest to the kinds of questions, issues, and themes that are at the heart of much of contemporary Jewish spiritual sensibility. Part one, "Discovering God in All Reality," is animated by one of the salient and common features of Kabbalah and Hasidism, namely, the confidence that divinity is both transcendent *and* immanent, both mystery beyond and mystery within. To be sure, this theme runs throughout the book, with a particular emphasis on the ways in which divine light/vitality/essence/being fills the world. The entire world is permeated, at its heart, with divine *shefa*, the "abundance" of God's energy and light. All of nature, every human being, every moment in time, and every sphere of reality are imbued with such light—no matter how concealed it may seem at present or in the life of any individual. As Jewish mystics have taught us for centuries: "There is no place in which God is not present" (*Tikkunei Zohar* 57). A corollary theme is that a deeper-than-usual human awareness is the critical vehicle by which to recognize and experience this light. Human beings, whose very essence is divine in nature, are uniquely capable of opening their hearts and minds to see that light and, in some manner or another, experience it deeply.

These themes and more inform the texts and reflections found in part two, "Spiritual Growth, Inner Transformation." In the first chapter in this section, "Approaching the Thick Cloud: Working with Obstacles in Our Spiritual Growth," Sheila Peltz Weinberg points to a fundamental truth about the spiritual life, namely, that it is a matter of work and continuous growth and transformation. Her reflections are based on a passage by the great Hasidic master Nahman of Bratslav dealing with obstacles or hindrances that people face in life, for example, anger or some other difficult emotion. Weinberg writes that while our natural tendency is to avoid confronting and dealing with such emotions, the willingness to confront them in a state of openness and heightened, mindful awareness is a spiritual strategy that Nahman's teaching encourages. Similarly, the other chapters in this section address various types of experiences that call upon us to grow in awareness and to be willing to transform ourselves in meaningful spiritual ways.

One of the most important features of contemporary Jewish spirituality is a (re)turn to the body and to embodied experience, which is explored in part three, "Embodied Spiritual Practice." Here Kabbalah and Hasidism serve as critical resources and inspiration. According to kabbalistic tradition, one of the central symbolic approaches to imagining God is by way of divine "anatomy." While God does not have an *actual* body, the various dimensions of the human body allude to and symbolize God's qualities. Thus, the ten *sefirot*, or qualities of Divine Being of the kabbalistic system, are understood, among many other ways, as representing the many "limbs" of God. What is more, God is gendered, as it were, possessing male *and* female dimensions of being. *Eros*, human and divine, is absolutely central to the kabbalistic conception of life.

Hasidism, in particular, cannot be properly understood without appreciation of the degree to which the body is to be employed in the quest to experience the divine light at the core of all reality. One of the key themes of Hasidism is that God can be discovered even in the realm of the material, including the activities of engaging in business, eating and drinking, and sexual relations. God can be served even with the so-called evil impulse, the *yetzer ha-ra*, by virtue of the conviction that *even* within such impulses there must be a divine spark waiting to be "liberated." As is well known, intense, ecstatic singing and dancing are central to Hasidic experience. Chapters in this section having to do with a woman's preparation of challah for the Sabbath, eating as a spiritual activity, and "loving God with the evil impulse" exemplify the importance of *integrating* the body and the spirit.

While many think of mysticism as having to do primarily with private or individual experience, the fact is that as often as not mystical traditions and practices have social and interpersonal dimensions. This is especially evident when it comes to Judaism, a religious culture in which the interpersonal is so crucial. In the history of Kabbalah and Hasidism, for example, there are numerous examples of specialized, intentional communities. Hasidism, of course, was traditionally structured along the lines of particular social communities organized around individual spiritual masters. As Barry W. Holtz comments in his essay "The Splendid Bird: Reflections on Prayer and Community," "In the Hasidic consciousness, the search for connection to the Divine was always rooted in the fellowship of others." Drawing upon the Jewish ethical tradition, Kabbalah and Hasidism have much to say about the way in which we should treat one another, and they have fostered a great range of special practices to promote proper interpersonal relations. Part four, "Compassion, Loving Others," includes a rich set of teachings about such ethical themes and practices.

We have already spoken of obstacles or "hindrances" and the spiritual life. In part five, "Prayer, Repentance, Healing," questions of personal longing and the search for personal redemption are further explored. Thus, for example, in his chapter "Spiritual Wounds," commenting on a passage by the eighteenth-century Hasidic teacher Avraham Yehoshua Heschel of Apt, Michael Fishbane writes:

> The Torah is not in heaven: it is ... addressed ... to the soul and
> its (inner) struggle for spiritual virtue.... [It is directed to] the
> seeker—in our case one who is on and off the way, whose soul
> is wounded by inadvertence, but who has become cognizant of
> that wound and wants to make repair. From the depths
> of ancient contemplative practices, our master provides a *tikkun*
> for such a person: a healing practice for their spiritual wounds.

We have already suggested that in Kabbalah and Hasidism spiritual
life has always been grounded in the ethical and ritual precepts that
compose the structure of Jewish practice. The life of the spirit and
the practice of Jewish law have always been inextricably tied to one
another. The *mitzvot* are intended to be the vehicle through which a
life of meaning, purpose, and holiness is realized. Kabbalists and
Hasidim, after all, were individuals who were completely committed
to the fulfillment of Judaism's religious precepts. But they invested
those precepts with profound spiritual significance and intentional-
ity. In part six, "Torah, *Halakhah*, *Mitzvot*," these questions are
explored.

Our volume ends with a fitting coda by Zalman Schachter-
Shalomi in a chapter titled "*Teyku*—Because Elijah Lives On!"
Reflecting on a passage by Levi Yitzhak of Berditchev, Reb Zalman has
these important words to say:

> Like Elijah the Prophet, the Berditchever was keenly aware of the
> need to provide his community with a vision of Judaism that was
> in deep dialogue with the past and responsive to the present. And
> like Hillel, he was a brilliant sage who understood that in his gen-
> eration the world needed a Torah of *hesed* [loving-kindness].

Arthur Green and His Contributions to Contemporary Jewish Mysticism and Spirituality

We take great joy in dedicating this book to our friend and teacher
Arthur Green. Art has been one of the most influential Jewish religious
thinkers and educators in the United States for the past several
decades. A leading scholar of Kabbalah and Hasidism, he has played a

key role in introducing the language and significance of Jewish mysticism and spirituality into American Jewish culture.

Art grew up in Newark, New Jersey, in a secular Jewish home but was educated in a more traditional Hebrew school and attended Camp Ramah of the Conservative movement. In 1959, he enrolled at Brandeis University, where he studied with Nahum Glatzer and Alexander Altmann. Upon graduation from Brandeis, he trained for the rabbinate at The Jewish Theological Seminary, where he was a close student of Abraham Joshua Heschel. Art was ordained in 1967 and returned to Brandeis to undertake doctoral studies in Jewish mysticism with Dr. Altmann.

A year later, he cofounded (with his wife Kathy and a group of friends) Havurat Shalom in Somerville, Massachusetts. The members of this intentional community sought to weave together insights from the Jewish mystical tradition—particularly that of Hasidism—and American counterculture. Havurat Shalom helped to birth the national Havurah and Jewish Renewal movements.

In 1973, Art joined the faculty of religion at the University of Pennsylvania, where he remained for over a decade. In 1979, he published *Tormented Master: A Life of Rabbi Nahman of Bratslav* (reprinted by Jewish Lights as *Tormented Master: The Life and Spiritual Quest of Rabbi Nahman of Bratslav* in 1992). With this book, he established himself as an outstanding scholar of Hasidism. Widely read by academics and lay readers, *Tormented Master* has since been translated into Hebrew, Russian, and French.

In 1984, Art became dean and then president of the Reconstructionist Rabbinical College (RRC) in Philadelphia. His move to the RRC was reflective of his commitment to the training of rabbis and his desire to unite scholarship and religious education. It was at the RRC that Art wrote his first theological book, *Seek My Face, Speak My Name: A Contemporary Jewish Theology* (1992; reissued as *Seek My Face: A Jewish Mystical Theology* by Jewish Lights in 2003). In this and in subsequent publications, he skillfully draws on the riches of the Jewish mystical tradition to articulate a creative vision for contemporary Jewish life.

In 1990, Art returned to his alma mater, Brandeis University, to become the Philip W. Lown Professor of Jewish Thought, the position once held by his mentor Alexander Altmann. While at Brandeis, he published the scholarly study *Keter: The Crown of God in Early Jewish Mysticism* (1997) and *The Language of Truth* (1998), a translation and interpretation of the Torah commentary of the renowned nineteenth-century Hasidic master Rabbi Yehudah Leib Alter of Ger (known as the Sefat Emet).[1]

In 2004, Art was named the founding dean of the Rabbinical School of Hebrew College. This new school is one of the few transdenominational Jewish seminaries in North America. Art's return to pluralistic rabbinic education is the fulfillment of a dream from his days in Havurat Shalom, which he originally envisioned as both a seminary and an intentional community. In 2007, he became rector of the Rabbinical School.

Art's most recent publication, *Radical Judaism: Rethinking God and Tradition*, builds upon his work in *Seek My Face* and a second theological volume, *Ehyeh: A Kabbalah for Tomorrow* (2003, Jewish Lights). The book explores the meaning of the classical concepts of God, Torah, and Israel in contemporary Jewish life, as well as the relationship of religion and science, the meaning of revelation today, and the complexities of American Jewish identity. Art draws on an array of biblical, Rabbinic, and mystical sources, while also speaking personally about his own experiences as a spiritual seeker, teacher, and scholar.

Art is now at work on two new books: one is a translation of the Yiddish and Hebrew writings of the early-twentieth-century mystical writer and journalist Hillel Zeitlin (a great influence on Art and his old friend and mentor Rabbi Zalman Schachter-Shalomi); the other is a two-volume translation of and introduction to the Torah commentaries of Rabbi Dov Ber, the Maggid of Mezritch (d. 1772), and several of his outstanding disciples (Jewish Lights). This latter project is a collaborative effort among Art and several of his own students.

In reading this brief overview of Arthur Green's career, it should be obvious why we have chosen to honor our beloved friend and teacher with the creation of this anthology of classical Jewish mystical texts and contemporary reflections. Art has inspired several generations of Jewish seekers and scholars to explore the great riches of the Jewish mystical tradition and its applications to life today. Through his teaching, writing, and public speaking, he has shared with untold numbers of people the teachings of Kabbalah and Hasidism, encouraging all of us to open ourselves to the theological, psychological, and ethical wisdom of these ancient and evolving traditions. Not only has he served as an expert translator and guide to the teachings of past Jewish mystical masters, but like his revered teacher Abraham Joshua Heschel, he has been courageous enough to add his own voice to this great chain of tradition. He has also been extremely supportive in encouraging his colleagues and students to do the same.

We hope that this book serves as a fitting tribute to Art as we seek to build upon his work, sharing a variety of Jewish mystical texts and contemporary reflections with a broad readership. We bless Art with many more years of health, happiness, and meaningful spiritual search and discovery.

Notes

1. In the world of traditional Jewish learning, great rabbinic personalities were often referred to by the titles of their most famous books. So, for example, Rabbi Yehudah Leib Alter of Ger is simply referred to as the Sefat Emet, and Rabbi Avraham Yehoshua Heschel of Apt is referred to as the Ohev Yisrael.

PART ONE

Discovering God in All Reality

Rabbi Nancy Flam is cofounder of the National Center for Jewish Healing and former director of the Jewish Community Healing Program of *Ruach Ami*: Bay Area Jewish Healing Center. She cofounded the Institute for Jewish Spirituality, was its founding director, and now serves as codirector of programs. She edited the Jewish Lights series of pastoral-care pamphlets, *LifeLights*, and writes and teaches widely on Judaism, healing, prayer, spirituality, and social justice.

"Pass Not Away"

Yearning for a Seamless Life of Connection

NANCY FLAM

In the Tractate *Shabbat*: "Rabbi Judah said in the name of Rav: 'The welcoming of guests is greater than greeting the *Shekhinah*,' for Scripture says, 'Pass not away, I pray you, from your servant' (Genesis 18:3). Said Rabbi Eleazar: 'Note that the ways of God are not those of man. Among people, a lesser person could not say to a greater one, "Wait until I come to you," but Abraham was able to say that to God.'"

We must understand this verse that says, "Pass not away." How could this be said with regard to the presence of God, since the whole earth is filled with His glory and there is no place devoid of Him? How then could one possibly say, "Pass not away," as though to assume that afterwards that place would not contain His glory? This is simply impossible. We must also understand how Rav's claim that making guests welcome is greater than greeting the *Shekhinah* can be proven from this passage. Might we not say that in the performing of that commandment one also evokes the presence of the *Shekhinah*? Commandment, after all, is called *mitzvah* because it joins together (*mitzvah/tzavta*) the part of God that dwells within the person with the infinite God beyond. It may be, then, that the *mitzvah* is not really greater than greeting the *Shekhinah*, but rather that it too contains the *Shekhinah*, and in fulfilling it one has both [commandment and presence]. We also have to understand Rabbi Eleazar's point here, that the lesser does not ask the greater one to wait, and yet Abraham did so. Could we not say that there too, in the greeting of the guests, there was a receiving of the *Shekhinah*? This is especially so since the righteous are called "the face of the *Shekhinah*" in the *Zohar*, as His presence dwells in them. When Abraham received the guests, that is, the angels who appeared to him in human form, surely that itself was an act of greeting the *Shekhinah*.

The truth is, however, that the real fulfilling of *any* commandment lies in the greeting of the *Shekhinah*, in becoming attached to God or joined together. Thus the rabbis said: "The reward of a *mitzvah* is a *mitzvah*," meaning that the commandment is rewarded by the nearness to God that the one who performs it feels, the joy of spirit that lies within the deed. This indeed is a "greeting of the *Shekhinah*," and without it the commandment is empty and lifeless, the body-shell of a *mitzvah* without any soul. Only when it is done with the longing of the divine part within it to be connected to its root, along with the divine part of all the rest of Israel, can it be called a *mitzvah*. In all service of God, whether in speech or in deed, both body and soul are needed to give it life. That is why the wicked are called dead within their own lifetime: their deeds are without life.

This is what really happened to our father Abraham. He was engaged in discourse with God ("greeting the *Shekhinah*"), as we learn from the verse, "The Lord appeared to him" [Genesis 18:1]. When he saw the guests coming, he asked of God that there too, while he was to be engaged in welcoming the guests, "Pass not away, I pray you, from your servant" [Genesis 18:3]. There too may I remain attached to You, so that this not be an empty *mitzvah*. Be with me so that I may perform the *mitzvah* in such a state that it too be a "greeting of the *Shekhinah*."

Now Rav's point that the welcoming of guests is greater than greeting the *Shekhinah* is proved by Abraham's action. Were this not the case, Abraham would hardly have left off a conversation with God to go do something of less certain value. This is especially true since "they appeared to him as Arab nomads"; they did not have a divine appearance. The *mitzvah* itself was very great even if it [was] not a "greeting of the *Shekhinah*." Abraham decided to fulfill this commandment with absolute wholeness. Therefore he said, "Do not pass away, I pray you, from your servant."

Now we also understand the point being made by Rabbi Eleazar. Indeed among people the lesser person cannot ask the greater to wait for him while he attends to some other matter. The greater one will not be present in that other place; if he is here he cannot be there! But of God it is said: "The whole earth is filled with His glory!" [Isaiah 6:3]. He asks that God not depart from him; "there too may I not be cut off from my attachment to You." He could say this only because wherever one goes he does not go away from God. He is there as He is here; Abraham only asked that he not be cut off from Him. Understand this.[1]

RABBI MENAHEM NAHUM OF CHERNOBYL, *ME'OR EINAYIM*

This exquisite teaching of Rabbi Menahem Nahum of Chernobyl (d. 1797) describes a compelling orientation and strategy for living a Jewish spiritual life. It clearly articulates and resolves a central tension facing contemporary Jewish spiritual seekers: how to cultivate an intense, personal devotional practice and remain steadfast to engaging actively in the world with kindness and with justice. Indeed, Menahem Nahum suggests that for the truly adept, they are one and the same practice.

Abraham is our model. The text provides us with a window into his inner life as a reflection of what ours might ideally become. We know Abraham as a person who speaks and listens directly to God. In the biblical scene before us, "God appeared to him at the terebinths of Mamre" (Genesis 18:1). We understand that God's "appearing" to Abraham means that he was engaged in conscious communion with

God, intercourse of some kind, what we might call "prayer" (understood most broadly). Clearly, Abraham's mind and attention were focused on *HaKadosh Barukh Hu* (the Holy One of Blessing). When the three visitors appear before him, walking toward his desert tent at the heat of the day, Abraham asks God not to go away while he runs to take care of his unexpected guests.[2] Menahem Nahum explores the oddity of such a plea (not only does a person of lesser status not make such a request of one greater than he, as Rabbi Eleazar notes, but where was God, the Omnipresent, to go, after all?) and realizes that Abraham's request was of a more subtle nature than might appear at first blush. Abraham was asking the Holy One to come with him on his mission so that he would continue to have a sense of God's presence even as he changed from engaging in one sort of *avodah* (service, devotion, worship) to another.

How compelling it must have been for Abraham to have been communing with God. No other pleasure compares. And yet, as soon as the visitors appeared, Abraham knew that he needed to turn his attention in their direction. The presentation of the *mitzvah* commanded him to action.

While Menahem Nahum refers specifically to the act of fulfilling a *mitzvah*, hoping to inspire his people through this midrashic polemic to engage in *mitzvah* observance with both body and soul, we can understand his teaching as an ideal to be realized in all our actions. This, we learn, is a high level of worship: to be actively engaged in the world through *mitzvot* or other acts of *hesed* (loving-kindness), *tzedek* (righteousness), and *emet* (truth) and, *in the midst of these very actions*, to experience our inner divine substance ("the divine part within," our soul) to be in connection with God, the soul of the universe.

The articulation of such an ideal was one of early Hasidism's greatest contributions to Jewish religious thought: *Bekhol derakhekha da'ehu*, "Know God in all your ways" (Proverbs 3:6). In the Hasidic worldview, *avodah* is no longer confined to the activities of Torah study and prayer:

> The Blessed One desires that we serve Him in every possible manner. How so? Sometimes a person might be walking and speaking with another person, and at that time he cannot

study [Torah]. Nevertheless, he must still cleave to the Blessed One and bring about unifications. And so it is when a person is walking along the road and is not able to pray or study as he is accustomed; he must nevertheless serve God in the other manners. And one should not be pained by this, because the Blessed One wants us to serve Him in all these different ways, sometimes in this one manner, sometimes in a different manner.[3]

The ideal of "serving God in all our ways" means that *avodah* must be connected to an act of consciousness. The question as to whether or not we are engaged in *avodah* is linked to the condition of our mind, our focus, our awareness (*da'at*). So long as we "still cleave to the Blessed One," any or all of our actions might be understood as *avodah*. In the Menahem Nahum text, Abraham clearly wanted not only to fulfill the *mitzvah* of greeting visitors with physical acts, but he wanted to do so "with absolute wholeness," as an act of *avodah*, connected to a sense of God's presence every step of the way. He wanted to stay connected (*zavta*), "cleaving" unto God, "greeting the *Shekhinah*," as he switched from one form of worship to another.

The cultivation of such an awareness seems similar to what Michael Fishbane calls the "praxis of theology" or "theology as a spiritual practice." In this sense, Fishbane speaks of theology not as an abstract or academic pursuit, but more as a form of contemplation:

As the exercise of theological thinking unfolds, it directs the human spirit toward an increasingly focused awareness of God as the heart and breath of all existence, and tries to sustain that focus throughout the course of life. Put differently, theology seeks to cultivate an abiding consciousness of God's informing presence in all the realities of existence, the infinite modalities of divine effectivity. Hence the world is both what we 'take' it to be, in all the moments of ordinary experience, and what we must 'untake' it to be, when we relate all things back to their ontological and primordial ground in God.... Spiritual attunement to this divine domain is an attentive God-mindedness in the course of life; and it is a task of theology to cultivate this attunement so that one may live in the everyday with God in mind.[4]

There are many ways to articulate this work of staying present to an awareness of God while engaged in the particularities of a life: maintaining *devekut* (cleaving to God),[5] doing everything with awareness (*beda'at*),[6] not turning to idols,[7] effecting "spiritual attunement ... , God-mindedness in the course of life." An important question presents itself to us in this exploration: what might this mean in practice for us Jewish spiritual seekers of the twenty-first century? Or, put slightly differently: how might we train ourselves to embody this awareness?

In Jewish tradition, there seem to be both exoteric and esoteric routes to such awareness. As Max Kadushin, scholar of Rabbinic theology, explains, Rabbinic Judaism encodes a densely articulated practice of "normal mysticism,"[8] accessible to all. For instance, the Rabbinic practice of offering *berakhot* (blessings) upon eating and afterwards, upon experiencing various ordinary and extraordinary pleasures of sight and sound, upon seeing someone we have not seen for a whole month, and so on for various occasions in the midst of a life, as well as upon occasions of performing *mitzvot* (such as studying Torah or lighting Shabbat candles) are all ways to link our specific sense experience in time to an awareness of the Creator of the world, a moment in which "we relate all things back to their ontological and primordial ground in God."[9]

But there are more subtle methods of cultivating such consciousness, as well—strategies of consciousness that depend more upon purely contemplative practice than upon the recitation of a *berakhah*. For instance, an early Hasidic teaching states that we might train ourselves to see God everywhere by constantly contemplating God as the place of the world (although this is certainly understood to be a "high level" and therefore not likely to be attained by many people). It is a matter of training our vision to see with the eyes of the mind. Rabbi Meshullam Feibush of Zbarazh transmits the teachings of the Baal Shem Tov and the Maggid of Mezritch:

It is a high level of spiritual attainment when someone is always aware of God's presence—that He surrounds him on all sides—

and his *devekut* with God is so great that he does not need to remind himself again and again that God, blessed be He, is there and present with him, but he sees God with the eyes of the mind, for He is the place of the world. What this means is that He was before He created the world, and the world exists within the Creator, blessed be He. A person's *devekut* with God should be so great that the essence of what he sees is God, blessed be He. It should not be that his vision is primarily of the world and then, by the way, of God. No, his sight should be essentially of God.[10]

Here we understand there to be a training of the sense of sight. As Rabbi Kalonymus Kalman Shapira (d. 1943) notes:

We can feel ourselves growing closer to God—enjoying His radiance, sensing His presence—but not only when we pray and do *mitzvot*. If we focus on holiness with clarity and strength for each and every moment, we can gradually take control of our sense perceptions. Commonly, our perceptions distract us: "You see the world, you observe materiality." Not only do we want to resist distraction; we want our sensual perceptions to come around to the perspective of the heart. We can actually see the presence of God, which infuses all creation. Each of us can see with our own eyes that we stand in paradise, in the palpable presence of God.[11]

Whatever the specifics of the practice of attaching ourself to God, Menahem Nahum's teaching suggests to me that we might learn how to do it in periods of personal practice and that we might then bring such awareness into our worldly interactions. Such a message is also clearly sounded in contemporary teaching of mindfulness meditation and yoga. For instance, we practice awareness of our mind's response to desire or aversion on the meditation cushion so that we might be more aware and skillful with these dynamics when they arise as we interact with our families, communities, and work partners. We practice moment-to-moment awareness of our minds and bodies in different positions on the yoga mat so that we might bring such awakened attention to any "position" we might find ourselves in during our lives, whether that be a position of ease or discomfort, freedom or con-striction, familiarity or surprise. Similarly, we might say that in our prayer we practice greeting the face of the *Shekhinah* so that we might see Her light in every subsequent human encounter that day. We inten-sively practice awareness of God in one form so that we might be able to be aware of God in all forms.[12]

For those who claim that people devoted to deepening their own spiritual lives are self-absorbed and solipsistic, this teaching provides a strong response. Fulfilling a *mitzvah*, responding to the real-life needs of others, engaging with the world with kindness and with jus-tice, actually trumps a particular moment of engagement with individ-ual spiritual practice. Rav's position is justified. If this weren't so, Abraham would not have broken off his conversation with God to respond to the needs of the visitors. Even if we are not capable of staying connected in our consciousness to God as we act in the world, we must act nonetheless. There are, in fact, no guarantees that one will stay connected, which is precisely why Abraham must make his plea.

Abraham asks God "not to pass away" from him. Toward the end of Menahem Nahum's teaching, we read that Abraham asks that when he turns to interact with other persons, that there, too, he "remain attached." Who, in the end, is responsible for the connection? Is the critical action God's "not passing" or Abraham's "remaining attached"? The two expressions provide insight into a central dialectic in the spiritual life. On the one hand, it is but folly to pray for God not to pass if we are not engaged in our own spiritual practice. We could only be understood to be naive or lazy to ask God to do all the work of the relationship. We must do the work of "letting God in," as in the famous Hasidic teaching of the Kotzker Rebbe: "Where may God be found? Wherever we let God in."[13] At the same time, even if we lead a life of dedicated spiritual practice, a life of regular prayer and contem-plation, practicing receiving the face of the *Shekhinah*, there is no guarantee that our efforts will provide results, even in the relatively simple context of private devotion. Ultimately, we are not in control of our experience of God's presence to us. In truth, we must both acknowledge not being in control—our dependence upon God's grace—and engage in regular, dedicated practice in an effort to experience the connection.

This teaching, recorded over two hundred years ago, transmits a surprisingly powerful message to our contemporary hearts and minds. Like spiritually serious Jews of all eras, we seek to deepen our sense of God's presence in our awareness, moment to moment, while at the same time staying connected to a life of obligation, relationship, and celebration in the world. Jewish tradition, after all, never created a system of monasteries and ashrams, unlike other religious traditions. The test of our spiritual practice is found in how we live in the world. Amid the many challenges of everyday life, we seek wholeness, the "complete wholeness" of Abraham, where every act and every moment of consciousness, no matter what the form, is filled with a sense of connection and presence. Perhaps we might make it a practice, as we conclude our final prayers of the morning, to call out the words "Pass not away!" as we turn ourselves to engage in the sacred work of worldly obligation.

Notes

1. Translation by Arthur Green, *Menahem Nahum of Chernobyl: Upright Practices, The Light of the Eyes* (New York: Paulist Press, 1982), pp. 135–37.

2. On the simple, narrative, *peshat* level, it would seem as if, read in context, Abraham addressed his words, "Please do not pass by" to the visitors who appeared at his tent. However, there is an ambiguity in the text. The verbs in this verse are all in the singular, making it appear as though Abraham is talking to only one person/being. In *Bereshit Rabbah* (48:9), Rashi and Ramban resolve this by understanding Abraham to be addressing the leader of the group, with the invitation extending to all three visitors. In addition, there is ambiguity with reference to the word *Adonai*, which may be translated either as "my lords" (referring to the guests) or as "my Lord" (referring to God). There is a difference of opinion among Rabbinic commentators, with Rashi and Ibn Ezra agreeing with the reading of *Adonai*, as plural, referring to the guests, and Maimonides understanding *Adonai* to be singular, referring to God. (See *The JPS Torah Commentary: Genesis*, ed. Nahum M. Sarna [Philadelphia: Jewish Publication Society, 1989], p. 129.)

3. *Tzava'at HaRivash* 3, English translation: *Tzava'at Harivash: The Testament of R. Israel Baal Shem Tov*, trans. Jacob Immanuel Schochet (Brooklyn: Kehot, 1998).

4. Michael Fishbane, *Sacred Attunement: A Jewish Theology* (Chicago: University of Chicago Press, 2008), p. 35. Similarly, he writes: "A primary task of theology is

thus to direct an ever-new attentiveness to the manifold impingements of sight and sound which happen roundabout; in response to these effects one may bring God's all-encompassing effectivity to mind. Everything depends upon one's focus or attention. To lose attention is to slip into a mindless habitude that disregards the mystery of the vastness; whereas to regain one's focus is to reprise the world as a sphere of value. The loss of attention is more than a deadness to the life-forms in our world. It also betrays God—the effective ground of all existence. Living theology regards this as a sin of omission. By cultivating an attentive conscious-ness, theology cultivates the soul and turns it toward God" (p. 41). Abraham's project, like ours, is one of directing his attention God-ward and worldward at the same moment.

5. The idea of cleaving to God is introduced in the Torah (Deuteronomy 4:4, 10:20, 13:5, 11:22, 30:20). Nahmanides taught about cleaving to God in the course of day-to-day life: "When you are walking on the way or lying down or rising up—until even where you are conversing with other people, in your innermost heart you are not with them but are in the presence of God" (Nahmanides to Deuteronomy 11:22). About this passage, pioneer of twentieth-century Kabbalah scholarship Gershom Scholem writes, "In Nahmanides' definition, there appears, for the first time, an element which has played no great part in the Kabbalistic doctrine of *devekut* ... but which was given great prominence by the Baal Shem, and even more by his followers. I am referring to the combination of earthly action and *devekut*. Of course, it was not Nahmanides' intention to say that *devekut* could be realized in social action and association too. But he clearly thought that it could be sustained even in social intercourse, although such inter-course in itself is considered rather as a hindrance which must be overcome by special effort. *Devekut* is a value of contemplative, not active, life. But Nahmanides' saying could be used to prove the possibility of the coincidence of the two spheres. A man might appear to be with other people, to talk to them, and perhaps even to participate in their activities, but in reality he is contemplat-ing God" (Gershom Scholem, "*Devekut*, or Communion with God," in *The Messianic Idea in Judaism* [New York: Schocken Books, 1971], p. 205).

6. Rabbi Efraim of Sudlikov, *Degel Mahaneh Efraim*, on the Torah portion *Kedoshim*: "Although this teaching is very deep, my feeble explanation is this: anyone who serves God in all his ways, seeking to fulfill the injunction 'know Him in all your ways' (Prov. 3:6) will do everything with awareness (or mind-fully): like eating, drinking, sleeping, engaging in conversation...."

7. Rabbi Efraim of Sudlikov, *Degel Mahaneh Efraim*, on the Torah portion *Kedoshim*: "'Do not turn to idols' (Lev. 19:4). Our sages interpreted this to mean, 'Do not turn to that which you conceive in your own minds' (*Shabbat* 149a). We can understand this according to the teaching of my grandfather [the Baal Shem Tov] regarding the verse, 'that you turn away and worship other gods' (Deut.

11:16). He interpreted this: 'that you turn away'—as soon as you turn your attention away from cleaving to the Holy One—'you will worship other gods'—it is as if you have become an idolater."

8. "We can perhaps now begin to recognize why the rabbinic experience of God can be thought of as normal mysticism. The ordinary, familiar, everyday things and occurrences, we have observed, constitute occasions for the experience of God. Such things as one's daily sustenance, the very day itself, are felt as manifestations of God's loving-kindness, calling forth *Berakhot*. *Kedushah*, holiness, which is nothing else than the imitation of God, is concerned with daily conduct, with being gracious and merciful, with keeping oneself from defilement by idolatry, adultery, and the shedding of blood.... And not only do ordinary things and occurrences bring with them the experience of God. Everything that happens to a man evokes that experience, evil as well as good, for a *Berakhah* is said also at evil tidings. Hence, although the experience of God is like none other, the *occasions* for experiencing Him, for having a consciousness of Him are manifold, even if we consider only those that call for *Berakhot*" (Max Kadushin, *The Rabbinic Mind* [Jacksonville, Fla.: Bloch, 1952], p. 203).

9. "Normal mysticism enables a person to make normal, commonplace, recurrent situations and events occasions for worship. The food he eats, the water he drinks, the dawn and the twilight are joined to *berakot* acknowledging God's love. These daily commonplace situations are not only interpreted in the act of worship as manifestations of God's love, but they arouse in the individual, in the same act of worship, a poignant sense of the nearness of God" (Max Kadushin, *Worship and Ethics: A Study in Rabbinic Judaism* [Westport, Conn.: Greenwood Press, 1963], p. 168).

10. *Likutim Yekarim* 54 (Jerusalem, 1974). A later Hasidic teacher, the Piaseczner Rebbe (Rabbi Kalonymus Kalman Shapira, d. 1943) taught in the same vein, but here providing a strategy for connecting back to our awareness of God at those times we have fallen away: "Make it a regular practice, as you go about your day, to notice your sense of distraction and despair as you remind yourself that the entire world is God. The specks of sand underfoot are God. The air in my lungs is God. Why am I flung from the Holy Presence to this distant exile, to become a separate entity, a kingdom of one? My will and awareness are encased in this body, my very spirit is subject to this materiality, God help me. *Ribbono shel olam*, draw me near to you because of your great goodness and my sincere desire to return" (*B'nai Mahshavah Tovah*, as translated in *Conscious Community: A Guide to Inner Work*, trans. Andrea Cohen-Kiener [Northvale, N.J.: Jason Aronson, 1999], p. 84). Here there is a recognition, even from one so great as the Piaseczner Rebbe, that continuous God-awareness is next to impossible. There will be times of focused attention on God's reality and times of distraction. Most important is to cultivate sufficient awareness to be able to know whether one is

connected or not and then to employ a strategy of reconnection, such as the above, when necessary. Perhaps there are only two prayers in this essential work of consciousness: "Pass not away" and "Help me return."

11. Shapira, *Conscious Community*, trans. Cohen-Kiener, p. 2.
12. Attachment to form can be a kind of idolatry, even when that form is a form of worship. Had Abraham been attached to the particular form of his solitary discourse with God as being "the real worship experience," he would have engaged in idolatry. The fundamental fluidity of consciousness that is required to move through the infinite forms and experiences of creation while maintaining awareness of their underlying unity is striking, and is a common feature of various kinds of mystical practice and expression across religious traditions.
13. Martin Buber, *Tales of the Hasidim: Later Masters* (New York: Schocken, 1948), p. 277.

Jeremy Kalmanofsky is rabbi of congregation Ansche Chesed in New York City. He was ordained at The Jewish Theological Seminary of America. His articles have appeared in a variety of Jewish journals, as well as in *Jewish Theology in Our Time: A New Generation Explores the Foundations and Future of Jewish Belief* (Jewish Lights). He serves on the editorial board of *Conservative Judaism*, and is a member of the Committee on Jewish Law and Standards of the Conservative movement.

Seeking the Sacred Self

JEREMY KALMANOFSKY

"I am amidst the exile" (Ezekiel 1:1).

The *I*—the interior, essential self, whether of individual or community—can only be revealed in accordance with its purity and sanctity. The inner identity can be revealed only in proportion to its heavenly strength, soaked in the pure light of heavenly radiance, burning within.

But we and our ancestors sinned. The first Adam sinned when he became alienated from himself, for he turned to the counsel of the serpent and destroyed himself. He became unable to respond to the divine question: where are you (Genesis 3:9)? For he did not know himself, and his essential identity eluded him. Israel sinned by worshipping alien gods, whoring after their seductions, abandoning its own identity, and deserting the good.

The land sinned, denying its essence, letting its strength wither, pursuing ulterior ends, looking towards externalities. It did not give forth all the goodness within itself, such that the taste of the tree itself would have been like the taste of the fruit.[1] The moon complained and lost track of its inner orbit, lost the true wealth of rejoicing in its own lot, and dreamed instead of receiving exterior regal glory (Babylonian Talmud, *Hullin* 60b). So the world goes, sinking in the obliteration of identity of every individual and every collective.

Learned teachers come along, looking at externalities, distracting others from their identities, and adding straw to the fire, giving vinegar to those dying of thirst, fattening up the minds and the hearts with all sorts of external things. And the *I* fades from memory more and more. And since there is no *I* there can be no *Him*, and certainly no *you*.

But "God's anointed is the breath of our nostrils" (Lamentations 4:20). The Messiah's greatness, glory, and might are that he does not exist outside of us. He is our breath. We seek *Adonai*, our God, and David, our king. We revere God and His goodness. We seek our *I*. We seek our selves. And we find.

Banish all strange gods (Genesis 35:2). Banish all aliens and bastards. And know that *I* am the Lord your God, who brings you out of the land of Egypt to be your God. *I* am Adonai.[2]

RABBI AVRAHAM YITZHAK HAKOHEN KOOK, *OROT HAKODESH*

Mystical human psychology, or sacred personhood, is a central concern of many mystic quests. In pursuing an encounter with God, spiritual seekers discover something not only about the infinite Divine Being but also about the mortal human one. To take a few steps along that path, I offer this selection from Rabbi Avraham Yitzhak HaKohen Kook (d. 1935), the mystic, poet, halakhist (legalist), and communal leader who shaped religious Zionism and who teaches us in this passage about the redemptive divine presence within ourselves.

People commonly repeat the Torah's phrase that we are "created in the divine image" or draw from the kabbalistic lexicon to say that we all contain a "spark" of divinity. While undoubtedly true, these have the ring of banal slogans, too metaphysically thin to point to real insight. Often we use these slogans only to mean that human beings are wonderful. But the logic of panentheism runs deeper, all the way to the ocean, and the ocean is never filled. Once we affirm that God is one and infinite and also that God's image is inscribed in all people (and all creation, for that matter), we find ourselves in deep waters.

Within the world's vast diversity, primal unity inheres. Infinite depths dwell within every finite crumb of matter. Mystical consciousness seeks insight into this transcendent mystery within the world of brute facts, atoms, and molecules.

Applying this panentheist awareness to human beings, we begin to intuit that we are not the little people we thought we were. The sacred depth of the human person is obscured through conventional consciousness, which affirms that each of us is a solitary, finite self, who knows itself through its own inner mental process. Once we introduce the idea that divinity sparkles within us, however, we can say none of these things simply. You cannot be solitary or finite, at least not ultimately; your limited aloneness dissolves as you participate in the universal life of God. And if the deepest part of yourself is the divine image, you cannot ever really get to the bottom of your own well. Your own heart will remain a mystery. But unless you intuit this unfathomable dimension within, you can never know who you are.

For these reasons, Jewish mystical spirituality holds the power to break down our sense of identity at first, on the way to imparting a deeper sense of holy personhood. Initially, the mystic learns to say, God exists and perhaps I do not. For as an individual, I am but a candle in the noonday sun, negligibly small before overwhelming divine light (Babylonian Talmud, *Hullin* 60b). But those who carry this insight further, into a deeper sense of personhood, become aware that the infinite, eternal God is the heart of their being, paradoxically manifest through a person's mortal individuality. The overwhelming divine light is neither in heaven nor across the sea, but is very near to me, in my mouth and in my heart. A primary goal for Jewish mystics is to overcome the obstacles that alienate us from ourselves. To discover God is to reveal this sacred presence at the depth of the self, and to lay bare the self is to reveal God.

Who am I? I am a "portion of God on high" (Job 31:2), a mortal manifestation of immortality, infinity within the finite. To borrow from the medieval Hebrew poet Yehudah HaLevi: God is closer to me than my own body and spirit.

Rav Kook's passage explores this dynamic of first losing then rediscovering God within the self. He treats this dynamic as it occurs in individual people, as well as in Israel as a nation and in the natural world, and looks forward to overcoming alienation by attaining a messianic consciousness. As with much of Kook's writings generally and the *Orot HaKodesh* ("The Lights of Holiness") in particular, this passage is gorgeous but grandiloquent, hopelessly unpunctuated, densely allusive, evocative more than expository. Still, the text's difficulties should not obscure the richness of spirit and thought within.

Beginning with an ingenious twist on the first verse of Ezekiel ("I am amidst the exile"), Kook takes up a dominant motif in Jewish mythopoesis: being forcibly exiled and making the long, arduous journey back to a promised homeland. Instead of the biblical verse's apparent semantic meaning, that the prophet is one of the Jews banished to Babylonia, Kook proposes that Ezekiel describes an inner alienation, in which the *I*, the self, suffers the condition of exile and seeks its way home. That is the paradigm that all the world follows, Kook suggests. Individual people, their societies, even the physical world itself rightly should manifest the Divine Presence within, which imbues them with incipient perfection and potential for cosmic integration. But all have run off course, into exile, becoming distorted, diminished versions of themselves.

Humanity began with sacred integration, when Adam and Eve lived in Eden, walking naked and unashamed. But they were unable to resist the snake's seductions and soon were driven from paradise to inhospitable wilderness. Rav Kook evokes a sense of inner alienation in this story by referring to God's resonant question, demanding that Adam account for his behavior: *Where are you?* But Adam cannot answer for himself. He hides. And we've been hiding ever since, unable to respond as God wanted: *I am here.*

As individual humans are driven from Eden into exile, so was the Jewish nation driven into Diaspora, a particularly important example to Rav Kook, the redemptive Zionist. And a parallel sense of alienation applies to an imperfect cosmos where the moon darkens each month. In Rav Kook's meditation, these are all types of homelessness, in which individual people, the Jewish nation, and the world itself could manifest an inner, authentic holiness if they could only find their way home to the true self, "soaked in heavenly radiance."

Exile comes upon people, societies, and the world, in Kook's account, because of their own failings. I suspect today's readers may be distressed by Kook's repetition of that nasty word *sin*. For some good reasons but largely due to cowardice, contemporary Judaism usually avoids such severe judgment. But any deep religious path must account for the rupture between the world as it is and the world that ought to be. Jewish spiritual quests cannot be all ecstasy and affirmation! Kook asks us to confront the inadequacy of our identities, of our ways of living, of the world around us. To take responsibility for that darkness, it is imperative that we admit the ways we worsen the world, corrupting ourselves and obscuring the divine depth within us that is our true identity.

The source of our sins, Kook suggests, tends to be egoistic self-assertion, a narrowing of the true self. The more we advance ulterior, indulgent interests, the more we lose ourselves. In terms of mystical psychology, one can say that the more we stress self-assertive desires, the less able we become to recognize the self-transcending divine within. On the individual level, this dynamic can be seen in Adam's "turning to the counsel of the serpent and destroying himself." As a nation, similarly, Israel turned to false gods "and lost its identity."

But I think Kook's subtlest exposition of this point comes when he expounds two vivid mythic-midrashic tropes through which he treats the sinful inclination of nature itself. To explain why the moon waxes and wanes each month, the Talmud tells a tale of a jealous moon, aggrieved at having to share glory with the sun, seeking first place in the sky (*Hullin* 60b). The moon tries to aggrandize itself, but measure for measure God responds, "Go shrink yourself." Because it sought greater sparkle, the moon is left less than it was created to be, exiled from its own natural powers, radiating no light of its own, merely reflecting sunlight. The other mythic image is particularly beautiful: Midrashic tradition records that the earth was created with such inherently full goodness that *all* its produce—not just fruit, but the very wood of trees as well—should be delicious and nourishing. But a selfish earth withheld its full measure of blessing, producing sweet fruit but dry wood (*Bereshit Rabbah* 5:9; Babylonian Talmud, *Sukkah* 35a). When the earth is exiled from its true self in this way, Kook suggests, divine blessing is manifest incompletely. A redeemed world awaits, on the other hand, when the earth exudes all the potential blessing within.

All these forms of exile are fundamentally parallel: people who cannot say where they are resemble a nation without a homeland, worshipping false gods, which is like the dry wood of an apple tree, and like a waning moon, giving no light of its own. Could we all but learn to give without jealousy, we would become ourselves as we were created to be.

Kook makes the particularly important observation, as apt in his own time as in ours, that religious education should cultivate awareness of the self-transcending sanctity within us. Only those who know their true selves a divine manifestation can have a relationship with God ("Since there is no *I*, there can be no *Him* ...") or another person ("... and certainly no *you*"). Yet Jewish educators often distract spiritual seekers, focusing on everything *but* inner sanctity. "Adding straw to the fire, giving vinegar to those dying of thirst," too many teachers stress externals, like rote performance and nostalgic traditionalism, instead of the inward. In Kook's own time, he would say, such narrow teaching would confine itself to defensively maintaining the age-old practices of the Diaspora, rather than opening the spirit to the possibilities of the restoration of prophetic Torah emerging in the Land of Israel.[3] In our day, in America, our anxiety at the eroding patterns of Jewish affiliation prompts many Jewish educators to want nothing deeper for students than recognizable Jewish behavior. Now, Kook certainly favored devoted and scrupulous practice, of course, and I join him in appreciating the spiritual discipline of *halakhah*. But this passage reminds us that the *telos* of religion is more than conformity to normative behavior; it is to clarify the divine image by refining the selves on which it is inscribed.

That would indeed be redemptive. So how do we attain it? In the final lines of our text, Kook points toward the identity transformation that ushers the self back from exile into the Promised Land. Having stressed that Adam became *estranged* (*nitnaker*) from himself, and that ancient Israel worshipped *alien* (*el zar*) and *strange* gods (*elohei neikar*), Kook suggests that it is their very strangeness that makes them false gods. But the true God, whose image we bear, is not alien to the self at all. Idolatry is not merely worshipping local deities or fetishes of wood and stone. Idolatry means treating God as alien to ourselves, thus denying the sacredness of the human personhood. But we, who are created in the divine image, must "banish gods who are strangers." Instead of strange deities, "we seek *Adonai*, our God ... we seek ourselves." That search constitutes a single spiritual quest, whose two components are inextricable from each other. That is, we should find the well of ultimate sanctity bubbling up within our hearts and seek the Divine by laying bare the true self, inscribed with God's image. And redemption comes in recognizing that the anointed redeemer, *Meshiah Adonai*, is none other than our own breathing spirit. "He does not exist outside us. He is our breath." The painful distortions of identity will not be overcome when a distant God sends a redeemer. We will be liberated from inner alienation by recognizing the sacred character of the deep self. When you sense the redemption of the Divine Spirit already breathing in your own nostrils, you will already be home.

The final line of Rav Kook's meditation on personhood is a master stroke. Recall that he began by citing Ezekiel to mean that the self, the *I*, is in exile. He concludes with reference to the Exodus, the paradigm of Jewish liberation. Having grasped the redemptive power within your own breath, grasping that there is no God beyond who is not simultaneously within, you stand ready to understand that the alienated self is restored by realizing its divine heart. Then this knowledge sets you free: "Know that *I* am the Lord your God, who brings you out of the land Egypt. *I* am *Adonai*."

Notes

1. Cf. *Bereshit Rabbah* 5:9; Babylonian Talmud, *Sukkah* 35a.
2. This passage brings together elements from Exodus 6:7 and Leviticus 22:35.
3. Abraham Yitzhak HaKohen Kook, *Igrot HaRayah* [Letters of Rav Kook], vol. 1 (Jerusalem: Mossad HaRav Kook, 1985), 124. See further discussions on this topic by, among others, Avinoam Rosenak, *Prophetic Halakhah* [Hebrew] (Jerusalem: Magnes Press, 2007), and Michael Z. Nehorai, "Halakhah, Metahalakhah, and the Redemption of Israel: Reflections on the Rabbinic Rulings of Rabbi Kook," in *Rabbi Abraham Isaac Kook and Jewish Spirituality*, ed. Lawrence J. Kaplan and David Shatz (New York: New York University Press, 1995).

Shaul Magid is the Jay and Jeannie Schottenstein Professor of Modern Judaism and professor of religious studies at Indiana University Bloomington. He is the author of *Hasidism on the Margin: Reconciliation, Antinomianism, and Messianism in Izbica/Radzin Hasidism* and *From Metaphysics to Midrash: Myth, History, and the Interpretation of Scripture in Lurianic Kabbala,* which won the American Academy of Religion Award for Excellence in the Study of Religion in the Textual Studies category.

Yitro, (Neo-)Hasidism, and a New American Piety

SHAUL MAGID

During this Shabbat I was in hiding.[1]

"And Yitro heard ..." (Exodus 18:1). Rashi asks, "What exactly did Yitro hear that made him 'come' to Moses?" He heard about the parting of the Reed Sea and the wars Amalek waged [against the Israelites].[2] There is a well-known question raised by my father, of blessed memory, as well as in other texts, "What is the nature of Rashi's question, 'What did Yitro hear that made him come to Moses?'" The verse itself is quite explicit when it states that "God brought Israel out of Egypt." Why then does Rashi answer [his question by saying] that Yitro heard about the parting of the Reed Sea and the wars with Amalek?

[In order to answer this] we need to note that the giving of the Torah was in the desert. Perhaps there is a hint to this in the Hasidic book *Beit Aaron* on Rashi to Deuteronomy 6:5, "Hear, O Israel.... You should love your God with all your heart, all your soul, and all your might." "One's heart should not be divided in relation to God [*she-lo yehei libkha haluk al ha-makom*]. R. Aaron [of Karlin] says with his holy tongue, 'Do not say in this place one can serve God but in that place it is simply impossible. Rather, one must serve God in every place.'"[3] Hence, if the Israelites had received the Torah in *Eretz Yisrael* they may have come to think that they could serve God only in their [own] place or in their dwellings and not when they are in exile and otherwise distracted. This is why God gave them the Torah in the desert, "on the way" (*ba-derekh*), in motion, so that they should know that it should be fulfilled in every place [they find themselves]. "One's heart should not be divided in relation to God [*she-lo yehei libkha haluk al ha-makom*]."

Now we can understand why Rashi asked the question he did about Yitro, "What did he hear to make him 'come'?" Why did he have to come at all? He could have stayed at home and asked Moses to send him an Israelite who could convert him and teach him Torah just like Yitro himself, who returned home [after visiting Moses in the desert] to convert his household. It is this question that brings Rashi to suggest [in his comment to Exodus 18:1] that Yitro heard about the parting of the Reed Sea and the war with Amalek. Amalek wanted to diminish [lit., "cool"] the Israelites' passion for God. Yet how could Amalek have thought this was possible after the Israelites witnessed the parting of the sea, the handmaiden seeing what even the prophet Ezekiel did not see?[4] Amalek surmised that since now the Israelites are in transit (*ba-derekh*), heaven forbid, he would succeed even though they were on such a lofty level. This is why he confronted them "on the way" (*ba-derekh*). Amalek was depending on that. This is why Yitro surmised, "It is not sufficient for me to receive the Torah only in my abode but I must go there and receive it in transit, 'on the way.' Only then will I be able to be a Jew [*Yehudi*] also in my home." That is, when Yitro heard that after the parting of the sea the Israelites faced the war with Amalek and that they persevered "on the way," he realized he also needed to journey and come to the desert in order to convert [that is, to receive the Torah].[5]

RABBI KALONYMUS KALMAN SHAPIRA, *ESH KODESH*

This very Yitro-centric *torah* (teaching) about the proper way of devotion, how to receive the Torah, is quite suggestive given Yitro's position as an outsider and the fact that he does not ultimately stay with Israel but returns to *his* homeland, to his old life now infused with a new sense of meaning and truth. Kalonymus Kalman suggests that Yitro's presence in the desert, however fleeting, and as important, his very *coming* to the desert, illustrate something fundamental about a human being's relationship to God. Below I suggest this approach teaches something about the nature of inside and outside and how each vantage point produces different results, the latter producing the conditions for renewal precisely in the way it subverts the ostensible inwardness intended in the former.

There have been numerous strong (re)interpretations of Hasidism in the last century. The first, calling itself neo-Hasidism, originated in Eastern Europe in such cities as Odessa, Warsaw, Vilna, and other urban centers in the late nineteenth and early twentieth centuries. Its main architects were secular and moderately religious Yiddishists and Hebraists (many of whom were reared in Hasidic or traditional families) who viewed Hasidism as an articulation of Jewish folk religion that aptly expressed the religiosity of the people. Many of these individuals were influenced by Tolstoy and other romantics who elevated the *Volk* as a central category of literary creativity. In some sense the most well-known, or most lasting, voices of this circle in America were Isaac Bashevis Singer, Shalom Aleikhem, Martin Buber, Shalom Asch, and to some extent Abraham Joshua Heschel.

The second articulation of neo-Hasidism took form in the mid- to late 1960s around Zalman Schachter-Shalomi, Shlomo Carlebach, Arthur Green, and others. In seminaries, universities, concert halls, and communal houses (*havurot*), these architects of what would become second-wave neo-Hasidism or Jewish Renewal used the American counterculture as a laboratory to reinterpret Hasidism, taking an inherited tradition that was externally foreign to, and largely incompatible with, modern American sensibilities and turning it inside out so that its spiritual nerve was exposed. While Schachter-Shalomi and Carlebach served as crucial transitional figures (Menachem Mendel Schneerson, the seventh Lubavitcher Rebbe, was perhaps the most seminal figure in this transitional generation in America), their first students were American, and most had no direct experience of the old-world Hasidism of Eastern Europe. Their experience was of postwar America as it was shaped by the Beats, the civil rights movement, the counterculture, the antiwar movement, environmentalism, and then feminism. They were not of the transitional generation but rather the first recipients of that generation's Torah on American soil.

The neo-Hasidism that emerged from this new generation, in many ways nurtured to maturity by Schachter-Shalomi, was a new form of neo-Hasidism similar in sentiment to the first wave but different in significant ways. One of the most prominent differences was that this new neo-Hasidism was unmoored from the language and ethos of what it was reconfiguring, only having the most indirect connections to the disappearing world of its origins. Its ethos was decidedly the progressive and even radical American sentiment of a culture founded on protest, experimentation, and perhaps most important, confidence in being American. It fundamentally came from the "outside" much more than did the subversive culture of first-wave neo-Hasidism, which had a direct experience with what it was undermining and thus in some way remained in closer proximity to it. Progressive America was the lens through which Hasidism was now revalued.

One could argue that this distance from the lived life of Hasidism was a disadvantage. In some ways that might be true, but it also served as an advantage in that it enabled Hasidism to bloom outside the limited, and limiting, frame of its own perspective. Its vision was not tainted by unfamiliarity with the culture in which it grew. As a result, many in this generation were less afraid to take this new interpretation of an old tradition in different, and even audacious, directions. While most in the transitional generation were radical in their thought, they often exhibited a tepid conservatism in their action—largely the product, one could posit, of memories of the untrustworthy world of their youth.[6] Their radicalism was largely a European radicalism expressed in historicism, criticism, and existentialism. For this new generation, however, America was home, and therefore they were more willing and better equipped to test the elasticity of traditional norms in ways an immigrant generation could not easily do. I want to read this new neo-Hasidism as a "Yitro-movement," a revision of tradition from the outside, from a place unbound and unfettered by the weight of tradition and preconceived notions of boundaries.

I suggest that this Yitro-centric approach has a prehistory articulated in the above passage by Kalonymus Kalman Shapiro of Piaseczno. It was well-known by some scholars of this second-wave neo-Hasidic community that some of the interbellum Hasidic masters in Poland had been sufficiently exposed to modernity to see through the veneer of lived Hasidism's social constraints. Hillel Zeitlin, an odd border crosser (*ish ivri*) who straddled the two worlds of Hasidism and the Jewish Enlightenment in interbellum Poland, had already found a small audience among these countercultural individuals. Kalonymus Kalman Shapira was a contemporary of Zeitlin. Both lived in the Warsaw Ghetto. Zeitlin was killed while being deported in July 1942. Shapira was killed in the Trawniki camp some months after being deported, most likely in November 1943. Kalonymus Kalman migrated to Warsaw in those heady interbellum years, yet unlike Zeitlin he remained closely aligned to the traditional world of his youth—due in part to his becoming the rebbe of the Hasidic court of his father while still in Piaseczno (a suburb of Warsaw) in his twenties. But in that conformist frame he managed to think beyond its borders. Posthumously found, collected, and published as *Esh Kodesh*, his ghetto homilies exhibit a remarkable understanding of human suffering and sympathy for humanity in the face of radical evil.

Citing Rashi, Kalonymus Kalman suggests that the very nature of Jewish worship from the perspective of Hasidism comes not from Moses but from Yitro. The midrash constructs Yitro as a man of spiritual substance, curious about and open to all manner of spiritual expression and experimentation. To take some license with Rashi as seen through Kalonymus Kalman's reading, I suggest it was not simply that Yitro heard these two events (the parting of the sea and the war with Amalek), but that while he heard these events as independent episodes, he came to see them as one, to realize something few knew; he came to realize why the Torah was given in the desert, "on the way."

Yitro's journey was one of receiving and giving. He knew he had to experience "on the way" in order to fully absorb the Torah's message of transience (internal and external) as a condition of devotion.

But he also taught Israel that while the promise of the stability of place may be true, the nature of the covenantal experience was not, and could not be, limited to *any* place. Inside the collective body of Israel it was *every* place. And, if I can insert a neo-Hasidic reading, being *every* place means it had to also extend beyond the collective body of Israel.

What did Yitro see that others could not? Coming from the outside, he saw something in the parting of the sea and Amalek that the Israelites could not see—that devotion requires motion; that focusing too intently on the comfort of a promise of stability is the *sitra ahra*, the Amalek that lurks inside the covenant. Amalek thought he could defeat Israel because, being "on the way," they were weak. In some way, he was right; without divine intervention he would have succeeded. But this was because Israel did not yet know that "on the way" was the very place where they meet God, in the desert. When Yitro realized this, he knew he had to "come," he had to show Israel that the real weakness was *inside* them. By coming to them, by traversing the desert, he taught them as well as himself. While tradition teaches that he "converted," he does not stay with the Israelite people (we never hear from him again after he apparently rejects Moses's plea to remain). Rather, he apparently returns home permanently. It is thus a strange kind of conversion, an individual and purely spiritual conversion, as opposed to one with a "national" character. In Kalonymus Kalman's reading, while returning to his home and leaving Israel to their fate in the desert, Yitro grasped the essential nature of human devotion to God as taught in the Torah. And it is his example via his realization of the linkage between the parting of the sea and the wars with Amalek that taught Israel a lesson they had not quite understood.

I suggest this second wave of neo-Hasidism embodied the ethos of Yitro described here, Yitro being the biblical referent of this new period of Hasidic flourishing. Like Yitro, this generation came from outside—not from Eastern Europe or ultratraditional homes—and they carried a kind of experimental spirit that could only be produced and nurtured in the free society of their birth. And as much as old-world Hasidism taught them and gave them a frame into which they could exercise that American spirit, they had a message for the Old World as well. They saw what the Old World, blinded by persecution and mistrust, could not see; what the ancient Israelites in the desert, blinded by the experience of slavery and overwhelmed by the promise of normalcy, could not see. They saw an expansiveness that was suffocating in the teachings of Hasidism, in Torah, and they began the arduous process of extracting that substance for new consumption.

This new generation argued *against* insularity as a devotional posture; even as they turned to Hasidism, they remained open to the world—its ideas, values, and perspectives. They came to see through their own particular lenses an expansive spirit that was bound and gagged inside the collective body of Hasidism, hardened by the social realities of history. Yet this new approach was not made of whole cloth. It was already realized by some Hasidic masters, Kalonymus Kalman Shapira being one of them. Ironically, the meeting of Hasidism's newest interpreters and some exceptional cases of the Old World did not arise from similar circumstances. Quite the opposite. This homily was given, or written, in hiding in a ghetto where Jewish life was precarious. Kalonymus Kalman's life in the ghetto exposed him to a level of persecution that far surpassed most of his Hasidic predecessors'. His sermons cry with the realization that "we" (he and his audience) would not survive, but that true devotion is not about survival; it transcends survival. Kalonymus Kalman came out the other side of forced insularity to realize the expansive spirit of his inherited tradition. It is almost as if the reality of death before death liberated him from the fear of death and allowed the life in him to pour out in its purest form. It is no wonder that the collection of Warsaw homilies, known as *Esh Kodesh*, became so popular in neo-Hasidic circles. Kalonymus Kalman was another kind of Yitro, or Yitro from another angle. He was so deeply inside that he discovered the perspective of the outside.

Yitro's discovery of serving God "in every place" can be read in conjunction with "on the way" to imply "every state of mind, every state of being." One of the most lasting, and daring, dimensions of this new generation's contribution to Hasidic history is how they were committed to translate Hasidism in a postparochial fashion. They made explicit what Buber mostly hinted at: "Hebrew humanism" (Buber's term) can be viewed as Hasidism liberated from its social and cultural confines of debilitating persecution. Yitro comes to Sinai, learns from Moses, exhibits something crucial in his very "coming"

(Rashi), and then returns home and educates his family, his generation, his world. The radical new thinkers of second-wave neo-Hasidism come to Sinai (old-world Hasidism) to learn from the masters of the transitional generation (Schneerson, Schachter-Shalomi, Carlebach, Heschel, and others), to reveal to the old school that here in America we needn't be afraid of the world outside, and then they return to their world—their readers and students of the next generation, in universities, seminaries, concert halls, and adult education forums—and offer their interpretation as part of the very chain of tradition (*shalshelet ha-kabbalah*). And so it became. Of course the next generation will break free of what they inherit and offer their own rendering. New Yitros will be born whose new outside perspective will offer a critique of the previous generation. And they will "come," "on the way," and be the next interpreters of Yitro's great contribution. Or so we fervently hope.

Notes

1. Uncharacteristically, Kalonymus Kalman Shapira writes this as a prelude to his homily. I am not aware of the specific condition of this situation.
2. See *Mekhilta, Mesekhta de-Amalek* 1, in *Mekhilta de-Rebbe Yishmael im Perush Meir Ayin* (Vilna, n.d.), p. 57; and Babylonian Talmud, *Zevahim* 116a.
3. R. Aaron of Karlin, *Beit Aaron* (Brody, 1875), p. 123d.
4. *Mekhilta, Parashat Shira* 3, in *Mekhilta de-Rebbe Yishmael im Perush Meir Ayin*, p. 37a.
5. Kalonymus Kalman Shapira of Piaseczno, *Esh Kodesh, Parashat Yitro*—January 27, 1940. For a different translation see *Sacred Fire: Torah from the Years of Fury, 1939–1942*, trans. J. Hershy Worch, ed. Deborah Miller (Landham, Md.: Rowman and Littlefield, 2002), pp. 38, 39.
6. I would exclude Zalman Schachter-Shalomi from this assessment. Despite his experience with the most egregious anti-Semitism in Jewish history, Schachter-Shalomi has exhibited an openness to the world that served as the basis for this new rendering of Hasidic spirituality.

PART TWO

Spiritual Growth, Inner Transformation

Sheila Peltz Weinberg was ordained by the Reconstructionist Rabbinical College and has served as an educator, activist, liturgist, and congregational rabbi. She has helped introduce meditation into the Jewish world as a form that can enliven and illuminate Jewish practice. She is a founder and outreach director of the Institute for Jewish Spirituality and the author of *Surprisingly Happy: An Atypical Religious Memoir*.

Approaching the Thick Cloud

Working with Obstacles in Our Spiritual Growth

Sheila Peltz Weinberg

"So the people remained at a distance, while Moses approached the thick cloud where God was" (Exodus 20:18).

If one spends one's entire life in materiality, and later on gets enthusiastic and wants to follow God's path, then the quality of judgment argues against that person, and doesn't allow him to follow God's ways and creates a hindrance for him. But God desires kindness and leniency and hides God's self, as it were, in that hindrance. And one who is aware looks at the hindrance and finds there the Creator, as it says in the Jerusalem Talmud (*Ta'anit* 1:3a): "If someone says to you, 'Where is your God?' you shall say to that person, 'In a great city in Aram.' As it says: 'God calls to me from Seir' (Isaiah 21:11)."

And one who is not aware, when one sees the hindrance, immediately moves away from it. The hindrance is like a thick cloud, for a thick cloud is dark and a hindrance is dark. [The words "darkness" and "hindrance," or that which holds back, share the same three Hebrew letters—*het shin kaf*], as it is written in Genesis 22:16: "You have not withheld [your son]." This is the meaning of the verse "So the people remained at a distance." When they see the thick cloud, namely the hindrance, they remain at a distance. But Moses, who represents the quality of awareness for all of Israel, "*approached the thick cloud, where God was,*" namely: he approached the hindrance, where the blessed God is actually hidden.

We heard more of this teaching directly from the holy [Reb Nahman], that God actually hides God's self in the hindrance. Scripture says: God loves justice. And God loves Israel. But the love with which God loves Israel is greater than the love with which God loves justice.

Thus when the quality of judgment argues against one who is not really worthy of coming close to God, because God loves justice, God is compelled, as it were, to agree to the arising of hindrances on the path. These hindrances are, indeed, the result of that person's evil deeds. After all, God cannot ignore just consequences, since God loves justice.

Because God loves Israel even more than God loves justice, what does God do? God is forced to agree to the hindrances for the sake of justice. However, despite this, the truest truth is that God wants that person to be able to draw close to God. So, God gives permission to place the hindrances in the way, but God hides God's self in the hindrances. One who is aware, more mindful, can find God in the midst of the hindrances themselves. There really are not any hindrances in the world at all, because in the hindrances themselves is found the Holy One. Through the hindrances themselves, in fact, one might draw closer to God because that is where God is hidden. And this is the meaning of "*Moses approached the thick cloud,*" that is, the hindrance, for that is "*where God was.*"[1]

RABBI NAHMAN OF BRATSLAV, *LIKUTEI MOHARAN*

I was immediately and viscerally struck by how much this teaching of Nahman echoed the teaching of mindfulness. In truth there was no reason to be so surprised. I have been teaching mindfulness meditation and yoga for the Institute for Jewish Spirituality for some time, and we often employ Hasidic voices to express the teachings of these practices. In this essay, I share my understanding of how this text can be applied by the mindfulness meditator and how the teaching of mindfulness can illuminate its meaning. In particular, this text deals with the issue of *meniot*, the obstacles or hindrances along the spiritual path. It suggests how to approach these *meniot* so as to reveal God's presence and lead to liberation, insight, and spiritual growth.

The first paragraph is a description of the spiritual seeker and a foretaste of the punch line of the whole passage. It introduces a person who has stopped finding meaning in the world of things. Maybe such persons realize that they have an inner life or that happiness depends on something other than accumulation and accomplishment. This pivot point is crucial. Something happens to prompt the turning. Nahman informs us that the desire to follow God's path is necessarily met with obstacles. Then he offers a way to move past these very obstacles.

I am reminded of people I have met over the years who come on meditation retreats. Many newcomers have a vague sense that something is missing in their lives. They are attracted to the idea of silence. Meditation has a romantic sound to it. They think it is going to be a relief from worry and stress—something like a Caribbean vacation— luxury style. However, what most often happens is that people are restless, sleepy, bored, and annoyed. They begin to doubt that this is a path for them. They are sitting with the contents of their own minds, and they see how difficult it is to be still. They realize that they have pursued distractions just for this reason, to be relieved of having to see how obsessive, fearful, greedy, and lonely they are.

In our text, the theme is struck from the outset that God's presence fills all reality, even the places we imagine are devoid of God: the places of delusion, constriction, resistance, and judgment. How could God be coming from Seir (a biblical place associated with temptation and violence)? Las Vegas? The Pentagon? You name it! The theological view that God *is* to be found in all these unlikely places is an approach to all spiritual practice. The invitation to the practitioner is to rest in this very moment. When we have the courage to release the struggle with what is, we see more clearly what is true. We then find ourselves more able to be in God's presence as it is revealed in this moment.

As Nahman says, if one is not cultivating awareness, the natural tendency is to move away from the *meniah*, the obstacle or hindrance.

In meditation it looks like this: I am sitting and anger arises. It may be an old or new story triggered by anything I see or hear or remember. There is no easy avoidance. I am sitting in silence. I can't reach for a drink or a magazine. Anger, like other unpleasant states, tends to trigger habitual reactivity. Following the trail of these unwholesome states without awareness can lead to more confusion and to acting unwisely. The tendency of the untrained mind is to get rid of the anger as best I can. This usually means moving away through various strategies such as judging myself or blaming another for this unpleasant and uninvited experience. In any case I move away from the actual arising of anger. Anger is the hindrance, the *meniah*. This moving away is itself a form of aversion that arises in relation to various stimuli. When we push against the hindrance or try to run from it, we notice that a struggle erupts in the mind and body.

When we get into an adversarial relationship with our own experience, we notice that the unpleasantness of the experience is exacerbated. It is like picking a scab. Awareness is restricted. The mind becomes more obsessed with the vague entity of "myself." "How am *I* doing?" "Why did they do this to me?" "Why am I not able to break out of this feeling?" These are the operative questions. A sense of self is solidified and it is small. Reality is narrowed and possibilities are collapsed.

One needs to explore this in one's own experience. It is not something to believe or take on faith. Meditation retreats and other spiritual practice environments set up the conditions to sit, without the usual distractions, and to observe the content and process of our own minds.

The practice of mindfulness is the alternative strategy pointed to in our text. We can choose to enter the frightening or difficult experience. We can choose to draw near, to not run away, and to resist the mental habits. Moses represents the quality of mindfulness, which is nonjudgmental awareness moment to moment. There is no pushing away and no holding back. Moses approaches the thick cloud that Nahman has identified with the *meniot*. Abraham, another model of courageous mindfulness, is remembered earlier in the text when the fusion of the word "darkness," along with "withholding" and "hindrance" is discussed. In the *Akedah*, "The Binding of Isaac," Abraham is willing to walk into the darkness of not knowing or understanding what God really wants of him. The average person needs a lot of practice to get to this stage.

In mindfulness practice there is reference to the five hindrances, sometimes referred to as the veiling factors: grasping, aversion, restlessness, sloth or torpor, and speculative or cynical doubt. Mindfulness is the primary way to work with these energies. When mindfulness is present, these *meniot* are revealed as a collection of conditions without any independent existence. The hindrances cloud the mind to what is true in this moment. They interfere with our clarity. The well-known mindfulness teacher Jack Kornfield writes:

> Open to it [the hindrance] and observe it without identifying with it or taking it as self. It is not "my restlessness" [substitute any of the *meniot*], but rather an impermanent state born out of conditions and bound to change. Like everything else, restlessness is a composite, a series of thoughts, feelings, and sensations. But because we believe it to be something solid, it has a great deal of power over us. When we stop resisting and simply allow it to move through us with mindful attention, we can see how transitory and insubstantial the state actually is.[2]

Is this not what Nahman is saying in our text when he declares that there really aren't any hindrances in the world at all? When we have the steadfast balance of Moses to approach any of the *meniot*, we enter into the darkness and the unknown in this moment. It is here we discover that the so-called obstacles are empty of form and substance. They are veils or garments that hide the light of the Divine Presence.

In the middle of our text Nahman adds an important dimension. He posits the reason that God hides, as it were, God's self in these hindrances. The hindrances represent justice. They are the lawful unfolding of certain conditions. This too is a dimension of God's presence in the world, a structure of cause and effect that must be respected and accounted for. It is in our willingness to approach the hindrances, with mindfulness, that we learn these laws of nature. In particular what is revealed is the insubstantiality of all forms of struggle and resistance and the emptiness of the concept of separate self. When we get close to the *meniot*, we see fluidity, aliveness, transparency. We see relationship and interconnection. We see the intimate partnership between light and darkness, as it says in the verse in Isaiah about coming from Seir: "Morning came, and so did night. If you would inquire, inquire. Come back again" (Isaiah 21:12).

Isn't this what Nahman is trying to teach us in this text? He is calling us out of the delusion that we can be safe by hiding from the darkness as if it were some other realm out of God's purview. He is inviting us to a nondual view of reality. It is our insistence on seeing ourselves as the center of the universe, isolated in our uniqueness, that locks us into the grip of suffering.

Here is Jack Kornfield again, maybe not such an unlikely disciple of Reb Nahman:

> To understand the nature of happiness and sorrow, to find freedom in our life, we have to be willing to face all the demons in our mind. Our journey ... is to learn a kind of mind control, a traveler's equilibrium. It is not the control of making something happen, but rather the ability to stay present, open, and balanced through all the experiences and realms of life.[3]

Our mindfulness practice and Reb Nahman invite us into the depths of our own minds and hearts, leading us to awaken to the truth of truths and to the depth of Oneness. We do not really have to get close. We only need to discover how close we are already. But for this we are asked to be fearless. We are asked to investigate and to know the light and the dark. Above all, we are asked to come back again.

Notes

1. Nahman of Bratslav, *Likutei Moharan* 1:115.
2. Joseph Goldstein and Jack Kornfield, *Seeking the Heart of Wisdom: The Path of Insight Meditation* (Boston: Shambhala, 1987), p. 53.
3. Ibid., p. 39.

Lawrence Kushner is the Emanu-El Scholar at Congregation Emanu-El of San Francisco and an adjunct member of the faculty of Hebrew Union College–Jewish Institute of Religion in Los Angeles. He is the author of numerous books on Jewish spirituality and mysticism, including *Honey from the Rock: An Introduction to Jewish Mysticism*; *The Way Into Jewish Mysticism*; and *I'm God; You're Not: Observations on Organized Religion & Other Disguises of the Ego* (all Jewish Lights).

"Who Am I to Go to Pharaoh?"

Lawrence Kushner

A *tzaddik* [holy person] who would serve God must be continuously aware of the spiritual level he has attained and that there is still a higher level above this that he has not.... And he knows that, once he attains this level, there will be yet another, higher one. There is no end to it. No matter how high he has ascended, he understands that completion is still beyond him. He is continuously aware of his deficiencies and his inadequacies.

As we read about even Elijah (*Tikkunei Zohar, Hakdama* 17a), "I don't know You at all." And just this is the choicest kind of service to God: That one is continually aware that he is still incomplete. And thus he craves and yearns to ascend to yet a higher level than where he now stands....

We can also explain this same dynamic with reference to God's Name of "I will be who I will be" (Exodus 3:14).

What someone attains now is for now, whereas God's Name of "I will be who I will be" [in the imperfect tense] alludes to that which can only be attained in the future. Such is the way of a *tzaddik*, one who is continuously aware of his deficiencies and trusts that God will help him attain this higher

39

level. And this is why God's Name is in the future tense, "I will be who I will be," implying a time yet to be, a future still to come. But, in the present, completion is unattainable—only in the future. And, of course, once he has reached this level, he knows that there will yet be another and another and that such yearning has no end. But still he trusts in God....

We have a teaching that comes to us in the name of the Baal Shem Tov. Punning on the odd language of Psalm 48:15, "He guides His worlds [al mut]," the Besht deliberately misreads it as, "He guides children."

It is like a father who wants to teach his child how to walk. As soon as the little one takes a few steps toward his father, the father intuitively steps back, thereby urging the child to take even more steps. And, no sooner does the child take a few more steps, than the father moves still farther away—all in order that the child would walk even more....

In the same way, *tzaddikim* are always aware of their inadequacies precisely so that they can improve themselves even more. Just this is the explanation of God's reply to Moses [when Moses asks God for some kind of sign] and God replies, "And this shall be for you the sign that I have sent you ..." (Exodus 3:12).

Moses, our teacher, asks, "Who am I that I should go to Pharaoh and lead the children of Israel out of Egypt?" (Exodus 3:11). From the great depth of his own piety, Moses was keenly aware of his own inadequacy and how much higher he had yet to ascend. In his own eyes he was convinced of his lowly state and his own deficiencies.

Indeed, this is why God said to him, "And *this* shall be for you the sign that I have sent you ..." for you, Moses, have attained such a high level of spiritual evolution that you remain convinced of your inadequacy and you continue to ask, "Who am I ... ?" Just this is the sign that I have sent you. Your asking, "Who am I?" is itself the sign that "I have sent you!"

This is the way of a true *tzaddik*, one who continually knows his deficiencies, who cannot even imagine ever attaining the goal of true divine service—just this is the sign of true prophecy: "The sign that I have sent you."[1]

RABBI LEVI YITZHAK OF BERDITCHEV, KEDUSHAT LEVI

Fear of Teaching

A few autumns ago, I was about to begin teaching a new class on an old topic and shared my anxiety with a friend. "I've been teaching for fifty years," I lamented, "and I still get nervous before the first session."

"My mother taught first grade her whole life," she replied. "And she was always a basket case at the start of each new semester. When I asked her why, my mother explained that, for her, her anxiety reminded her that she respected her students. 'The day I'm sure this will be a piece of cake is the day I quit.'"

Alas, some professions just seem immune to any amount of prior experience or self-confidence. No matter how well prepared or how good (you think) you are, you always feel inadequate, unworthy—perhaps none of them more than the tightrope act of impersonating a rabbi.

Kedushat Levi

No matter how old you are, it always seems you're never quite old enough to be a rabbi. No matter how much you know, you're never wise enough. No matter how devout, you're never religious enough. Tough job, the rabbi thing.

Rabbi Levi Yitzhak ben Meir of Berditchev (c. 1740–1810), in his *Kedushat Levi*, like many teachers among the early generations of Hasidism, is particularly interested in crafting the job description of a would-be rebbe or *tzaddik*. And this, not surprisingly, leads him to what may be the ultimate ordination scene in the *Tanakh*, the one at the burning bush where God commissions Moses to lead the Jewish people out of Egyptian slavery. (Now that's *my* idea of an ordination. I'm *musmakh* from God; who ordained you?)

After a very close reading of the biblical text, however, the Berditchever notices an apparent lacuna in the story. In brief: God says to Moses, I want you to free the Jews from slavery. To which, Moses, not unreasonably, replies, "*Mi anokhi ki eilekh el Paro?* Who am I to go to Pharaoh?" Then God answers, "Don't worry, I will be with you;

v'zeh l'kha ha-ot ki anokhi shelahtikha ... and this shall be for you the sign that I have sent you ..." (Exodus 3:11–12).

It's a powerful scene. There's only one problem: God never tells Moses what the sign is, leaving Moses and us wondering how someone is supposed to know he or she is a fit leader. And that is where we pick up Levi Yitzhak of Berditchev's explanation. It has four parts.

Where Are You?

A *tzaddik*, says the Berditchever, must constantly be aware of the spiritual level he has attained even as he must also be aware that there is a still higher level that he has not yet attained. Indeed, no sooner does a *tzaddik* attain one level than he becomes aware of the next. There is always another, higher level yet to attain. And there is no end to it. No matter how high one ascends, completion will always elude him. He is perpetually and painfully aware of his deficiencies and inadequacies. He must endure a continuous state of incompleteness.

Levi Yitzhak cites a tradition in *Tikkunei Zohar* that even Elijah himself confessed, "I know nothing of You at all!" (*Hakdama* 17a).

But just this, the Berditchever teaches, is the highest form of serving God: "One is continually aware that he is still incomplete. And thus he craves and yearns to ascend to yet a higher level than where he now stands...."

I am reminded of a comment made by Rabbi Jerome Malino, his memory is a blessing. Malino was one of the great ones of the generation. Rabbi of Danbury, Connecticut, faculty of Hebrew Union College–Jewish Institute of Religion, president of the Central Conference of American Rabbis. A man of extraordinary depth and literacy. Well into his eighties, he was asked, at a communal luncheon meeting marking his retirement from teaching rabbinic students, what he intended to do now. He rose to his feet and without hesitation, in all seriousness, replied, "I intend to continue my *preparation* for the rabbinate."

Are We There Yet?

Levi Yitzhak now invites us to examine the grammar of God's Name as revealed to Moses only a few verses later in our story. Moses says to God, "When the Jews ask me who sent you, what name shall I give them?" God replies, "*Ehyeh asher ehyeh*" (Exodus 3:13–14).

But that Name does not, as it is frequently mistranslated, mean "I am that I am." That is static and present tense. And *ehyeh* is clearly future (or imperfect—that is, the verbal idea is not yet "perfected" or completed). *Ehyeh* means, in effect, "I will be" and alludes to an unfinished future and what might only be attained then. Indeed, a cumbersome but accurate translation of *Ehyeh asher ehyeh* would be "I am not yet who I am not yet." Which means, therefore, that if God is not done yet, then neither are we.

Such is the way of a *tzaddik*, says the Berditchever, someone who is continuously aware of her deficiencies yet trusts that God will help her attain a higher level in the future. Indeed, if the Name of your God is "I am not yet who I am not yet," then you too get to keep learning and striving and growing.

My own beloved teacher Arnold Jacob Wolf, whose memory is a blessing, used to mischievously complain that his problem was *not* that God was silent. "My problem," he would insist, "is that God won't shut up. Now what do You want? Leave me alone. I did that *mitzvah* last week. What do you mean, you want it again and better?"

One More Step

For his third observation, Levi Yitzhak turns to a frequently cited teaching in the name of the Baal Shem Tov. The Besht used to pun on an odd term in Psalm 48:15, *al mut*, usually rendered as either "until death," *al mavet*, or "worlds" or "evermore," *olamot*. Thus: "He will be our guide until death," or "He guides worlds." The Besht, however, following Rashi, deliberately misreads the phrase as, "He guides *al mut* / children."

It is like a parent, Levi Yitzhak explains, who wants to teach his child how to walk. No sooner does the little one take a few steps toward his mother or father, than the parent intuitively steps back, thereby urging the child to take yet another step. And, once the child takes a few more steps, the parent moves still farther away. And why? All in order that the child might walk even more.

Our self-dissatisfaction, our stumbling, our failures, our fear that we are inadequate to or unworthy of the holy task, in other words, are nothing more than God's loving ever being one more step just beyond reach. And it never ends.

Rabbi Adin Steinsaltz, arguably the wisest Jew of this generation, echoes this same theme. He reminds us, "Jewish thought pays little attention to inner tranquility and peace of mind.... The very concept of the Divine as infinite implies an activity that is endless, of which one must never grow weary." Indeed, Steinsaltz continues, "The Jewish approach to life considers the man who has stopped going [on]—he who has a feeling of completion, of peace, of a great light from above that has brought him to rest—to be someone who has lost his way."[2]

Who Am I?

Levi Yitzhak now returns to the textual lacuna where Moses asks his original question, "*Mi anokhi?* Who am I to go to Pharaoh?" and God cryptically replies, "*Zeh l'kha ha-ot* ... This shall be for you the sign ..." without apparently specifying the sign.

God *does* give Moses a sign, says the Berditchever. And it has been right there in plain sight all along; we just didn't notice it. From his native humility, Moses cannot imagine he is worthy of such a holy task. This is why he says, "Who am I that I should go to Pharaoh and lead the children of Israel out of Egypt?"

But precisely this fear of inadequacy is the source of his true spiritual authority. It is not an expression of unworthiness; it is a necessary qualification and precondition for the job of any would-be Jewish leader. Your fear that you are unworthy makes you worthy.

God, in effect, says to Moses, "Dummy! Your asking, 'Who am I?' *is the sign* that I've sent you!"

Who Are You?

I conclude with a true story of my first official task as the rabbi of my own congregation. It was over forty years ago and took me to the hospital.

We had just moved into a one-bedroom apartment in Marlborough, Massachusetts. It must have been late July. I dutifully called the president to inform him of our arrival. He welcomed me and, in the course of our conversation, said that he had heard through the grapevine that a member of the congregation was in Massachusetts General Hospital. She was a young mother who he heard was terminally ill. So I put on my rabbi suit (my only suit), drove into Boston, found MGH, and walked into her room. One of Boston's great physicians was just concluding a counseling session with her. He motioned kindly for me to take a chair and listen in.

The woman said, "But how can I be a mother? I can't even get out of bed anymore."

But, to my astonishment, he only scolded her. "Is that what you have to do to be a mother?" he asked. "Is being a mother just cooking and chauffeuring and playing?"

"No, I guess not," she whispered. "A mother is supposed to love and to teach."

"So, *nu?*" he replied, "Be a mother. Maybe you want to teach them about faith and about courage. Maybe you have an opportunity to love and to teach few mothers will ever understand."

She wept. He wept. I wept.

"Oh, thank you, doctor," she said.

He kissed her, nodded to me, and left.

I sat motionless, astonished, dumbfounded in the corner.

Startled, she turned to me and said, "Who the hell are you?"

Notes

1. Levi Yitzhak of Berditchev, *Sefer Kedushat Levi,* s.vv. "And this shall be for you the sign that I have sent you ..." (on Exodus 3:12).

2. Adin Steinsaltz, *The Thirteen Petalled Rose* (New York: Basic Books, 1980), pp. 131–32.

Judith A. Kates teaches Hebrew Bible and Jewish interpretive traditions at the Rabbinical School of Hebrew College and in many programs of adult learning. She is the coeditor (with Gail Twersky Reimer) of *Reading Ruth: Contemporary Women Reclaim a Sacred Story* and *Beginning Anew: A Woman's Companion to the High Holy Days.*

The Cry of Redemption

Judith A. Kates

It came to pass in the course of those many days that the king of Egypt died. The children of Israel sighed because of their bondage, and they cried out, and their cry rose up to God because of the bondage.

Exodus 2:23

My grandfather and teacher commented that until the king died they were so deeply sunk in exile that they did not even feel it. But now the process of redemption began, and they became aware of their exile and started to sigh. This is also the meaning of [the verse:] "I will bring you forth from beneath the sufferings of Egypt" (Exodus 6:6), meaning that [Israel] will no longer be able to put up with the ways of Egypt.

Surely there are several rungs in each exile. "He brings forth the prisoners"; "He delivers the humble"; "He helps the poor"—these are three different aspects [of redemption from exile].

The middle rung [comprises] those who are prisoners in exile; they are unable to broaden out that point of divine life that is within them. They need to be brought forth from that prison. "The humble" are the righteous; they themselves are not really in exile, but they remain there only for the common good. Such was the case with Moses, who had already been a shepherd. He was prepared for redemption. In essence he was no longer in exile at all, but was there just to redeem Israel. The same was true of the light in those seventy souls who came into Egypt; they were there just to make for redemption. This is "He delivers the humble." But "He helps the poor" refers to those lowly ones who do not yet even feel their exile; they are in need of the greatest salvation. This is the beginning of redemption: "I will bring you forth from beneath the sufferings of Egypt."

This is why there are four terms for redemption [mentioned in the Torah. Those are three, and the fourth is] "I will take you as My people" (Exodus 6:7). This is the purpose of redemption, the uplifting that was the reason for the entire exile.

Something like this is true of every exile. But more than that, all these rungs seem to exist in every person as well. Every Jew has some inner place in which he is a free person. This is especially true since we have already come out of Egypt: now there is surely something free in every Jew. This helps the person to prepare for redemption. That which is true of the people as a whole is true of each individual person as well.[1]

RABBI YEHUDAH LEIB ALTER OF GER, *SEFAT EMET*

Here the Sefat Emet responds to the questions implied in the classic midrash on this passage in Exodus (*Shemot Rabbah* 1:34–35): Why does the Torah, after two full chapters narrating the oppression and destruction wreaked on the people of Israel by the death-dealing king of Egypt, suddenly let us hear their response? Why is the notice of the king's death immediately followed by their "groaning" and "crying out"? And why does this generate a response from God? What has changed in an apparently endless unfolding of deadlocked time (*bayamim harabim hahem*, "during those many days" [Exodus 2:23])?

In the midrash, the Rabbis imagine a series of external events so extreme that the people are driven to the anguished groans of those wounded unto death (Ezekiel 30:24). When we are told that the king of Egypt "died," it really means that he was struck with *tzara'at* (skin scale disease), which in Numbers 12:12 is described as being "like a dead person." The cure prescribed by the king's magicians: bathing in the blood of 150 newly slaughtered Hebrew children every morning and evening. This horror generates the outcry of a heretofore silent people. This in turn arouses an entirely gracious response from God. God not only miraculously cures Pharaoh, ending the slaughter, but also turns God's full attention to the suffering people. God begins the work of deliverance despite the fact that they were at this point unworthy of salvation.

According to *Shemot Rabbah* and other classical midrashim, the people "could not appeal to any good deeds for the sake of which they merited deliverance."

The Rabbis suggest that the people's silence under oppression has reflected not only endurance of what has become long-standing trouble (*tza'ar*), but even acceptance. They take no initiative (the midrashic phrase is literally "there were no good deeds in their hands") to counter the regimen imposed on them. Nor can they even envision a moral universe in which the term *ma'asim tovim* (good deeds) could have meaning.

In the midrashic imagination, what jolts them from passivity is the torturers' extremity. When they experience themselves as in their death throes, they call out in a way that arouses God. Yet the emphasis remains on powers external to the people. God is the only subject of a powerful series of verbs that lead from perception to understanding to intimate knowledge and experience (*va-yeida Elohim* [Exodus 2:25]), the basis of God's saving acts.

The Sefat Emet, quoting his grandfather Rabbi Yitzchak Meir, moves the response to the midrashic questions inward. The people's silence, for him, reflects apathy—an inability or unwillingness to feel. He suggests that if we allow ourselves to feel at all, that will inevitably involve feeling pain, unsatisfied desire and longing, and loss, all of which he considers as *galut* (exile). The ultimate exile is an exile from all those dimensions of ourselves that register as feeling, perhaps even consciousness (they were so deeply sunk in exile that they did not feel that they were in exile). Such is the condition of "the poor," those most fully suffused with the condition of exile, who require "the greatest salvation."

The Sefat Emet also presents this as a stage in the process of redemption revealed in the Torah narrative. This is where the children of Israel began, not "feeling" the exile. What changes? Why the juxtaposition of "the king of Egypt died" and "the children of Israel groaned"? Ingeniously, he suggests that the death of the king of Egypt can be understood as the death, the pushing out of existence, of the kingship of Egypt, the dominance of that state of apathy or perhaps fear of feeling that prevents what Avivah Zornberg calls "conscious alienation."[2] To become aware of the pain of one's existence, to resist assimilation into one's condition of need, pain, or suffering, is to begin a process of change.

The Sefat Emet calls this opening of awareness "a little bit of redemption" (*k'tzat g'ulah*). What seems especially daring and powerful to me here is precisely this naming of the inner movement that he sees in the Torah's narrative. When they (we) discern, become conscious, aware (*heivinu*) of the condition of *galut* (exile), the response is to take on the pain of that awareness, to take it in, to feel it in its fullness (he uses a reflexive form of the verb for groaning used in the Exodus verse—*hitanhu*). And this, he claims, is already a "little bit" of redemption. It is a small step of redemption that occurs within the self, the collective self of *b'nei Yisrael* (the children of Israel) in the Torah and all subsequent generations of their descendants, but also, as the Sefat Emet tells us explicitly, within every individual.

This inner movement is mirrored in God's movement toward us. The Sefat Emet juxtaposes to our verses Exodus 6:6, "I will bring you forth from beneath the sufferings [*sivlot*] of Egypt." His psychological reading of this verse—I will bring you out from your ability or willingness to endure (*lisbol*) the ways of Egypt—suggests an intimate connection between God's action (I will bring you out) and the inner reshaping of the human psyche.

But the sequence of verses in chapter two, which guides the Sefat Emet's teaching here, suggests, in his reading, that the inner transformation within the self is what arouses and enables the redemptive "help" of God. A willingness to take into the self the full awareness of what we lack, of our deficiency, our limitation, our vulnerability, our suffering, is the necessary first step in the process of redemption. What I find especially profound here is what seems almost paradoxical in twenty-first-century America, obsessed as we are with control and technological "fixes." The Sefat Emet's formulation is that genuine absorption of our fundamental condition of being in need, unable to control the world or to fix it in accordance with our desires—our "groaning"—is in itself *k'tzat g'ulah*—not simply the beginning of the process, but a small redemptive movement in itself.

He tells us that this applies to us both collectively and individually. I hear in this an essential teaching about what makes it possible for us to imagine a different, better condition and to undertake what is even more difficult—actually to desire change, to overcome the fear of change. His insight that it is possible to be so settled into inner exile as not to feel it as exile resonates on every level of our existence, from personal relationships to national and international politics.

Yet, while deepening the meaning of exile even beyond the horrors of the Rabbinic imagination, he also offers a larger scope for our own capacity for liberation. Hope in this *Sefat Emet* comes from a source different from the gracious, undeserved compassion of God asserted in many Rabbinic midrashim. Rather than coming from the external movement of God's mysterious attention to us, hope for divine redemptive energy is intimately connected to human struggle. We, in our very vulnerability and suffering, can have the capacity for an inner transformation that can arouse response from God.

Notes

1. Rabbi Yehudah Leib Alter of Ger (d. 1905), *Sefat Emet, Shemot* 1 (2:18), trans. Arthur Green, *The Language of Truth: The Torah Commentary of the Sefat Emet* (Philadelphia: Jewish Publication Society, 1998), pp. 81–82.
2. Avivah Gottlieb Zornberg, *The Particulars of Rapture: Reflections on Exodus* (New York: Doubleday, 2001), p. 33.

Reb Mimi Feigelson is an Israeli Orthodox rabbi. She is the *mashpiah ruchanit* (spiritual mentor) and lecturer in Rabbinic literature and Hasidic thought at the Ziegler School of Rabbinic Studies of American Jewish University in Los Angeles. She is the former associate director of Yakar in Jerusalem and is an international teacher of Hasidism and spirituality.

"All This and Maybe"

The Doubting Servant

MIMI FEIGELSON

"And God spoke to Moses, saying: Take [*naso*] also the sum of the sons of Gershon ..." (Numbers 4:21–22).

And those that erected the Place [the *Mishkan*, the Tabernacle] were Gershon, Kehat and Merari, Moses, and Aaron and his sons. The sons of Kehat are the Masters of the Torah, for they carried the Ark; for they knew the law of the Torah in every situation they confronted. The sons of Gershon are the Masters of Trepidation, for they carried the fabrics that covered the *Mishkan* like the sky, and the hooks that appeared in the *Mishkan* like stars, and this alludes to trepidation. The sons of Merari are the Masters of Commandments [*Mitzvot*] and Good Deeds, for they carried the planks of the *Mishkan*, which allude to practical *mitzvot* that every Israelite has an under-standing of.... And though they all had of these good qualities, each one of them stood out in one quality more than his fellow.

The reason for "also" regarding the sons of Gershon, which is different than the sons of Kehat, is because *naso* alludes to outstandingness [in Hebrew the root *n-s-a* can mean "to count, lift up, elevate"]. The sons of Kehat reached a sense of pride, for they put themselves in doubtful and trying situations. As it says, "and to the sons of Kehat he did not give, for they carried their holy service on their shoulders," meaning they experienced endurance by virtue of putting themselves in doubtful situations.... But the sons of Gershon, their lot was to be in a state of trepidation in the presence of God and to distance themselves from doubt. Any place where they encountered something that was not clear they would withhold from action. They always walked in assurance, therefore it says "also." God testifies that they also have endurance by virtue of removing themselves from doubt, and they too render outstandingness....

Regarding the sons of Kehat and Merari it says "by the hand of Moses" but in regard to the sons of Gershon it does not say "by the hand of Moses." For Moses alludes to clear wisdom and intention for the sake of Heaven. The integrity and strength of the sons of Kehat was drawn from their good intentions. The integrity and strength of the sons of Merari was drawn from the clarity of their actions to all that observed them. But there is a lack of clarity regarding the sons of Gershon. Their lot was that of trepidation and they always removed themselves from doubtful situations. But, perhaps they are holding back in a place where God has actually commanded action. It is for this that at the conclusion it is said in regard to all of them, "in the hand of Moses," that they are all refined according to God's will.[1]

RABBI MORDECHAI JOSEPH LEINER, *MEI HASHILOAH*

Rabbi Mordechai Joseph Leiner of Ishbitza (d. 1853),[2] also known by the title of his book, *Mei HaShiloah*, has maintained his reputation as a radical antinomian, as a noted iconoclast, and as an uncompromising determinist since the publication of his commentary on the Torah and the Talmud.[3]

While there is no doubt of his place in the Hasidic library, and the Ishbitza-Radzhin dynasty as a community that continues to thrive even today, it is noteworthy that the vocabulary he uses is not common in the Hasidic milieu. It is not that you will not find him touching upon *devekut* (cleaving to God) or *kavanah* (contemplative intention), for example, but it is rather the uniqueness of concepts such as *safek* (doubt) and *ratzon HaShem* (God's will) that claim centrality in the Ishbitzer's theology and therefore demand our attention.

The conviction that underlies both of these terms steers us away from what can be considered as normative Rabbinic Judaism: a system that is founded on a collective revelation at Sinai, and hence a collective obligation to manifest the specific divine calling as it was given. The Ishbitzer Rebbe diverts us from a normative mode of behavior based on Torah and *mitzvot* (commandments). Similarly he diverts us from a system that enables community to evolve around a given body of knowledge and set of rules, as well as social hierarchy based on Torah knowledge and definable piety.

For the Ishbitzer Rebbe, *safek* and *ratzon HaShem* immediately remove us from the realm of the collective and position us in the heart of the individual, the intellectual, emotional, intuitive domain of each and every person as a unique manifestation of God. The basic understanding and fulfillment of the *mitzvot*, the realm of the religious life that we all share, is only the *beginning* of the religious quest. It is never, for him, the goal of this religious endeavor. The ultimate questions that the Ishbitzer *hasid* (disciple) must ask include, among others: "What is God's will at this moment?", "How does God perceive this specific situation, and how am I asked to respond right now?", and "Why am I confronted with this encounter, and what is it that God is really showing me?"

Ratzon HaShem symbolizes a divine revelation that is personal, continual, ever evolving, and changing! The consistency in adherence that is called upon in this school of thought is flexibility, not rigidity. The source of authority is individual, as it is derived from a personal understanding or intuition of God's will. It is not rabbinic and collective. The biblical figure of Jacob's son Judah symbolizes, in the Ishbitzer's reading of the Torah, the one who manifests such a practice. He is the one who continuously looks up to God to understand what is being asked of him at any given moment. Even in the realm of sin and transgression a person can experience the fulfillment of God's ultimate will!

Though the Ishbitzer does not use the kabbalistic/Hasidic formula "There is no place empty of Him and the whole world is filled with His glory" (*Leit atar panui minei u'melo kol ha'aretz kevodo*), he presents a radical theocentric philosophy in which all that the human experiences is but a prism of God's will. Even that which we experience as free will only has existence in the realm of human consciousness, but never in the domain of the divine reality!

It is from within the understanding of the parameters of such a theology that the centrality of *safek* (doubt) emerges. More often than not, doubt is something that needs to be overcome when engaging in a relationship with God. The fact that we are commanded to believe in God (according to some readings of the 613 *mitzvot*) means that doubt can be seen as sinful. But for the Ishbitzer Rebbe doubt appears as an inevitable and necessary state in which to be. Doubt is the outcome of the human condition and the limitations of our minds—minds that are not able to hold on to duality or to the paradoxical as the definitive nature of the world. Rabbinic tradition chastises Jacob for attempting to live in a state of peace of mind. This is undesirable to God in our earthbound lives. It is from within the realm of the not-knowing that God becomes known!

It is from within the process of questioning that God's inner intentions are unearthed. A common term that the Ishbitzer Rebbe appears to have adopted from *Sefer Yetzirah* 1:5 (The Book of Creation) is *omek* (depth). Embracing a life defined by *omek* introduces a subterranean power that is seldom visible to the human mind and eye. The religious journey is one that contains more doubt than certainty and more questions than answers. It is not about reconnecting to a moment in history that represents God's true manifestation in the world, but rather demanding that we seek a new voice of God and a new path that has never been taken. The paradoxical existence that the Ishbitzer hurls us into is his expectation that we do this while simultaneously living a life of unwavering commitment to Torah and *mitzvot*.

The time has now come to meet the three primary representatives of our teaching, the three sons of Levi: Gershon, Kehat, and Merari. Each one of them manifests a different way to serve God. These three individuals, as read by the Ishbitzer Rebbe, are manifestations of different elements of a human being. They are external representations of different aspects of our being. The three sons of Levi were responsible, the Torah teaches us, for the transporting of the *Mishkan* (Tabernacle) from place to place as the Israelites wandered through the desert. The Ishbitzer sees a direct correlation between the part of the *Mishkan* that they were carrying and the manner in which they carry their relationship to Torah and *mitzvot*. He is asking us to ask ourselves questions about the way we carry ourselves and our relationship with God. How do we walk with God in God's world? How do we wander through the desert of life? Though the Ishbitzer offers equal representation to all three brothers, it is clear that there is one that he favors and one that he sees as more challenged.

Kehat, the Master of Torah, is the son who can be seen as a true Ishbitzer *hasid*. His sons are the ones who carry the Ark containing the Torah on their shoulders without the help of oxen (oxen were given to his brothers to transport their appointed parts of the *Mishkan*). Kehat symbolizes those who have learned and refined themselves to the point that they do not need mediators in the attempt to understand God's will in different situations. They are the ones who have mastered the Torah in such a way that regardless of the situation in which they find themselves, they will always have a Rabbinic solution. No matter what the situation appears to be, they will always be able to decipher God's will in that moment. They derive their strength from being able to function in the realm of doubt; they are strengthened by walking in uncharted territories. They proceed with assurance that they will always be able to claim God's will.

Merari is the Master of the *Mitzvot* and Good Deeds. His sons carry the poles of the *Mishkan*. They carry the part that holds the foundation in a way that is revealed to all. Merari is the son who lives life at face value. He does not put himself in questionable situations, but nonetheless will take advantage of what life has to offer as it naturally unfolds. You will never find yourself puzzled as to what Merari is doing. He follows the *halakhah* (Jewish law) with a sense of ease. There is no magical ecstasy in Merari's religious life, but there is no agony either. The children of Merari do what they are told to do but do not go beyond appropriate boundaries. Their assurance is derived from their knowledge that they have shunned the realm of doubt and walked simply in the presence of God.

Gershon, the third son, is the Master of Trepidation. He lives in a state of spiritual anxiety. His sons carry the fabrics that (likened to the sky) cover the *Mishkan* and their hooks (likened to the stars). They represent those that live in utmost fear of transgressing the *mitzvot*, of not fulfilling God's will as expressed in the Torah. The sons of

Gershon are those who will never venture into the world for fear of what they will find, for fear of not knowing what to do. Ironically, in their attempt to steer away from doubt, they are plagued with doubt. They question whether they are holding back in a place where God is really asking them to take action.

As one who has lived most of her life in Israel, where "everyone who is anyone" makes their way to India after the army or before college, I love to use the following example when thinking of the paradigm presented here. The Kehat travelers are the travelers who go off by themselves, carrying with them a sack of assurance that no matter where they are, they will be all right. They will know what kind of questions to ask regarding the food preparation in the vegetarian restaurants so they will have no problem regarding eating kosher food. They know to identify what they regard as idol worship in a way that will enable them to avoid certain places. They will know how to manage on Shabbat. The Merari travelers say, "It cannot be that God created a beautiful and fascinating place like India that I should not see it, but I will go on an organized kosher trip. This way the organizers will take care of kosher food, we will not go to questionable locations, and we will all stop at the right time and in the right location for Shabbat." And our Gershonites will, clearly, stay home, since they know that once you are on the road, there are no promises as to what you will find and what kind of compromises may be asked of you.

Alongside the theological and religious realm there are many ways to apply the Ishbitzer's paradigm and adapt it to our lives.[4] One may ask whether this is a matter of temperament. Are we born as one or the other, or perhaps is it evolutionary? In our spiritual journey, do we evolve from one identity to the next? Do we start out as Gershon and work our way through Merari until we reach the promised peak of Kehat? Do we vacillate in different chapters of our life between these different modes of being?

I believe that there is one place where these three types truly do meet. They meet in the realm of doubt! They *all* carry a sense of existential doubt regarding the manner with which they walk in God's world and serve their Creator. Throughout his writing, the Ishbitzer Rebbe warns us to not put ourselves, from the outset, in questionable situations. The Kehat state is something that "falls upon us," not something to be sought out. It tells us that there too danger is lurking. It is possible that Kehat will not know what to do. It is possible that Kehat will actually fall, albeit unwillingly, into the pit of transgression. This is his doubt.

The doubt of his brothers we have already seen. Merari's angst and self-doubt are fueled by virtue of living a life that knows no struggle and questioning. Merari asks, "What is the value of such a life? What will happen when I am confronted with a Kehat moment—will I know what to do? If my life is so obvious and explainable to anyone who observes it, where is my uniqueness and individual voice?"

The Ishbitzer voices Gershon's doubt. "Am I holding back in situations in which God truly wants me to participate?" One can imagine Gershon plagued by Rav's statement (Jerusalem Talmud, the last lines of Tractate *Kiddushin*): "One will be accountable in the future for all that their eye has seen and they did not eat from." In his comment on a verse from Leviticus 26:3 ("If you follow my laws and faithfully observe my commandments ..."), the Ishbitzer Rebbe leaves us with no doubt as to the essence of doubt in a created world. If there is something that we share with our Maker it is that we both dance with doubt! From our perspective, the Ishbitzer tells us that even if a person was to observe all of the *Shulhan Aruch* (the sixteenth-century code of Jewish law), they still would not know if they aligned themselves with the depth, the *omek* of God's will. That is the human "*if*." From God's perspective, God sits in prayer, praying that we understand the depth of God's will. God too, in God's encounter with human beings, sits in doubt as to the nature of the encounter. God asks, "Will I be seen, will I be understood?" It is in the music of the doubt that God and human beings dance together.

Rabbi Mordechai Joseph leaves us with more questions than answers. How does such a perspective influence our theology? How does it alter our religious path? What does it mean to never truly know in regard to the One who cannot be known? How do we participate in community even as we embrace a life of doubt?

Notes

1. The first volume of *Mei HaShiloah* was published in 1860; the second volume appeared in 1922 and was described by Leiner's grandson as the more radical in

content of the two. All references are to the edition published in New York by Sentry Press, 1984. This passage is found in portion *Naso*, p. 47.

2. Rabbi Mordechai Joseph was introduced to the Hasidic world by his teacher Rabbi Menahem Mendel of Kotzk (d. 1859). At first they spent five years together in Tomashov, after which they were together for nine years under the tutelage of Rabbi Simcha Bunim of Peshischa. Upon the latter's death, Leiner continued to study with the Kotzker Rebbe until they parted in 1840. In Ishbitza he held his own "court" until his death. Upon his death, his son, Rabbi Ya'akov Leiner, inherited his position and moved the community to Radzhin.

3. For further reading, see Morris Faierstein, *All in the Hands of Heaven: The Teachings of Rabbi Mordecai Joseph Leiner of Izbica* (Hoboken, N.J.: Ktav, 1989), as well as Shaul Magid, *Hasidism on the Margin: Reconciliation, Antinomianism, and Messianism in Izbica/Radzin Hasidism* (Madison, Wisc.: University of Wisconsin Press, 2003).

4. I have in mind, for example, different styles of parenting, from exceedingly strict parenting to an approach that allows for a great amount of autonomy. Or, for example, with respect to different ways that people deal with obesity, these three models can be translated as a means to deal with their situation. Kehat says, "I've read all the books; I know how to create a diet for myself that will work." Merari will go to Weight Watchers, counting points as a way of asserting independence within a structure. Gershon will go to Overeaters Anonymous and swear to abstain from sugar for the rest of his life.

Yehonatan Chipman, an Orthodox rabbi, lives in Jerusalem, where he works as a professional translator of academic Jewish texts. He is currently writing his first book on Jewish religious thought.

Rabbi Nahum of Chernobyl and "Second Maturity"

YEHONATAN CHIPMAN

Our Sages taught: "There is no difference between the first *Adar* and the second *Adar* except for the reading of the *Megillah* and gifts for the poor" [Babylonian Talmud, *Megillah* 6b].[1] For in man's physical being there is the matter of first gestation and second gestation, first maturity and second maturity. The first gestation occurs in his mother's womb, for there too godliness is with him; as our Rabbis said: "There is a candle lit over his head, and he sees from one end of the world to the other ... and he is taught the entire Torah" [Babylonian Talmud, *Nidah* 30b]. But once he emerges into the air of the world, even though he reads [Scripture] and studies [Mishnah], he is still considered a minor until he is thirteen years and one day, when he is called an adult in every respect ... for he does not attain complete knowledge [i.e., religious consciousness] until he is thirteen years and a day. For even though there are minor children who are very astute and have extraordinary knowledge of Torah, in any event this is not considered [true] knowledge until they have attained the years of maturity—and this is called first maturity ... for the essence of knowledge is to know the Creator, may He be praised, and to be able to unite the blessed Holy One and His *Shekhinah*....

But even though a person attains his [formal] majority in the thirteenth year, this is not true maturity, for he subsequently falls away from this knowledge, for "seven times the righteous man falls and gets up" [Proverbs 24:16]—but thereafter he returns to his former knowledge. And this is called second maturity. But this second maturity is never truly complete, for a person always falls down and then returns to this second knowledge.

But in the future that is to come [i.e., the Eschaton], second maturity will be complete, for "the earth will be filled with knowledge of the Lord [like water running down to the sea]" [Isaiah 11:9]. As our Rabbis said: "The world to come is not like this world. In this world I [i.e., My Name] am written with YH and I am pronounced with AD [i.e., the name Adonai used in our prayers and Torah reading]; but in the future to come, I shall be written with YH and pronounced with YH" [Babylonian Talmud, Pesahim 50a]. For in this world we do not have full knowledge, as of the second majority; even though there are righteous men in every generation by whose means the Creator, may He be praised, imbues His Shekhinah among us, through the knowledge that they have; their knowledge is incomplete to understand and to know God clearly. For they do not attain the essence of His unique Name, but only in the sense of His being the Lord, that He is great and masterful, the essence and root of all worlds, powerful and sovereign over all. But we are unable to understand the true meaning of His unique Name; the mind cannot apprehend it at all. But in the future to come, "they shall see eye to eye when God returns to Zion" [Isaiah 52:8]....

Now this first gestation and maturity is called the first Adar, and this second gestation and maturity is called the second Adar—that is, the first Aleph dar and the second Aleph dar [reading the name of the month as Aleph—i.e., God, the Aleph of the universe; dar, dwells—i.e., the Divine dwelling within man]. For wherever he goes, God is with him, even in the time of his first minority and smallness; and concerning this our Rabbis said: "A candle is lit over his head ... and he is taught the entire Torah." All the more so once he has emerged into the world and learns the letters of the Torah, and thereafter when-

ever he learns and understands the Torah, even in the days of
his second smallness when he has fallen from knowledge.[2]
RABBI MENAHEM NAHUM OF CHERNOBYL, ME'OR EINAYIM

Religious growth—the winding and often unpredictable path leading to God-consciousness and to awareness of one's own task in
life—is a central concern of Hasidic thought. These issues are high-
lighted in the passage above from Rabbi Nahum of Chernobyl's *Me'or
Einayim*. R. Nahum Twerski (d. 1797), a disciple of both the Baal
Shem Tov and the Maggid of Mezritch, was one of the most incisive of
the early Hasidic masters, as well as the forebear of several Hasidic
dynasties.[3]

The Rabbi of Chernobyl presents here a fascinating model of religious growth. From a strictly halakhic viewpoint, the child is considered an adult at the age of thirteen, obligated to perform *mitzvot* and
considered an autonomous legal personality. From that point on, his
formal obligation remains the same throughout his life. But Hasidism
is concerned less with formal legal categories and more with religious
experience and consciousness, *da'at*. Hence, formal obligation in
mitzvot, religious behavior, is merely a beginning.

Rabbi Nahum presents a map in which all of adult life is seen as
"second gestation," a time of constant ascent and descent: the person
attains a certain level of religious consciousness, but then falls from
that level; from there he attempts to ascend again, gradually integrating the knowledge and insights he has attained to reach an ever higher
level. This unending process is often referred to in Hasidic and kabbalistic texts as *ratzo va'shov*, "running back and forth" (Ezekiel 1:14).
But, hopefully, religious life is not merely an oscillation between highs
and lows, but also a process of gradual growth, a slow upward spiral,
in which each stage in the process leads to a new insight, a new stage.
The ultimate goal, called "second majority," is never fully reached in
this world, but is an eschatological goal—a target that may be envisioned, but only attained in the days of the Messiah.

In the second half of this passage, R. Nahum elaborates upon this
future messianic consciousness. His central metaphor is the Rabbinic
saying that, whereas today God's name is spoken differently than the
manner in which it is written, in the future it will be spoken as it is

written. Today, the holy name of *YHVH* is never pronounced, but in the synagogue we use the name *Adonai*. The euphemism *Adonai* used today in worship addresses God as Lord and Master; our religious consciousness is based upon seeing Him as a king or father figure, the supreme authority who commands and judges, who metes out reward and punishment, life and death. Thus, I would add, obedience is the paradigmatic religious virtue, as implied by the very semantics of the word *mitzvah*, meaning "commanded action."

In messianic consciousness, by contrast, the model is based upon the name *YHVH*. The Chernobyler describes the meaning of this holy, unique name as beyond human comprehension. I think that the Chernobyler is suggesting that this ineffable name (containing no consonants) alludes to the notion of God as Being: the name *YHVH* is derived from the root *hvh*, "being." The implication is that God is everywhere, that God Himself encompasses all of Being. Perhaps, then, the messianic insight to which the master hardly dares allude is the mystical consciousness of God as Being: one that is attained by only a very few righteous people possessing sublime consciousness, and even then only imperfectly—but, in the future, it will be the legacy of all.

But what is it about this consciousness that the Chernobyler finds too dangerous to say explicitly? Judaism, as a path deeply rooted in and expressed in law, is filled with distinctions: Sabbath and weekday, meat and milk, man and woman, permitted and forbidden. If one fully embraces the radical unity of all Being, then these distinctions themselves become relative: the same God who made Israel also made the gentile nations; He who made the pure also made the impure; and He who created the Torah with its numerous commandments also, in the final analysis, created the delight inherent in certain acts of sin! The prophet Isaiah dared to say that God "makes peace and creates evil" (45:7), but the Rabbis, in adapting this phrase for the prayer book, softened it to "creates everything."

Such an approach can easily slide into antinomianism; moreover, we must remember that R. Nahum lived barely a hundred years after the Sabbatian movement, and fifty years after the openly antinomian Frankist movement, so that the great upheavals these created in Jewish life were much with him.[4] Hence, to maintain a traditional understanding of Torah as law and discipline, as an ethical approach to life, while accepting an all-embracing monism in which even the differences between good and evil become blurred, requires a very special type of consciousness possible to only a very few.

Therefore, for R. Nahum and his Hasidic colleagues, *halakhah* (as the root meaning of the word *hlk*, "to go," indicates) is seen as the guide along the winding road of life of the God seeker. If Judaism, like the ladder in Jacob's dream, is grounded in the earth but reaches up to the heavens, *halakhah* serves both to ground our worldly existence and to help us ascend to the heavens. *Halakhah* aids people in refining themselves and in participating in the creation and sustenance of sacred community. It is in this context that one seeks to expand his consciousness (*da'at*), recognizing God not only as *Adonai*, but also as *YHVH*. This ongoing, spiraling journey to "second maturity" is our life's work; it is an undertaking whose complete fulfillment necessarily remains beyond our grasp, but which offers us glimpses of the mystery, beauty, and complexity of Being.

Notes

1. *Adar* is the sixth month of the Jewish year. In leap years, a second month—a second *Adar*—is added to the calendar.
2. Rabbi Menahem Nahum of Chernobyl, *Me'or Einayim, Parashat Terumah* (Jerusalem, 1968), p. 116f.
3. See *Menahem Nahum of Chernobyl: Upright Practices, The Light of the Eyes,* ed. and trans. Arthur Green (Mahwah, N.J.: Paulist Press, 1982).
4. For information on these two antinomian movements see Gershom Scholem, *Sabbatai Sevi: The Mystical Messiah, 1626–1676,* trans. R. J. Zwi Werblowsky (Princeton, N.J.: Princeton University Press, 1973); and Pawel Maciejko, *The Frankist Movement in Poland, the Czech Lands, and Germany, 1755–1816* (New York: Oxford University Press, 2003).

PART THREE

Embodied Spiritual Practice

Gordon Tucker is senior rabbi of Temple Israel Center in White Plains, New York, and an adjunct assistant professor of Jewish philosophy at The Jewish Theological Seminary. He produced *Heavenly Torah: As Refracted through the Generations*, a translation of and commentary on Abraham Joshua Heschel's work on Rabbinic theology.

Taking in the Torah of the Timeless Present

GORDON TUCKER

"Remember what Amalek did to you...." (Deuteronomy 25:17). The holy Torah admonished us concerning four remembrances. That is, we are obligated to remember at all times four things that are at the root and basis of the faith. The first is to remember constantly and at all times the assembly of the chosen at Mount Sinai. [The other three are Miriam's punishment for her slander of Moses, the Sabbath, and the treachery of the Amalekites.] That is, each Jew must consider each and every moment as the one at which he is standing at Mount Sinai to receive the Torah. For people are subject to past and future, but with respect to the Blessed One there is no such distinction. And so each and every day God is giving the Torah to God's people Israel. Thus, whenever a person opens any holy book in order to learn from it, he must then recall the assembly at Mount Sinai and imagine that he himself is receiving the Torah from on high. In that way, he will come to a state of fear and trembling—just as the Torah was given in fear and trembling, as it is written: "All the people who were in the camp trembled" (Exodus 19:16). Indeed, a person should feel trembling in all his 248 organs, which are collectively called "the camp," as it is written, "Let your camp be holy" (Deuteronomy 23:15).

"Amalek came and fought with Israel at Rephidim…. But Moses's hands grew heavy; so they took a stone and put it under him [*tahtav*]" (Exodus 17:8, 17:12). It is written in the book *Asarah Ma'amarot* that had the Israelites not said to Moses, "You go closer and hear all that the Lord our God says, and then you tell us" (Deuteronomy 5:24) "lest we die" (Exodus 20:16), and had they rather listened to the Ten Utterances from the Blessed Presence directly, as it were, they would then not have had any need for the tablets of stone. Instead, the Blessed Presence would have bestowed on them a flow of great and pure wisdom, and such great insight that the very hands of Moses themselves would have virtually become two tablets. And then his ten fingers, five on the right side and five on the left, would have illuminated everything for Israel. In that way they would have been able to apprehend the complete Torah. But since they rejected this out of hand and wished to hear God's word through an intermediary, their insight was diminished, and they then needed two stone tablets.

In light of this, we can now give an explanation of the phrase "But Moses's hands grew heavy." It means to say that the Israelites introduced a burden and a heaviness into Moses's hands by their not wanting to hear directly from the Blessed Presence. That is, had they heard from the Blessed Presence directly, then Moses's hands would have illuminated them, as noted above. But now that they refused to do so, they introduced a heaviness into Moses's hands, and they came to need the two stone tablets. This is why it is written "they took a stone"—that is, the stone tablets—"and put it under him [*tahtav*]"—that is, *in place of his hands*, as also noted above. This also explains [the Talmud's statement (*Sanhedrin* 106a) that the name Rephidim means] "they slackened [*riphu*] their hands from holding the words of Torah." The explanation is this: "the hands *of their master Moses* became too weak; for they should have been able to apprehend all of the words of Torah from his hands."[1]

RABBI AVRAHAM YEHOSHUA HESCHEL OF APT, *OHEV YISRAEL*

In these related texts (both of which, interestingly, juxtapose the gift of Torah with the treachery of the Amalekites), the *Ohev Yisrael* makes two far-reaching points concerning the revelation of Torah.

The first of these—contained in the commentary on *Parashat Ki Tetzei*—concerns the question of whether the revelation of Torah was a unique moment in the history of the world. One of the standard themes of Rabbinic tradition has been that the words *kol gadol ve-lo yasaf* (Deuteronomy 5:19) are to be understood as meaning that at Sinai there was "a mighty voice that did not endure." Moreover, even such seemingly innocuous words as *eileh ha-mitzvot asher tzivah YHVH et Moshe ... be-har Sinai*—"these are the commandments that the Lord gave Moses ... on Mount Sinai" (Leviticus 27:34)— were glossed (in both the Talmud and the *Sifre*) to carry the meaning, "no new prophecy may be introduced from this time forth." Notwithstanding this prevalent and normative view, the Apter Rebbe informs us here that revelation, as an event between God and human beings, can have no privileged time or place. This is a consequence of his fundamental insight, stated with deceptive simplicity, that God, unlike human beings and every other creature of the physical world, is not subject to time. But note well: this is not simply an assertion that God is *sempiternal* (i.e., always exists, at every past, present, and future point in time). That would still allow the possibility that the always-existing God chose a particular moment of time to reveal the divine will. Rather, the assertion here is that God is *eternal*, in the sense of being independent of time, of being timeless. Our human memory may construct for us what we take to be unique moments in our history, with which we associate our great narratives of humans encountering God. But God's eternity (in the strong sense put forward here) entails the impossibility of excluding all other points in the human time line (and, it would seem, in human space as well) from hosting revelatory encounters. In other words, and to paraphrase S. Ansky only slightly: "every spot where a man raises his eyes to heaven is the foot of Mount Sinai," and "every day in a person's life is the day of revelation." This is consistent with the alternate understanding of *kol gadol ve-lo yasaf*—already ventured in Babylonian Talmud, *Sotah* 10b—as meaning "a mighty voice that did not *end*." And it clearly has significant implications for the idea that prophecy ceased as a mode of encountering God at some point in time.

The reality of prophecy is present here in another way as well. The first text ends with a startlingly vivid description of what a "Sinai experience" should be like. It should make "the entire camp tremble," which our teacher here takes to mean that it should penetrate one's entire person, one's entire body. And this is our transition to the second far-reaching idea about revelation, which is primarily contained in the second text, the commentary on *Parashat Beshallah*. Here the use of strikingly corporeal language to describe true revelation continues. The Ohev Yisrael paraphrases Rabbi Menahem Azariah of Fano's words in *Asarah Ma'amarot (Ma'amar Hikkur Din* 2:16) that if only the Israelites had been willing to listen more directly to God, rather than asking for an intermediary, the Ten Commandments would have gone directly into their ten fingers, just as they had into the ten fingers of Moses, and from there into their very existence and substance. They would have apprehended an intuitive truth, as it were (Menahem Azariah, in the passage paraphrased here, refers directly to Jeremiah's promise [31:33] that God's teaching would be "in our innermost being and inscribed within us"). The *embodiment* of revelation that is offered us in these remarkable depictions reminds us of the descriptions—in both Scripture and in later sacred literature—of the physical effects of prophetic encounters. This was to have happened, we are taught, with the Israelites at Mount Sinai. But it did not happen as it was intended to. Instead, our ancestors at Mount Sinai asked Moses to be their intermediary. And because of this unwillingness to listen to God directly, they made themselves dependent on inscribed tablets of stone. How different inert stone is as a receptacle for God's Torah from the living organic "innermost being" of the human receiver encountering the eternal and timeless! So this is how the Ohev Yisrael allegorized the narrative, in Exodus 17, of the struggle against the Amalekites. This apparently military tale leads us, after all, into *Parashat Yitro*, which in turn tells the story of the assembly at Mount Sinai. And thus, the Amalekite battle is taken here to be the background necessary for understanding why that sacred assembly resulted in a written Torah. During the battle, which took place at Rephidim, Moses's hands became unbearably heavy, and so they placed a stone *tahtav*—presumably "under him." But the word *tahtav* can also mean "in place of." And here comes the sweeping lesson. Moses's hands, which should have been the *model* for all Israel of how to embody God's word (in a person's ten fingers, and ultimately in the 248 organs), became too heavy to lift. For the Israelites, by demanding an intermediary, were asking those hands to do what *God* was supposed to do—to be the radiating source of Torah to every body and soul. And so they had to take stone—the stone tablets—and use them in place of the hands—their *own* hands, their *own* beings, their *own* intuitions, which should have been their true vehicle for understanding God's will. And that's how God's will ended up being imperfectly written on stone tablets.

We ought to read the *Ohev Yisrael* texts here as a reminder that an unyielding and uncompromising suppression of intuitive, prophetic encounters—no matter how "normative"—is in the end an undermining of the religious spirit and a thwarting of the divine will. Michael Fishbane has powerfully drawn our attention to the importance of distinguishing between God's all-encompassing, timeless Torah—the *torah kelulah*—and the written (and oral) projections of that heavenly Torah that are a necessity for human life, but cannot be timelessly true. He echoes our texts quite faithfully when he writes of the "ever-happening voice of God's *torah kelulah* saying, 'Here I am, also here.'"[2]

The double juxtaposition we have seen here of Amalek and revelation is meant to remind us of the dangers that lurk when we fear or dismiss religious experience, when we close our bodies off to the intimacy of feeling the Divine Presence, and when we are satisfied with intermediaries—be they great leaders or great texts.

Notes

1. *Sefer Ohev Yisrael* on *Parashiyot Ki Tetzei* and *Beshallah*.
2. Michael Fishbane, *Sacred Attunement: A Jewish Theology* (Chicago: University of Chicago Press, 2008), p. 160.

Chava Weissler is the Philip and Muriel Berman Professor of Jewish Civilization in the Department of Religion Studies at Lehigh University. She is the author of *Voices of the Matriarchs: Listening to the Prayers of Early Modern Jewish Women* and is completing a book on the Jewish Renewal movement in North America.

Holiness in the Kitchen

CHAVA WEISSLER

"As the first yield of your baking, you shall set aside a loaf [*hallah*] as a gift" (Numbers 15:20).

May my *hallah* be accepted as the sacrifice on the altar was accepted. May my *mitzvah* be accepted just as if I had performed it perfectly. In ancient times, [the offering] was the portion of the High Priest,[1] who caused the sins to be forgiven. So also may my sins be forgiven with this act, and may I be like a newborn child. May I be able to honor my dear Sabbaths and holidays. May God grant that I and my husband and my children be able to nourish ourselves. Thus may my *mitzvah* of *hallah* be accepted: that my children may be fed by the dear God, be blessed, with great mercy and great compassion. May this *mitzvah* of *hallah* be accounted as if I had given the biblical tithe. As I perform my *mitzvah* of *hallah* with might and main, so may the blessed God guard me from anguish and pain.[2]

SARAH BAS TOVIM, *SHLOYSHE SHEORIM*

As often as I can, especially on Fridays, I begin the day by mixing a teaspoon of yeast and a little sugar or honey into a cup or two of warm water in a large bowl. For about five minutes, the mixture sits on the counter, quiescent, and then suddenly it erupts into life. The dormant yeast, softened by the warm water and awakened by the sweetener, starts to metabolize the sugars. There is an ongoing burst of bubbles as the yeast cells create the substances—alcohol, carbon dioxide—that later will enable the bread to rise. Now it's time to add the flour, and from here, the recipes diverge. Will I bake a chewy, dark, multigrain bread plump with softened wheat berries? A fragrant honey-oatmeal sandwich loaf? On Fridays, which hallah recipe will it be? A sweet hallah rich with eggs, oil, and honey? A spicy Turkish pumpkin hallah, especially for Rosh Hashanah or Thanksgiving weekend? Or my favorite, the crisp-crusted, light-crumbed *churek* traditionally prepared for the Sabbath by the Jews of Rhodes?[3]

Taking *Hallah*

Whatever my choice, there is a holy moment that comes after the dough has risen, just before I shape the loaves. Like generations of Jewish bakers, women and men, I put my hands on the warm, living dough and say a blessing:

> Blessed are You, Lord our God, Ruler of the universe, who has made us holy by Your precepts, and commanded us to separate out the *hallah* portion from the dough.

Then, I scoop out a little piece of dough, about the size of an olive, and set it aside on a sheet of aluminum foil to be burnt later in the oven, a remembrance of the portion of baked goods given to the priests in biblical times. This portion is called *hallah* (a biblical Hebrew term for "loaf"), no matter what sort of bread dough it comes from.[4] Most home baking through the ages was done by Jewish women, who paid particular attention to this *mitzvah*. Separating the *hallah* portion of the dough became known as one of the three "women's commandments"; the other two are kindling the Sabbath lights and observing the menstrual purity laws within marriage. In the books of Yiddish prayers for women known as *tekhines*, published beginning in the late sixteenth century, the women's commandments, including the "taking of *hallah*," were an important subject.[5] Sarah bas Tovim, an author of *tekhines* who lived in Poland in the eighteenth century, explains to her readers that the laws of *hallah* are based on the biblical system of offerings and tithes given to the priests and to the poor. Since the destruction of the Temple, the practice of taking *hallah* is one of our few links to these ancient holy rituals. She specifies that the dough must be made with at least two quarts (some editions say three quarts) of flour to qualify for the *mitzvah*, and she gives the Hebrew blessing for the performance of the commandment. After a short Hebrew prayer asking God to rebuild the Temple, Sarah continues with the prayer cited at the beginning of this essay (translated from Yiddish).

What did this *mitzvah* mean to Sarah, and what might it mean to us? Sarah's prayer conveys the sense that by taking *hallah*, a woman can continue the ancient system of sacrifices and tithes and identify herself with those ancient Israelites who brought sin offerings and gave tithes to the poor, the priests, and the Levites. Can our act of taking *hallah* connect us to the holiness and splendor of the Temple in Jerusalem? Can this be another way of making our homes, kitchens, and dining tables "miniature sanctuaries," as suggested in the midrash (Rabbinic legend and teaching)? Also, in ancient times, properly performed sacrifices could ensure God's forgiveness for sin, but, as Sarah suggests, the taking of *hallah* can now substitute for those sacrifices. The moment of taking *hallah*, then, is a moment to take stock of ourselves, a moment to look back on where we have fallen short and to make a new beginning, "like a newborn child."

Because special attention is paid to bread (and all food) for Sabbaths and holidays, Sarah's prayer asks for the ability to honor these festive and holy times. In the eighteenth century, when this text was written, many Jewish families lacked the economic wherewithal to purchase special food for the Sabbath and could barely sustain themselves during the week. Bread (usually a whole-grain mixture of rye and wheat on weekdays) was literally the staff of life, the central food and most important part of the meal. Taking *hallah* is an essential part of preparation of all bread. Thus this *tekhine* prays for abundant food for the family and recognizes God as the source of all sustenance.

This sentiment is expressed in many contemporaneous texts from the Hasidic tradition that speak of the need to recognize the divine force that animates all life. Like Sarah bas Tovim, the Hasidic masters call us to pay close attention to the sacred dimension of our physical existence. The anonymous author of *Tzava'at HaRivash* (no. 109) articulates this point as follows: "In making use of your clothing, food, or other physical objects, seek to derive benefit from the divine force inherent in each of these things. For without this essential vitality, nothing could exist."

Recognizing that we depend on God for our nourishment is, for me, the heart of the *mitzvah* of taking *hallah*. For most of us, luckily, getting enough to eat is something we take for granted. But taking off a piece of dough and burning it in the oven reminds us of the point of sacrifices: to recognize that our bounty is a gift from God and that the conditions of our lives are ultimately beyond our control. My usual practice is not to burn the *hallah* completely, but to bake it in the oven, and then toss it into the backyard, where it can become food for squirrels, birds, or ants. I give back a little of my copious nourishment to other living creatures; this is my way of giving it to God.

Baking Bread

There is a midrash that the biblical matriarch Sarah separated dough for *hallah* and kindled Sabbath lights that burned from one Friday evening to the next. While she was alive, there was blessing in the dough and the lights, and the Divine Presence hovered at the entrance to her tent. After her death, the blessing and the Divine Presence departed. Only when Rebecca arrived as Isaac's bride, took up residence in Sarah's tent, and resumed Sarah's practice did they return.[6] An anonymous *tekhine* from the seventeenth century recalls this generational transition when speaking of the dough of Sarah and Rebecca.

This she says when she puts the Sabbath loaf into the oven:

> Lord of all the worlds, in Your hands is all blessing. I come now to honor Your holiness, and I pray You to give Your blessing on what I bake. Send an angel to guard the baking, so that everything will be well baked, will rise nicely, and will not burn, to honor Your holy Sabbath (which You have chosen that Your people Israel may rest thereon) and over which one recites the holy blessing—as You blessed the dough of Sarah and Rebecca our mothers. My Lord God, listen to my voice, for You are the one who hears the voices of those who call upon You with the whole heart. May you be praised to eternity![7]

The woman who speaks these words turns to God with her whole heart, asking for the blessing that has rested upon the bread of generations of Jewish women, descendants of Sarah and Rebecca. She understands the domestic task of baking bread as a sacred act, shared with the ancient matriarchs and guarded by angels. Can we, too, sense the holiness of our mundane kitchen chores and our connection to our forebears?

Baking bread is miraculous each time. We feel the life of the worlds under our hands in the living dough, a life in which we participate but that goes far beyond ourselves. We see the yeast come to life, feel the dough develop as we knead it, watch it grow and rise, and smell the wonderful aroma of the loaves in the oven. But baking bread is also a practice, and it takes practice. We have to learn how to judge the proportion of liquids and flours, the texture of the developing dough, the moment that the loaf is baked and not overbaked. This is a skill to master even now, when we have recipes, standardized yeast cultures, and ovens with thermostats.

Consider how much riskier baking bread was when none of those existed, and how much more it depended on years of practice, on a tradition of baking handed down from mother to daughter. Consider as well that baking bread, in the past, was not the occasional treat it may be today, but part of the time-consuming chore of food preparation for the family day in and day out. Most of us no longer devote our full days to food preparation for the family but squeeze it in among many other tasks. Can we still feel the miracle of the creation of sustenance in the daily rush to get dinner on the table or the weekly struggle to make *Shabbos*? Are we able to see our kitchens as holy, a place of blessing, worthy of angels? Can we turn, wholeheartedly, in the midst of the hurry, to praise God for the daily miracles of cooking, eating, and family gathering?

Notes

1. In fact, it was usually given to any local priest.
2. Sarah bas Tovim, *Shloyshe Sheorim* [The Three Gates], undated eighteenth-century edition, Jewish National and University Library, Jerusalem, *tekhine* pamphlet collection R41 A460, vol. 8, no. 26. For more on Sarah bas Tovim, see Chava Weissler, *Voices of the Matriarchs: Listening to the Prayers of Early Modern Jewish Women* (Boston: Beacon Press, 1998).

3. The recipe for pumpkin hallah is found in Gilda Angel, *Sephardic Holiday Cooking: Recipes and Traditions* (Mt. Vernon, N.Y.: Decalogue Books, 1986), p. 22; the recipe for *churek* is found in Maggie Glezer, *A Blessing of Bread: The Many Rich Traditions of Jewish Bread Baking around the World* (New York: Artisan, 2004), pp. 163–65. There are many recipes for sweet, rich *hallot*.

4. A discussion of the history and laws of "taking *hallah*" is beyond the scope of this essay. A good summary, from an Orthodox perspective, is found in Glezer, *A Blessing of Bread*, pp. 317–22. Most Orthodox authorities state that a large volume of dough made with about five pounds of flour and mixed with water or other specified liquids is required for the blessing to be halakhically necessary. I do not follow this requirement, and I separate *hallah* with a blessing from smaller amounts of bread dough. Also, I separate *hallah* just before shaping the loaves, while others do it as soon as the dough is mixed, before kneading and rising.

5. The Yiddish term *tekhines* is derived from the Hebrew word *tehinot*, which means "supplicatory prayers." To learn more about these prayers for women, see my *Voices of the Matriarchs*. To read translations of selected texts, see *The Merit of Our Mothers: A Bilingual Anthology of Jewish Women's Prayers*, ed. Tracy Guren Klirs (Cincinnati: Hebrew Union College Press, 1992); and Devra Kay, *Seyder Tkhines: The Forgotten Book of Common Prayer for Jewish Women* (Philadelphia: Jewish Publication Society, 2004).

6. *Bereshit Rabbah* 60:15.

7. *Tekhines* (Amsterdam, 1648), 5a.

Joel Hecker is associate professor of Jewish mysticism at the Reconstructionist Rabbinical College. He is the author of *Mystical Bodies, Mystical Meals: Eating and Embodiment in Medieval Kabbalah* and is currently preparing a translation of the *Zohar* on Song of Songs, Ruth, and Lamentations for volume eleven of *The Zohar: Pritzker Edition*.

Eating as a Spiritual Ecosystem

JOEL HECKER

"Moses spoke to the heads of the Israelite tribes … : If a man makes a vow … he shall not break his pledge; he must fulfill all that has come out of his mouth" (Numbers 30:2–3).[1] We begin with the teaching of the sages, of blessed memory, with regard to the nazirite: "'[The priest] shall make expiation on his behalf for the guilt that he has incurred …' (Numbers 6:11). But against whom did the person [nazirite] sin? Against himself: for he afflicted himself by abstaining from wine" (Babylonian Talmud, *Bava Kama* 91b). It is well known that the whole world and its contents "were created through the word of *YHVH* and all of its hosts through His breath" (Psalm 33:6), for it is through [divine] speech that all of reality—all things large and small—were created…. [*YHVH*] maintains and sustains them, as is written, "And You sustain them all" (Nehemiah 9:6).

If not for the *hiyyut* [life force] within an object, it would not exist….[2] [All things] come from the words that fell into this lower world as a result of the shattering [of the vessels] … from the sin of Adam. In the succeeding generations as well, there are countless sparks of fallen souls, garbed in the things of this world: in foodstuffs, drink, and the like…. For there is nothing in this world that does not bear a spark of holiness within, emanating from the speech of the blessed Holy One, sustaining it.

This [spark] is the taste—sweet to the palate—within the food, as is written, "Taste and see that *YHVH* is good" (Psalm 34:9). When you taste and see that something is good: that is *YHVH!* For He is the holy spark within that item, garbed in it. This is self-evident: After a person has eaten a certain food, the *hiyyut* remains within while the waste is cast out, without any *hiyyut*—it is useless and foul. For the essence of food nourishing a person, providing added energy, is the holy spark within that particular food, and *it* is the good taste that a person tastes in food and drink. Consequently, when a person eats a certain food, that spark is united to his *hiyyut,* and energy is added to it.

When one believes with … total faith that this spiritual food *is* divinity … and cleaves with all of one's being [to the] additional *hiyyut* supplemented through the holy spark that has come into the body … one brings that previously fragmented and exiled spark back to God…. [And] this brings Him great delight…. For this is the essence of our worship: to bring all of the holy sparks from the shells where they reside in fragmented form back to the domain of holiness, attaining holy ascent from their fragmented state.

This should be done especially [with regard to one's prayer and Torah study, for] all prayer and Torah uttered as a result of this [added] energy and life force are received from the taste of the food—the holy spark…. And when one unites one's speech to the holy speech, there is an ascent for that spark, for it, too, is the word of *YHVH*…. Everyone who worships *YHVH* must look at an object's inwardness so that all of one's actions will be done for the sake of heaven, in eating and drinking as well. This will raise the sparks of holiness from their fallen state—the dimension of slavery and exile—back to supernal holiness. This is achieved through the blessings uttered for that … food in which one accepts the sovereignty of the Creator….

Similarly for all things of this world, such as business matters, taking profits—it is all delight that comes from those same sparks designated for that person, garbed in the matter that has come before him…. A person may not impinge upon [a spark] prepared for one's fellow, for sparks appropriate for one person's soul root can only ascend by means of the person for whose soul root they are fit; for they are truly an aspect of that person's soul. This is the reason that one person has to travel to such-and-such a place while another person travels to another place—because of the conduct of the Creator.... [God] knows that spark fragments appropriate to one person's soul are garbed in a particular piece of food, or in a particular business deal, and the Creator ... causes events to transpire so that one will go to that certain place. [The Creator achieves this by] placing a desire in one's heart, cloaking the cause, necessitating travel to that place. The essential intention: one should eat, drink, or conduct business there, and through that action those sparks will ascend....

Therefore, everyone must pay attention, directing one's heart to see, for this is the mystery of the verse, "Know Him in all your ways" (Proverbs 3:6).... When a person pays attention to this matter he will know how the blessed Creator actually sustains him with divinity, as it is said. This is as is written, "... A human being does not live on bread alone, but may live on every utterance of YHVH" (Deuteronomy 8:3). This is the aspect of Speech that is garbed in that very thing and in that bread.... If this is the case, one who afflicts himself and causes himself distress by refraining from the goods of this world is called a sinner, as there is an opinion in the Talmud that one who sits fasting is called a sinner. For it [enjoyment of this world] is also service of YHVH just like Torah study, prayer, tefillin, and all of the commandments because it was through the Torah that the blessed Holy One created the world and through the Torah that He conducts the world. There is Torah in everything ... and each person who has faith must believe that there is nothing beyond service of Him, ... as long as it is according to the Torah, that which the Torah permits to eat and drink. As long as they are done for the sake of their Maker and not for personal enjoyment, but rather in the manner described—then this is all called pure worship.[3]

RABBI MENAHEM NAHUM OF CHERNOBYL, *ME'OR EINAYIM*

Divine Words descend, morphing into food, providing life-sustaining energy, which in turn transmutes into words, sustaining divinity itself. This teaching portrays a spiritual ecosystem in which the spiritual seeker can participate in a continuous cycle, sending the holiness embedded within our reality back upward with the proper spiritual intent.

Menahem Nahum Twerski of Chernobyl (d. 1797) was a student of the Maggid, Dov Ber of Mezritch, and the founder of the Chernobyl line of Hasidim. The passage above teaches about the practice of *avodah be-gashmiyut*, "worship through materiality." *Avodah be-gashmiyut* is the Hasidic term that refers to the mystical act of raising sparks contained within the physical world and restoring them to their source within the realm of divinity. Many Hasidic texts dealing with the topic refer to three areas in particular in which *avodah be-gashmiyut* can be practiced—eating, sexual relations, and commerce—but the vast majority explicate the dynamic regarding eating rather than the other two. The technical aspects of this approach to the material world originated in Lurianic Kabbalah, which stressed the importance of redeeming sparks trapped in the material realm, but in that context it was mostly in the course of ritual acts.[4] The material world was regarded as a world of *kelipot*, shells or husks that obscured the holiness within. Hasidism expanded the arena in which these holiness-redeeming practices could be performed to include all of material reality, excluding foods or practices deemed forbidden in Jewish law.

In Rabbi Menahem's text, the details of the practice are spare, but the meaning is front and center: through our most basic activities, with eating as a prime example, we are able to participate in the flow of Divine Being that underlies all of reality. The text begins by implicitly comparing our speech (the Torah portion of *Mattot* opens with the arcane details of uttering a vow) to God's, the medium for the creation of the world. Genesis 1 teaches that the world came into being through God's speech: "Let there be light," "Let there be a firmament," etc. Through the lens of Lurianic Kabbalah, the cosmic catastrophe engendered by Adam's sin caused the holy words that undergird reality to shatter, ultimately being cast into the materiality of this world.[5] It is at that point in the story of the creation of the cosmos that the Chernobyler interjects the anti-ascetic stance of the Rabbis. They assert that the sin offering brought by the nazir at the end of his tenure is commanded as an atonement for his refraining from enjoying wine, part of God's bounty in this world. As the text proceeds to explain, abstaining from wine signifies not only a rejection of material goods, but also marks a rebuff of divinity residing within this world.

The shattered words are the very life force, the vitality that animates all of creation. In their form as holy sparks, they inhabit and sustain all things—living and inanimate. In a potent assertion about the mysticism of eating, Menahem Nahum explains the line from Psalm 34:9, "Taste [ta'amu] and see that YHVH is good." The Hebrew word ta'amu bears an equivocal meaning, corresponding to both "taste" on the one hand and "consider" or "understand" on the other. The Hasidic writer capitalizes on the visceral meaning, stressing the experiential encounter. In a bold pronouncement, he states that the experience of the sweetness of the food is *itself* the experience of God. Holiness, divinity, and redemption are all realized when a person eats. There is a wide range of positions within Hasidism about the relationship of God's Being with the world, but it can often be described as a moderate pantheism, in which divinity and mundane reality are not poles apart; rather, our this-worldly reality barely conceals the holiness lying behind its veils. According to this perspective, all of reality contains holy sparks, or *hiyyut*, the sustaining divine power that courses through creation. Upon eating, a unification occurs within the body—for animals as with humans—in which the *hiyyut* contained within the food bonds with the *hiyyut* already residing within the diner's body. The spark of holiness that originated within the food boosts the eater's energy, providing continued sustenance, while the waste that is generated, lacking that holy life force, is cast out.[6]

Rabbi Menahem turns the simple act of eating into a spiritual practice by emphasizing that a transformation in the cosmos itself is achieved when eating is performed with the appropriate consciousness and faith. The practitioner must direct her attention to the flow of divine energy from the food into her body, thus causing an ascent of the holy spark within the food to its point of origin in God. The text elaborates how this system works. Words of speech, particularly that of prayer and Torah study, energized by the *hiyyut* in the food's sweetness, unite with divine speech located in the initial holy spark, causing that spark to ascend. Ultimately there is an identity of divine speech and human speech, with human speech participating in the continued circuit of holy overflow, proceeding downward, inward, outward, and upward.

Expanding the scope of our spiritual engagement with the world, the Chernobyler explains that *all* of our activities bear holy sparks, specifically designated for each of us alone. On the one hand, this suggests a high level of determinism—God is directing our every act, ensuring that appropriate sparks stream our way. From a religious existentialist perspective, however, this means that we must regard each moment of the day as uniquely ours, the one that we must crown because we are bound to it.

This is why the Rabbis frown upon the nazirite's asceticism, for such a person has neglected to participate in the spiritual ecosystem, the continuous and circuitous flow of holy language that sustains all things. In the mind of the Chernobyler, as in the mind of the literary artist, language is the ultimate vehicle of creation, instilling and sustaining Being itself. We are enjoined to attend to the linguistic substratum of all of existence, the holy language that underlies all, in order to bind ourselves to holiness at every turn. "Pay attention," Menahem Nahum is saying, "there is holiness inhabiting everything: your food, your drink, your job, your commute ..." The circle of holiness pervades not only every aspect of your daily activity, but the very fiber of your existence. The circle itself, though, depends on your attention, on your investment, on your mindful engagement at every moment.

Passive living is certainly possible, as we are all the beneficiaries of divine grace, and in our inevitable lapses of attentiveness to the blessings around us we are sustained nonetheless. When we heed the luminous letters and words that infuse our being, however, our own inwardness fuses with the divine inwardness that is shot through all of reality. When Hasidic thought speaks of raising sparks, part of the intent is that our consciousness as well as our surrounding environment be enhanced and expanded. Indeed, it is through this kind of engagement that, to use Martin Buber's language, our interactions cease to exist in the realm of I–It, now transpiring in the realm of I–Thou. Each moment becomes an opportunity for reflection upon the nature of our relationship to that item.

One way that this reflection can proceed concerns the economic and environmental nature of my relationship to this food. Regarding this apple before me, whose inner spark is personalized, belonging to me and me alone: How much gas was used to transport it to my kitchen? What kinds of labor practices were employed? Was the apple grown in a way that fosters the earth's sustainability, or is its main feature the grower's bottom line? How has this apple been manipulated to prolong its shelf life, and how does that impact its taste and nutrition? If, however, we're talking about my third piece of cake or "a last drink before hitting the road," a different series of questions will have to be asked, on whether the sparks in the cake and the drink do ultimately belong to me. Looking at the world in this way fosters not only spiritual consciousness but also an enhanced sense of responsibility for oneself, one's environment, and ultimately the world. Recognizing the depth that is treasured away in every bite and every sip, we must pause, give thanks, and note the wealth that surrounds and even pervades us.

The Chernobyler includes a rhetorical flourish—"There is Torah in everything"—as part of a picture of unmitigated devotion: "Each person who has faith must believe that there is nothing beyond service of Him." The conclusion of that same sentence, one that seems to herald a near-pantheistic picture, in which the world is saturated with Torah, divinity, and service of God, sounds a cautionary note: "as long as it is according to the Torah, that which the Torah permits one to eat and drink. As long as they are done for the sake of their Maker and not for personal enjoyment, but rather in the manner described—then this is all called pure worship." He enjoins us to remember that this discourse began with a sin offering and operates within a sensibility in which a moral order operates. There is holiness everywhere, he declares, but our behavior cannot be untrammeled. With a nervous look back at Sabbatianism,[7] Menahem Nahum is fully aware of the dangers that a hedonistic approach could bring to the practice of *avodah be-gashmiyut*. In our contemporary society, most of us live in a world unconstrained by the four ells (bounds) of the *halakhah*, certainly not enforced by civil or community authorities. We are left to our own devices as we seek to expand the realms where we discover holiness, while remaining conscious of the dangers of intoxication, recognizing that not all sparks are ours to be redeemed.

Notes

1. A note regarding gender in the translation: the present text was written by a Hasidic rebbe with a male audience in mind. I have attempted to limit the gender-specific references in the text but retained the masculine form when necessary to prevent awkward formulations.

2. The term *hiyyut* connotes the vitality that animates a person but also all things in this material world. It is common to all of reality and is a central feature of Hasidic pantheism.

3. Menahem Nahum of Chernobyl, *Sefer Me'or Einayim, Parashat Mattot* (Slovita, 1798), 92a.

4. The idea of eating as an avenue to knowledge of God can be found in earlier mystical literature, particularly that of Zoharic Kabbalah. See Joel Hecker, *Mystical Bodies, Mystical Meals: Eating and Embodiment in Medieval Kabbalah* (Detroit: Wayne State University Press, 2005). In early modern Kabbalah and Hasidism, see Louis Jacobs, "The Uplifting of the Sparks in Later Jewish Mysticism," in *Jewish Spirituality from the Sixteenth-century Revival to the Present*, ed. Arthur Green (New York: Crossroad, 1987), pp. 99–126. The most complete study of this theory and practice is Tsippi Kauffman, *In All Your Ways Know Him: The Concept of God and Avodah be-Gashmiyut in the Early Stages of Hasidism* [Hebrew] (Ramat-Gan: Bar-Ilan University Press, 2009).

5. Lurianic Kabbalah treats the formula of "Adam's sin" as shorthand for the cosmic catastrophe that is otherwise called the "breaking of the vessels." In other words, the story in Genesis 3 is not about the first transgression of God's will in the Garden of Eden; it is to be understood in symbolic terms, referring to the very possibility of this world withstanding God's Being.

6. One might contend that waste could also be recycled, but that's not how the author conceptualizes human waste.

7. In the 1660s much of the Jewish world was swept up in the belief that Sabbatai Zvi was the Messiah. His strange acts, including a range of violations of normative practice performed in the belief that it was time for the most hidden sparks to be redeemed, culminated in his forced conversion to Islam. This did not quell his most hard-core devotees who believed that this, too, was a sign of his commitment to raising holiness concealed. His spiritual heirs, most particularly the cult surrounding Jacob Frank, participated in a slew of forbidden hedonistic behaviors, relying on the same justification. The magisterial treatment by Gershom Scholem remains unrivaled: Gershom Scholem, *Sabbatai Sevi: The Mystical Messiah, 1626–1676* (Princeton, N.J.: Princeton University Press, 1973).

Daniel Matt is a scholar of Kabbalah with a particular expertise in the literature of the *Zohar*. He has published numerous books, including *The Essential Kabbalah*; *Zohar: The Book of Enlightenment*; *God & the Big Bang: Discovering Harmony between Science & Spirituality* (Jewish Lights); and *Zohar: Annotated & Explained* (SkyLight Paths). He has completed six volumes of the widely acclaimed annotated translation *The Zohar: Pritzker Edition*. This work has received various awards, including the Koret Jewish Book Award.

Loving God with the Evil Impulse

DANIEL MATT

[Rabbi El'azar said, *"You shall love YHVH your God]* with all *levavekha, your heart* [Deuteronomy 6:5]—with two hearts, namely, two impulses: one, the good impulse [*yetzer ha-tov*]; the other, the evil impulse [*yetzer ha-ra*]....

"How can a person love the blessed Holy One with the evil impulse?... Well, this is a greater service of the blessed Holy One, when the evil impulse is overturned by the love that one feels for [Him].... [T]his is true love of the blessed Holy One, since he knows how to draw that evil impulse to His service.

"Here is a mystery ... : [A]ctually, [the evil impulse] is doing the will of his Master! This may be compared to a king who had an only son, whom he loved exceedingly....

"In the king's abode, outside, was a harlot.... [T]he king said, 'I want to see my son's devotion to me.' He called for that harlot and said to her, 'Go and seduce my son.'...

"That harlot, what could she do? She went after his son and began embracing him, kissing him, seducing him with all kinds of enticements. If that son is worthy and obeys his father's command, he rebukes her, pays no heed to her, and thrusts her away from him. Then the father rejoices in his son and brings him into his palace, giving him gifts and presents and great honor. Who caused all this honor for that son? You must admit, that harlot!

"And that harlot, does she deserve praise for this or not? Surely she does, from every aspect. First, because she carried out the king's command; and second, because she brought upon the son all this honor, all this goodness, all this love of the king toward him....

"Were it not for this accuser, the righteous would not inherit those supernal treasures reserved for them in the world that is coming.... Therefore, the righteous should be grateful to him."[1]

ZOHAR 2:162B–163A

Rabbi El'azar quotes the famous line from the *Shema*: "You shall love *YHVH* your God with all your heart." In this verse, the word *levavekha*, "your heart," is spelled with a double *vet*, instead of *libekha* with one *bet*. Rabbi El'azar paraphrases the teaching of the *tanna* Rabbi Me'ir, who explains this peculiar spelling as indicating that you should love God "with both your impulses: *be-yetzer tov uv-yetzer ra* [with the good impulse and with the evil impulse]."[2]

But what can it possibly mean to love God with the evil impulse? The early Rabbinic sources do not clarify this provocative remark, but Rabbi El'azar says that by overcoming the evil impulse, you demonstrate your love for God and actually "draw that evil impulse to His service." Then he proceeds with a parable.

The king tests his son's love for him by sending a prostitute to try and seduce the prince. By thrusting her away, the son demonstrates his love for the king and his worthiness, thereby gaining a reward. But the son isn't the only one deserving of praise; the prostitute too has performed admirably, not only by obeying the king and fulfilling his command, but by testing the prince and enabling him to prove his virtue.

Similarly, you should be grateful to the evil impulse because it tests you, enabling you to wrestle with temptation and hopefully triumph over it. The appreciation of the evil impulse is, of course, limited: its value lies in the possibility of subduing it. You can express love for God with the evil impulse by defeating it. Yet the positive tone is remarkable. It is not enough to simply ignore or avoid the evil impulse; you have to face it and contend with it. Otherwise your love of God is incomplete.

We find a positive aspect of the evil impulse in earlier Rabbinic texts as well. For example, on the verse "God saw all that He had made, and behold, it was very good" (Genesis 1:31), Nahman (quoting Rabbi Shemu'el) comments, "*Behold, it was very good*—this is the evil impulse. Now, is the evil impulse *very good*? I am astounded! Well, were it not for the evil impulse, a man would never build a house or marry a woman or engender children." A variant reading adds: "... or engage in business."[3]

Here *yetzer ha-ra* is roughly the libido, expressing itself as desire, passion, and ambition, without which the world would remain unproductive and rather boring. Whereas the *Zohar* (although praising the evil impulse) recommends rejecting it, here it seems, rather, that you can serve God by drawing on the power of the evil impulse and channeling it creatively. Raw passion can animate the spiritual life. As one eighteenth-century preacher wrote, "*Yetzer ha-ra* is like fertilizer for the soul. As manure fertilizes the field, improving its produce, so the fruit of the righteous person, that is, *mitzvot*, are improved by *yetzer ha-ra*. This accords with the well-known principle *with all your heart*: with both your impulses."[4]

It is not enough to simply fulfill the commands of Torah. Only by pouring primal energy into religious practice can we animate the *mitzvot*. The wild flavor of *yetzer ha-ra* is an essential ingredient of holiness. This radical notion appears in a Hasidic interpretation of a passage from the Talmud: "The blessed Holy One said to Israel, 'My children, I created *yetzer ha-ra*, and I created Torah as its seasoning'" (*Kiddushin* 30b). Here in the Talmud the point seems to be that Torah can temper the dangerous effects of the evil impulse or serve as its antidote. But the Maggid of Mezritch (d. 1772) finds a more radical meaning: "The metaphor does not fit! Seasoning is added to meat, and the meat is the main dish, not the seasoning. Yet here God says that Torah is the seasoning! And so it is: *yetzer ha-ra* is the main thing. One has to serve God with the ecstasy drawn from *yetzer ha-ra*."[5]

The challenge is to convey passion and ecstasy without harming yourself or others. If *yetzer ha-ra* is libido, then perhaps *yetzer ha-tov* is conscience. To serve God with both impulses is to find the balance between libido and conscience—not simply repressing *yetzer ha-ra*, yet not allowing it to dominate. Too much spice can ruin any dish.

Let's turn back to the parable in the *Zohar*. Despite the positive aspect of *yetzer ha-ra*—that it enables a person to demonstrate his love of God—the message here is clearly to overcome this impulse. One must withstand its seductive power, not draw on it. The provocatively positive depiction of the prostitute does not disguise the fact that she must be rejected.

So, how should we deal with the raw power of *yetzer ha-ra*—by thrusting it away or by incorporating it? We find a clue in another Zoharic theme, an elaboration of a midrashic teaching about Satan and Yom Kippur. In the original ritual of Yom Kippur (described in Leviticus 16), one goat is sacrificed as a purification offering to God, while a scapegoat bearing the sins of Israel is sent off into the desert for the demon Azazel. According to a remarkable midrash, the goat of Yom Kippur is intended to preoccupy Satan: "They gave him a bribe on Yom Kippur so that he would not nullify Israel's sacrifice."[6]

The *Zohar* develops this one midrashic line and applies it to numerous other rituals and activities. By providing a portion to the demonic force, we ensure that it will be occupied, assuaged, and deterred from interfering in the realm of holiness.[7] What applies to the demonic personality Satan applies as well to the evil impulse, since according to the colorful Talmudic figure Resh Lakish, "Satan and the evil impulse ... are one and the same" (*Bava Batra* 16a).

I would suggest that there are different strategies for dealing with *yetzer ha-ra*. Sometimes, its seductive power must be rejected outright. At other times, its wild energy can be sublimated into virtuous action or creativity, thereby channeling its passion to goodness. In other cases, it should be "bribed" and pacified—given its due so that it no longer hinders virtue. None of these strategies is always ideal, and none can always succeed. It is too easy to justify bribing *yetzer ha-ra* by giving in a little, when selfish motives determine the whole transaction. Sometimes, sublimating an urge is impossible, and instead you are overtaken by it and dragged down. Sometimes repressing or subduing *yetzer ha-ra* is the best option, but if this becomes your only response, then such piety may turn into neurosis.

Learning how to wrestle with *yetzer ha-ra*—to deal with our desires, passions, and ambitions—is not an easy process, nor is it ever completed. All we can do is to keep trying: to practice loving and living with all our heart, with all our impulses. By employing various strategies, we can gradually learn what works and what doesn't, thereby cultivating practical wisdom. Through failing, we can discover how to succeed, because this is one of those things that "one cannot understand ... unless one has stumbled over them."[8]

Notes

1. *The Zohar: Pritzker Edition*, vol. 5, trans. and ann. Daniel C. Matt (Stanford, Calif.: Stanford University Press, 2009), pp. 439–43.
2. See *Tosefta Berakhot* 6:7; *Mishnah Berakhot* 9:5.
3. *Bereshit Rabbah* 9:7. The reference to engaging in business appears in the Paris and Oxford manuscripts, the first printed edition, and *Yalkut Shimoni*, Genesis 16.
4. Eliezer Lipman, *Tal Orot im Migdal David* (Vienna, 1792), 162b.
5. Cited in the name of the Maggid of Mezritch by Avraham Hayyim of Zlotshov, *Orah la-Hayyim* (Jerusalem, 1960), 25a.
6. *Pirkei de-Rabbi Eliezer* 46. Cf. *Sifra, Shemini* 1:3, 43c.
7. See *The Zohar: Pritzker Edition*, trans. Matt, vol. 5, p. 102, n. 291.
8. Babylonian Talmud, *Gittin* 43a, speaking of "words of Torah."

PART FOUR

Compassion,
Loving Others

Rabbi Jonathan P. Slater was ordained at The Jewish Theological Seminary of America and has a doctor of ministry degree from the Pacific School of Religion. He is author of *Mindful Jewish Living: Compassionate Practice*. He is codirector of programs at the Institute for Jewish Spirituality, as well as an instructor in meditation at the Jewish Community Center in Manhattan.

"A Better Way of Being in the World, a Way of Compassion"

Jonathan P. Slater

In the Talmud [Babylonian Talmud, *Shabbat* 33b] we read the lengthy story of Rabbi Shimon bar Yohai and his son who were hidden in a cave [for twelve years, studying Torah and subsisting on water and carob pods]. When they learned that they were safe and came out of the cave, they saw people "forsaking eternal life to engage in transient concerns." Whatever they looked at was consumed in fire. They aroused destruction in the world, and a heavenly voice came forth and said, "Do you wish to destroy My world? Return to your cave." Twelve months later they emerged with compassion, and wherever they went they brought blessing to the world.

Initially, R. Shimon bar Yohai and his son were convinced that the only practices that constituted *avodah* were Torah study, prayer, fasting in tears, and the like. Therefore, when they saw that people were not engaged in these practices, they were enraged and said, "They forsake eternal life to engage in transient concerns." Their intolerance increased anger in the world, until a divine voice told them to return to their cave. They then sensed that this was to teach them a better way of being in the world, a way of compassion. The path of compassion is to serve

God through every aspect of every act, giving heed to the fact that the Holy One is there too.[1]

It appears to me from what I have received from my teachers and colleagues that this is how to behave with compassion toward all others. Even when you see something ugly or unbecoming in another person, you should turn your heart to thinking that the Holy One dwells there too, since there is no place devoid of Him. It is therefore for your good that you have seen this, since you have some aspect of this same ugliness in you as well, and this will move your heart to *teshuvah*. Even if you should be distracted from your study of Torah or prayer by someone's conversation, you should pay attention and consider that this is for your good, either because you were not praying or studying properly, or so that you will bring a different intention to your service. In these ways you will come to accept this situation as good, and ultimately that it truly is for your good....

When Psalm 16:8 says, "I have placed God before me [*l'negdi*] always," it means that even when there is some sort of opposition [*negdiut*] that might cause me to desist from Torah or prayer, I can understand that this comes from heaven for my good. It comes from the side of compassion, as in the continuation of the verse, "He is at my right hand, I will never be shaken," which is love [*hesed*] and compassion [*rahamim*].[2] Thus, the psalm continues, "So my heart rejoices," since everything is for my good; in this manner compassion is aroused in the world, and all beings can be at ease: "my body rests secure" (Psalm 16:9).[3]

RABBI YA'AKOV YOSEF OF POLNOYE, *TOLDOT YA'AKOV YOSEF*

I have loved these texts from the first time I studied them. It is so gratifying and inspiring to me to read a Jewish text that makes behaving with compassion toward all beings an unambiguous priority. And, it is important to me that the value of compassion is not only identified, but also grounded in practice. It is not surprising that we are dealing here with a Hasidic text. The movement from which it emerged taught that through practice (*avodah*, "worship"), you could develop a greater awareness of God's presence in all existence and thereby experience more directly and more constantly God's faithful love. Through practice (*teshuvah*, "repentance"), you could learn to let go of the constraining dictates of the ego, to live with greater honesty and integrity. Through practice (*tefillah*, "prayer"), your perception of reality shifts, so that you might more fully trust in God's loving goodness and so be liberated to love all beings as well. To be a *hasid*, then, might be understood to have two components: to be a person who is attuned to God's limitless and constant love toward all creation (*hesed El kol ha-yom*, "God's love is ceaseless" [Psalm 52:3]); and to be a person who has developed the capacity for *hesed* (love) in your life, expressing it toward God and all creation.

Toldot Ya'akov Yosef was the first Hasidic book to be published (1780), authored by Rabbi Ya'akov Yosef of Polnoye, one of the more prominent students of the Baal Shem Tov. It is not surprising, then, to find these themes here. Indeed, the message of these passages is repeated a number of times throughout this rather large work, as well as in his subsequent books. It is clear that this lesson was important to R. Ya'akov Yosef, and its significance is even greater in that he regularly attributes it to his teacher (as above). A central teaching of the Baal Shem Tov was that God fills all creation and no place is devoid of divinity. He meant this absolutely, so that nothing—no place, no person, no being, no act—was outside the realm of the divine, empty of God's enlivening force. Realizing this, learning to perceive God in all moments, inspires a deep, passionate connection to all things and engagement with other people, as well as joy. As a further consequence of this view, the Baal Shem Tov and his successors were wont to misquote Lamentations 3:38 to express their belief that "woe does *not* come out of God's word."[4] Therefore, everything that takes place must ultimately be good, as God's intention and action are only for the good. This view also demanded and fed a profound sense of faith. Seeking God in all things and all events was not only a form of devotion—connecting the manifest world back to its divine source—but an act of faith, offering consolation that even in suffering God's goodness is present.

Faith is a personal, internal experience. It shapes perception and prompts action in response. Faith, however, is not fixed or permanent.

Challenged by suffering and frustration, it weakens; confirmed in ease or affirmation, it is energized. This ebb and flow of a sense of connection to God is a natural element of the spiritual life, but it can also be confusing and frustrating. The Baal Shem Tov and his successors taught their students and followers to pay attention to this dynamic, employing it positively to deepen their faith. They framed this dynamic as a form of *teshuvah*. With each return to faith, to awareness of God's presence and goodness in all things, you grow in spiritual capacity and quality, gaining greater stability in your faith. This return to faith is fundamentally a return to God. To truly wake up to God's presence in any given moment or act is to become aware of where you are: if you have gone wrong or if you are on the right path. Coming to know either makes it possible to return to awareness of and connection to God.

Recognizing the Good in All

These themes play themselves out in our text. R. Ya'akov Yosef teaches that when we see someone whose behavior is unbecoming—"ugly" or even sinful—we are to strive to resist our habitual negative judgment. Instead, we are to pause and recognize that despite our perception of someone as "ugly," God is still present in this person. Seeing God in this person, from whom we would otherwise turn away in disgust, calls us to remain connected, to pay even closer attention. The consequence is that we will see our own "ugliness" reflected in this other person, and we will become aware of our own flaws. We will then turn to God in *teshuvah*. This movement has three components: (1) we need to do *teshuvah* for having (mis)judged our fellow; (2) we need to do *teshuvah* for having failed to notice and so previously rectify our own flaws; and (3) we need to do *teshuvah* for having, if only momentarily, forgotten that God is present in all things, even in that which we deem unbecoming or "ugly."

The process described here is virtually all internal: the first awareness of a reaction to something "ugly"; the pause to assess the judgment; the shifted awareness to God's presence in this other; the impulse toward *teshuvah*. Yet, its implications are interpersonal and transpersonal. Instead of turning away from the other person and cutting them off from us—and also, in a sense, from God's world—we turn to reconnect, to find in them God's image. Rather than reacting in anger or disgust, we are moved instead to compassion. The source of the compassion is not only in our own hearts, in the end. It is the product of connecting as well to the Holy One in that other person. The compassion we feel toward the other is God's compassion, and it is available to us as well. And, it leads us to act differently, to behave with more love.

This is made clear when R. Ya'akov Yosef gives an additional example of circumstances that require a response of compassion: when we are interrupted in Torah study or prayer by someone else's conversation nearby. We might at first blame this other person for disrupting us, for interfering in our private endeavor. Yet R. Ya'akov Yosef points out that if our attention has been distracted, it is because of a failure in our own concentration. We were not studying or praying properly—with true, selfless, focused attention—or our intention was misplaced. We were either studying or praying out of egotistical motivations or out of a mistaken understanding of how prayer and study connect us to God. If we were truly connected to God, aware of God as filling all creation, we would not be susceptible to distraction or interruption. With our hearts fully attached to God, everything would manifest as God-in-the-world, and nothing would appear as interruption.

If every instance of distraction, interruption, or aversion—which otherwise is disruptive, frustrating, or infuriating—can be a moment of returning to awareness of and connection to God, then our hearts may become less constricted and our lives more spacious. We will have to devote less energy to recovering from anger or resentment. We will have more energy to be loving and compassionate. This is the import of the concluding paragraph of our text. When we are able to find God in all moments, we are less likely to be thrown off balance by untoward events. Indeed, both the good and the bad will seem equal to us, as all circumstances will be to us an invitation to meet God. It is in this sense that R. Ya'akov Yosef remarks that we will find all eventualities of life "for our good": they are "good" insofar as they turn us to God, connecting us to the source of love and compassion. This is an occasion for joy, as we come to experience all as good, all the true unfolding of divine intention. We are liberated from our constricted self-interest to give attention to the needs, indeed the existence of all other beings, who are no less bearers of divine vitality than we are. We rest secure in the "goodness," the rightness of what is in this moment, our hearts turned toward God, free to "behave with compassion toward all others."

Living Torah through Compassion

What Ya'akov Yosef transmits in these texts is a fundamental teaching of the Baal Shem Tov. That this is true is clear in the following text, where it is attributed to his teacher:

> Therefore we recite before beginning the morning prayers: "Behold, I take upon myself the positive commandment 'Love your neighbor as yourself'"—to acknowledge that all existence is one unified whole, similar to a Torah scroll, which is one unity made up of the combination of all the individual letters. Therefore, even when you see something bad in your fellow, you must despise only that bad thing so that you can love the holy portion in him as yourself. The Baal Shem Tov said: A perfectly righteous person, in whom there is nothing bad, cannot see anything bad in another person. But, if you see something bad in your fellow, consider it as if you were looking in a mirror: if your face is filthy, you will see it in the mirror, but if your face is clean, then you will see no blemish at all. And so, what you see is who you are. This, then, is the meaning of "love your neighbor as yourself": "as yourself"—if you know that there is nothing bad in you, then you will not despise yourself, even if you despise whatever bad you might discover there. You will then also relate to your fellow in this way, since all is truly one unified whole. After all, doesn't your fellow also have a portion of divinity in her, just like you, and doesn't she also have her own unique letter in the complete, unified Torah?[5]

This passage shares with ours the concern that we not remain blind to our own flaws and failures. But, it is not so concerned with the outcome of waking up to this fact. While we are not to despise our fellow, only the bad in them, we are not instructed in the ways of compassion. While we are encouraged to remain connected to the other, our love for her is out of the love we have for ourselves. God is not so present, compassion is not a priority, and equanimity and joy are not an outcome.

The difference is telling. In our two versions of this teaching, R. Ya'akov Yosef is focused on promoting—and living—"a better way of being in the world, a way of compassion." He presents this "way of being" in the context of the story of R. Shimon bar Yohai and his son. Their demanding ways, uncompromising and lacking in self-reflection and compassion, were destructive. They had to learn how to live with people in a loving, compassionate way. Telling the story in this manner reflects R. Ya'akov Yosef's particular understanding of the Baal Shem Tov's teaching.

It is tempting to see this version as his reflection on his own life path.[6] Martin Buber offers a version "of how the Baal Shem gained for his disciple Rabbi Jacob Joseph."[7] In one story, R. Ya'akov Yosef is depicted as short-tempered: "It is well-known that he was very particular and quick to fly into a temper." In this story, the Baal Shem Tov interfered with R. Ya'akov Yosef's familiar daily rhythm, distracting his beadle from his work and the people of his town from attending morning prayers on time. "'What do you think you are doing!' shouted the Rav. 'Keeping people from prayer!' 'Rabbi,' said the Baal Shem calmly, 'it does not become you to fly into a rage.'" The lesson R. Ya'akov Yosef learned in this story is that people will be more willing and able to pray, to truly engage in their lives, when their leader "slackens the reins" and is more attendant to their needs with compassion.

In another story, the prophet Elijah appears in R. Ya'akov Yosef's study hall and proceeds to interrupt him, particularly asking the latter about his life and livelihood: "The Rav could no longer endure this empty talk. 'You are keeping me from my studies,' he said impatiently. 'If you fly into a temper,' said the other, 'you curtail God in making His living.'" Elijah explains that Jews who meet and speak of their lives and livelihood, constantly praising God by saying *barukh HaShem* (praised is God), provide God with livelihood, as God is "enthroned on the praises of Israel." "'But you, who do not talk to anyone, you who only want to study, are curtailing God's living.' The Rav was taken aback. He wanted to reply, but the man had vanished. The Rav went back to his book, but he could not study. He shut the book and went into the Baal Shem's room. 'Well, Rav of Szarogrod,' he said smilingly, 'Elijah got the best of you, after all, didn't he?'"

In the end, R. Ya'akov Yosef takes on the ways of the Baal Shem, angering his community to the point of being ousted from his position as *rav*. "Soon afterward, Rabbi Jacob Joseph became *rav* in the city of Rashkov. He issued a proclamation far and wide that he would return all fines he had ever received, and there had been many. He did not rest until he had distributed all the money he had. From that time on, he used to say: 'Worry and gloom are the roots of all the powers of evil.'"

In these stories we see R. Ya'akov Yosef's anger creating division, rancor, and suffering. He is so affected by the teachings of the Baal Shem Tov that he is moved to personal transformation and engages in his own form of *teshuvah*. We might suggest that in R. Shimon bar Yohai and in the person who is distracted in prayer or study we see the former R. Ya'akov Yosef. "The way of compassion" is the only way to equanimity, joy, and a true connection to God. This is not to negate the importance of Torah study or the performance of the commandments. But, the reason that a person studies is now transformed.

We see this in a parallel passage:

> "If you see your fellow's ox or sheep gone astray, do not ignore it; you must take it back to your fellow. If your fellow does not live near you or you do not know who he is, you shall bring it home and it shall remain with you until your fellow claims it; then you shall give it back to him" (Deuteronomy 22:1–2).
>
> "If your fellow does not live near you or you do not know who he is": that is, if you have investigated your own behavior to find some small way in which you share in the sin you have observed in another person, such that you do not find him "close" to you, as your "brother [fellow; *ahikha*]," then "you shall bring it home and it shall remain with you until your fellow claims it." This is, as in a lesson I once heard, "if you search (for a reason for your suffering) and cannot find one, attribute it to neglect of Torah study" [cf. Babylonian Talmud, *Berakhot* 5a]: you have neglected Torah study and therefore lack knowledge of what truly constitutes a sin. Therefore, you should study

Torah, and in that manner find the sin (by which you can make the other your brother, and thereby raise him up).[8]

Torah study (and all spiritual practice) cannot be done to gain honor or out of self-interest. It cannot be a distraction from the world. True spiritual practice must connect us to other people, opening our hearts in self-awareness and compassion.

Jewish Spiritual Practice for Today

As we enter the twenty-first century, it is even more important to reclaim these texts (and those like them) to revive Jewish life in America. It is even more necessary to demonstrate how Jewish practice—as spiritual practice—is "the way of compassion." All of Jewish religious practice has the potential to—and is fundamentally intended to—wake us up to the connection among all beings, within all existence. It is meant to challenge the idolatry of the separate self, to release the hold of egoistic fears and urges, so that we might act with greater wisdom and love. R. Ya'akov Yosef, before he became a disciple of the Baal Shem Tov, held beliefs and behaved in ways that were destructive to his own health and well-being and damaging to the life and well-being of his community. We, today, are obligated to change, just as he did, to revive contemporary Jewish life through spiritual practice, so that as Jews we can more fully work to prevent the destruction of life on earth as we know it, and to promote the health and well-being of all creatures. When we come into contact with our own hearts with love, we are liberated to act with compassion and wisdom, for the sake of all existence, with joy, equanimity, and peace.

Notes

1. Rabbi Ya'akov Yosef of Polnoye (d. 1784), *Toldot Ya'akov Yosef, Vayetzei 5,* edited translation.
2. Jewish mystical symbolism identifies love with the right side of the Divine. Compassion, which results from the balance of love and limitation, inclines toward the right side.
3. *Toldot Ya'akov Yosef, Hayyei Sarah 2,* edited translation.
4. The actual verse says, "Is it not at the word of the Most High that weal and woe befall?"
5. *Me'or Einayim, Hukkat,* s.vv. *zot ha-torah adam ki yamut ba-ohel.*

6. Ya'akov Yosef does not make this connection directly, and the narratives in Buber's *Tales* (see below) are suspect as historical records. Yet the personality of R. Ya'akov Yosef presented in these stories and the nature of the change called for by the Baal Shem Tov are so aligned with these teachings that it seems fair to make such a connection.

7. Martin Buber, *Tales of the Hasidim*, vol. 1 (New York: Schocken Books, 1978), pp. 56–59.

8. *Toldot Ya'akov Yosef, Ki Tetzei* 3.

Rabbi Everett Gendler was ordained at The Jewish Theological Seminary of America. After serving congregations in Mexico City; Rio de Janeiro; and Princeton, New Jersey, he was rabbi for many years at Temple Emanuel in Lowell, Massachusetts, while also serving as Jewish chaplain and instructor in philosophy and religious studies at Phillips Academy in Andover, Massachusetts. He has written widely on Judaism and the environment, nonviolence, social justice, and liturgical innovation.

Rabbi Nahman's "OD"

An Ode of Human Redemption

EVERETT GENDLER

Know that you must judge every human being favorably, even one who seems wholly wicked. You must search to find some bit of goodness in that person, to locate the small portion that is not evil. For by finding that bit of goodness and judging the person favorably, you thereby truly elevate that person to a state of merit to which he can turn in repentance. Thus the meaning of Psalm 37:10 ["a little merit, and there is no wicked person"] is: This *od m'at*, this touch of goodness, can initiate the process of redemption for the wicked; hence when you look at the place previously occupied by a wicked person, no wicked person is to be found. No matter how evil the person appears, you must search ceaselessly for that bit of goodness that is not tainted by evil. For after all, how is it possible that any existing person shall not have done at least one good deed during those years of existence? Because you so insistently search to find that touch of goodness untainted by evil, and because you judge her favorably, you thereby elevate the person to a true state of goodness from which full repentance follows. Thus, however diligently you may search, there is no wicked person now to be found in that place where previously a wicked person could be found.[1]

RABBI NAHMAN OF BRATSLAV, LIKUTEI MOHARAN

Both in English and in Hebrew, the word "ode"/*od* is a short, simple monosyllable. Small in sound, however, it is large in significance. In English it first denoted a poem intended or adapted to be sung, and later a rhymed lyric, often in the form of an address, generally dignified or exalted. From Pindar to Keats to Wordsworth to Tate, ever so many poets known for their odes come to mind. In Hebrew *od* connotes duration, persistence, continuity, surplus. Here, too, numerous examples could be cited.

Let's focus on two: Psalm 37:10, *v'od m'at*, and Psalms 104:33 and 146:2, *b'odi*. The former is regularly translated "and yet a little while"; the latter, "while I live," "while I have being." Those are plain meanings and not to be denied. But they are not the only possible meanings. If one were to construe *od* as a noun, a noun that points to a pure part of a human being, that draws our attention to a meritorious aspect of a human being, then suddenly these phrases assume a different meaning. *V'od m'at* of Psalm 37:10 now means "a little merit," and *b'odi* in Psalms 104:33 and 146:2 means "with the meritorious part of my being." Unlike any previous commentary that I know of, this is Rabbi Nahman's startling rendering of *od*, with spiritual consequences that we shall now consider.

Especially worth noting is the context that Psalm 37 provides Rabbi Nahman for his approach to the eradication of evil among humans. The psalm is often characterized as a meditation on the problem of evil, the painful fact that, all too often, the wicked prosper on this earth while the pious suffer and languish. The psalmist appears to counsel patient waiting, repeatedly assuring the meek, the humble, the wholehearted, the righteous that in the course of time, God will ensure their future while cutting off the seed of the wicked. Those who faithfully hope for/wait for God will ultimately be vindicated, while the wicked will perish. The psalm includes the verse in the Grace after Meals that we whisper or sing ever so softly: "I have been young, and now am old; yet have I not seen the righteous forsaken, nor his seed begging bread" (Psalm 37:25). Sometimes referred to as a psalm expressive of *anavim*, "piety"—the faithful, patient waiting of the meek for God's justice to appear—the psalm appears to recommend quietism rather than activism in relation to the world's woes. "The meek shall inherit the earth" is promise rather than praxis, a state of affairs that will come about directly through the intervention of God, not through humans.

Rabbi Nahman startlingly changes this scenario. As he interprets *od m'at*, human activity can, indeed, intervene to change the state of affairs. By identifying the barely visible hint of goodness hidden among the evident evil deeds of the wicked, then actively appealing to that element of goodness, a fellow human being can initiate the process of personal transformation so that, in truth, when you look anew for the wicked person in her former location, you see not a wicked but a decent human being. "Yea, thou shalt look well at his place, and he [the wicked] is not" (Psalm 37:10).

A full discussion of human transformation is beyond the limits of this brief essay, but a few contemporary examples should help us grasp the vast implications of this teaching. One vivid, lived example of Rabbi Nahman's approach in practice I find in Martin Luther King Jr.'s stirring words addressed to recalcitrant resisters of equal justice for all:

To our most bitter opponents we say: We shall match your capacity to inflict suffering by our capacity to endure suffering. We shall meet your physical force with soul force. Do to us what you will, and we shall continue to love you. We cannot in all good conscience obey your unjust laws, because noncooperation with evil is as much a moral obligation as is cooperation with good. Throw us in jail, and we shall still love you. Bomb our homes and threaten our children, and we shall still love you. Send your hooded perpetrators of violence into our community at the midnight hour and beat us and leave us half dead, and we shall still love you. But be ye assured that we will wear you down by our capacity to suffer. One day we shall win freedom, but not only for ourselves. We shall so appeal to your heart and conscience that we shall win *you* in the process, and our victory will be a double victory.[2]

King is here referring to love as *agape*, selfless concern for the other, "understanding and creative, redemptive goodwill for all men." This stands in contrast to *eros*, aesthetic or romantic love, and *philia*, "a reciprocal love and the intimate affection and friendship between friends." King's articulation of the power of agape includes, also, a strong emphasis on the transformative power of self-suffering. I cannot say whether this voluntary self-suffering motif is prominent in Rabbi Nahman's teachings; such "redemptive suffering" seems different from Rabbi Nahman's own depressive suffering.[3] Yet without claiming Rabbi Nahman as a nonviolent activist in the modern sense of the term, I do think that we can best understand the practical implications of his teaching by examining examples of the work of such modern figures as Gandhi, King, and the Dalai Lama.

Decades before King, Gandhi insisted that we must always distinguish the person from the deed:

> Whereas a good deed should call forth approbation and a wicked deed disapprobation, the doer of the deed, whether good or wicked, always deserves respect or pity, as the case may be. 'Hate the sin and not the sinner' is a precept which, though easy enough to understand, is rarely practiced, and that is why the poison of hatred spreads in the world.... It is quite proper to resist and attack a system, but to resist and attack its author is tantamount to resisting and attacking oneself.[4]

Along with this principle that Rabbi Nahman would surely recognize as akin to his, both Gandhi and King did, of course, use many other nonviolent techniques to coerce as well as persuade the opponent. Yet for each of them, the ultimate goal was that agape, selfless love, successfully address and draw into action the capacity for decency in every human being, so very like Rabbi Nahman seeking the *od m'at*, the element of goodness in even the greatest sinner.

The Dalai Lama also exemplifies this approach of Rabbi Nahman. His emphasis on compassion translates into advice such as this:

> The appropriate response to someone who causes us to suffer
> ... is to recognize that in harming us, ultimately they lose their

peace of mind, their inner balance, and thereby their happiness. And we do best if we have compassion for them, especially since a simple wish to see them hurt cannot actually harm them. It will certainly harm us, though.[5]

The three of them would concur, I believe, with Rabbi Nahman: by appealing to the latent, hidden decency in every human being, the errant human being can be so moved toward goodness that we, looking for the sinner previously seen, are startled to discover that now *ein rasha*, "there is no sinner" (Psalm 37:10), so effective has been the appeal to the *od m'at*.

The profound societal implications of this teaching invite—in fact, demand—further consideration. Do not all religions contain this teaching in some significant form? How far can this principle be applied? Are there limiting cases, such as Scarpia in Puccini's *Tosca* or, in the real world, Hitler or Stalin? These questions come to mind immediately.

Following his remarks about looking for the good in others, Rabbi Nahman now asks, if this applies to the other, what about the self? Shouldn't this approach apply to every individual, including myself? His answer is the following:

> Just as a person should judge others charitably, even the wicked, finding in them certain good points, and by these truly bringing them from culpability to worthiness, as in the cited verse ... [it is] exactly so with the person himself: he must judge himself charitably, to find an existing good point, thereby strengthening the self so that he does not despair completely, God forbid. All the more should the person revive herself by rejoicing in the bit of good which she finds in herself: a good act, a commandment properly fulfilled. Then the person should seek additional examples of goodness within the self, even if they are mixed with unworthy elements as well. And as this process of gathering examples of goodness proceeds, and the good is distinguished and extracted from the evil, melodies are made ... melodies and songs exalted and holy.... These melodies and songs prevent the person from succumbing to despair, and so the person revives ... and is again able to pray

and sing praises to God ... and again feel near, not distant from the Divine.[6]

This attention to the self is not surprising for one who suffered such constant inner pain from feelings of personal unworthiness as did Rabbi Nahman. Hence the importance of the above formula (*etza*) for overcoming feelings of personal unworthiness that lead to depression and despair. Introspection, serious self-searching, though essential for fully aware and responsible living, can be demoralizing. In the process, we are likely to identify with Jeremiah's pained cry: "The heart is deceitful above all things, and it is exceedingly weak—who can know it?" (17:9).

Mixtures of motives, doubts about intentions, and the ultimate unknowability of ourselves can, indeed, unnerve us. If not Rabbi Nahman's despair, vertigo, at the least, is likely to be our reaction as we contemplate the depths of our being. In dramatist Georg Büchner's words,

> Every human being is an abyss,
> it makes one dizzy
> to look down into it.[7]

Or as Gerard Manley Hopkins vividly portrays our plight:

> O the mind, mind has mountains; cliffs of fall
> Frightful, sheer, no-man-fathomed. Hold them cheap
> May who ne'er hung there.[8]

Small wonder that Rabbi Nahman searches with equal zeal for the *od*, the goodness within oneself. To find that is to find footing against what could otherwise be a precipitous, despairing plunge into depression or despair.

Rabbi Nahman now finds support for his interpretation in another psalm where *od* can be construed as substantive. While the words from Psalm 146:2 are usually translated, "I will sing praises unto my God while I have my being" (see also Psalm 104:33), Nahman renders these words as "by means of my merit [*od*] that I find within myself," as previously cited, with "just a bit of merit, there is no wicked person now to be found."

Hence, Psalm 146:2/104:33 is best understood as "I am able to sing praises to my God because I have discovered that bit of merit, of goodness, within me." And "I will sing" is to be taken literally, referring to the liturgical songs and wordless melodies that emerge from collecting those elements of goodness.

Based on his own experience in overcoming despair, Nahman is confident that the natural human reaction to feelings of self-worth will be an overflow of gratitude to the Creator, expressed in heartfelt words of praise and melodies of exaltation.

> And our rabbi was very insistent that we follow this teaching [*torah*], for it is the fundamental basis for anyone who wants to approach the Divine.... For the majority of human beings who feel remote from the Divine, the essential cause is despair, depression, bitterness of spirit due to feelings of worthlessness. They see within themselves the corruption that taints their deeds; they feel heartbroken. And from this follow the feelings of worthlessness that prevent their praying or doing whatever of value they might otherwise be doing. Therefore each person must be vigilant not to succumb to those dark, bitter feelings. Instead, all must follow this teaching of searching for, and finding, the element of goodness that assuredly exists within each person. Encouraged by this, each should then find and collect additional elements of goodness within. And so each person comes to life again, feels joy, and can once more anticipate redemption. And in that state of morale, the person can truly utter heartfelt prayers of gratitude. Thus is fulfilled the meaning of "I will sing praises to my God by virtue of my *od*, the worthiness that I find within me."

While this may appear repetitive to us, the scribe here is following Rabbi Nahman's explicit instruction to reemphasize this fundamental method for overcoming despair and avoiding depression. Rabbi Nahman's prescription should not be confused with facile, just-feel-good-about-yourself nostrums. His advice emerges from the depths of having experienced the very despair that he is eager to help us counter. Critical self-scrutiny is an essential part of worthy living. That such introspection be constructive, not destructive, uplifting, not depressing, is Rabbi Nahman's goal; the repeated teaching is his urgent recommendation for achieving this positive outcome.

Ever since I happened upon this passage ever so many years ago, *Azamer lelohai b'odi*, "I will sing praises to my God with my *od*"—recited daily in traditional morning prayers as well as weekly on Sabbath afternoons between Sukkot and Pesach—has reverberated with these overtones sounded by Rabbi Nahman. His profound expansion of the meaning of *od* has, at the same time, freed me to understand *od* in its plain, simple sense of "more, additional." More what? As applied to the human being, I suggest that aspect of ourselves that appears to further the life ascent of all creatures: consciousness, self-awareness. We cannot, with certainty, deny this quality to other animals; which of us, after all, has successfully entered the mind of a fellow creature? Yet we do comprehend that our natural endowments exceed those necessary for simply staying alive. Imagination and creativity, artistry in all its forms, accumulated learning and scholarship—simple survival does not require these, yet they are prominent features of our existence. They represent, indeed, an *od*, a "more," an "addition," a "surplus." It is from this abundance that we play, pray, sing, dance, draw, design, think, and build. Perhaps this superfluous endowment is the godlike quality called *tzelem Elohim*, "the divine image," in the great creation epic of Genesis.

Might this personal extension of Rabbi Nahman's teaching be faithful to the spirit of his comments? If so, Robinson Jeffers, a somewhat surprising witness, joins Rabbi Nahman in affirming this quality of excess as godlike. In his stirring poem "The Excesses of God," he boldly asserts, "Is it not by his high superfluousness we know / Our God?" He then provides several illustrations of mere physical needs being met in ways that quite exceed the bare necessities: rainbows over rain, iridescent coatings on seashells, blossoms on weeds, music from birds. These represent, in his words, "the great humaneness at the heart of things, / ... extravagant kindness."[9]

This, perhaps, is another way of articulating the underpinning and ultimate source for the *od* of which Rabbi Nahman so movingly speaks. We, too, might see ourselves as recipients of that "extravagant kindness." Rabbi Akiba implies something of the sort, I believe, when he remarks, "Beloved is the human being, for he was created in the image of God. It is yet greater divine love that makes known to us that we are created in the image of God."[10]

This, too, is an *od*, an addition to our being, isn't it? In ever so many areas of our lives, recognition of the *od* may, indeed, revive our morale and rejoice our spirits.

Ode/*od*: a single syllable both in English and in Hebrew. Yet what vast horizons it can open, and what profound introspection it invites. With that ode/*od* on our tongues, perhaps we, too, shall be able to sing, with renewed conviction and intensity, the fullness of God's praises.

Kein y'hi ratzon. Be this God's will.

Notes

1. Nahman of Bratslav, *Likutei Moharan* (Jerusalem, 1969), 1:282.
2. Martin Luther King Jr., "Loving Your Enemies," in *Strength to Love* (New York: Harper & Row, 1963), p. 39.
3. Arthur Green, *Tormented Master: A Life of Rabbi Nahman of Bratslav* (Tuscaloosa, Ala.: Alabama University Press, 1979), pp. 28, 164ff.
4. Mahatma Gandhi, *The Essential Gandhi: An Anthology of His Writings on His Life, Work, and Ideas*, ed. Louis Fischer, rev. ed. (New York: Vintage Books, 2002), p. 93.
5. Dalai Lama XIV, *Ancient Wisdom, Modern World: Ethics for the New Millennium* (London: Abacus, 2000), p. 113.
6. *Likutei Moharan* 1:282.
7. Georg Büchner, from his opera *Wozzek*: "Der mensch ist ein Abgrund / es schwindelt Einem / wenn mann hinunterscaut."
8. Gerard Manley Hopkins, *Poems and Prose*, ed. William H. Gardner (Middlesex, U.K.: Penguin, 1956), p. 61.
9. Robinson Jeffers, *Selected Poems* (New York: Vintage, 1965), p. 62.
10. *Pirkei Avot* 3:18.

Lawrence Fine is the Irene Kaplan Leiwant Professor of Jewish Studies and professor of religion at Mount Holyoke College. He is the author of numerous books, including *Judaism in Practice: From the Middle Ages through the Early Modern Period* and the award-winning *Physician of the Soul, Healer of the Cosmos: Isaac Luria and His Kabbalistic Fellowship*. He teaches widely in the Jewish community, including at the Institute for Jewish Spirituality.

Spiritual Friendship

"Go Among People Who Are Awake and Where a Light Shines Brightly"

Lawrence Fine

I have seen among the writings of the holy Rabbi Shalom Dov Ber of Lubavitch, the memory of the righteous is a blessing, that there are many categories of sleep. There is a sleep that is no more than a light nodding, when the sleeper is half-awake. There is the category of real sleep. There is the category of slumber. And there is the category of fainting, far worse, God forbid, where it is necessary to ... revive him with every kind of medicine in order to restore his soul.... And there is a category of still deeper unconsciousness that is known as a coma where, God forbid, only a tiny degree of life still remains in deep concealment.... In this age we are in this deepest state of unconsciousness. To be sure, there are still holy individuals among us who are still alert.... Now, when a person becomes aware that he is falling asleep and begins to nod and he is afraid that a strong, heavy sleep may overcome him, the best advice for him is to request his friend to wake him ... or that he should go among people who are awake and where a light shines brightly. But when he is on his own who can wake him? My meaning is that he should obtain a mentor, a friend who will converse with him from to time to time on matters having to do with the fear of God. These words are in the category of a seed, the holy words they speak being sown in the heart. Even though he may not be aware of it at the time, yet later he will become conscious of it.… This was the way of the disciples of the holy Baal Shem Tov, that each encouraged the others and that is why they attained to such lofty spiritual stages.[1]

RABBI AARON ROTH, *HITRAGSHUT HA-NEFESH*

Much of what we know about friendship and interpersonal relations in the history of Jewish mystical tradition comes to us in the context of community, or more precisely within the context of *intentional* communities. In reflecting upon the nature of spiritual companionship in the *Zohar*, Arthur Green remarks that Rabbi Shimon bar Yohai's group of companions (*havrayya*) "is one of a series of such circles of Jewish mystics, stretching back in time to Qumran, Jerusalem, Provence, and Gerona, and forward in history to Safed, Padua, Miedzybozh, Bratslav, and again to Jerusalem."[2] But in addition to communal and collective friendship, we also have important examples of practices having to do with one-on-one relationships (although it is perhaps obvious that even these occur more often than not within the social framework of fellowships or communities as well). The practice described by Rabbi Aaron Roth (d. 1944), a Hasidic teacher born in Hungary, is but one striking example of the way in which Hasidism encouraged intimacy and connection between individuals.[3] Rabbi Aaron (or Reb Arele, as he was called), drawing upon the teachings of Rabbi Shalom Dov Ber, the fifth Lubavitcher rebbe, gives us a fascinating phenomenology of states of consciousness, ranging from those who are fully "alert" to those who are in a deep "coma" such that only "a tiny degree of life still remains in deep concealment"!

Reb Arele's approach to living in an age in which "we are in this deepest state of unconsciousness" is to encourage individuals who fear that they are "falling asleep" to "go among people who are awake," to seek out a friend who will speak with him and commune with him. He sets down two basic conditions for success. First, the friend who is to awaken him should be at least more awake than he is! While this may seem quite obvious, R. Arele is reminding us that not everyone from whom we seek support is equally up to the task. We need to be discerning—even in our not-so-awake state—to seek out companions who are themselves spiritually vibrant, rather than rely on those who are "also half-asleep." For the main thing is for one's friend to be more alert than he is, that is, "more burning with fire for the service of the King." If we cannot find such a person, though, we must nevertheless make sure that we have a loyal friend through whom we can gain some degree of support.

The second condition is that this friend ought to be fully cognizant of the critical consequences of spiritual torpor and fully appreciate how urgent it is to arouse a person in such circumstances: "He must know, therefore, how essential it is for one to wake up the other, namely by means of the words they speak to one another, and these should be for the sake of heaven, to encourage one another...." Interestingly, R. Arele cautions that one must find a friend whose intentions are not self-serving or egoistic, for such a person will have no effect on his own heart, to say nothing of the heart of his neighbor. One's only motivation should be to offer encouragement, so that "the *Shekhinah* [the Divine Presence] will rest upon their friendship with one another." For "when holy Israelites come together for the purpose of encouraging one another, the Holy One, blessed be He" pays attention to the words they speak.

The language of sleep and wakefulness is central to kabbalistic and Hasidic traditions, something that is no more obvious than in the *Zohar* itself.[4] Here is one classic example: An old man, Yeiva Sava, encounters two of Shimon bar Yohai's companions while journeying on the road. One of the companions initially dismisses him as being a mere donkey driver who speaks nonsensical riddles. But after he offers profound teaching, the companions are amazed and dumbstruck, upon which Yeiva Sava announces the following:

> "Enough companions!... I, Yeiva Sava, have stood before you to awaken your awareness of these words." They rose as if awakened from sleep and threw themselves down in from of him, unable to utter a word.[5]

More generally, the *Zohar*'s companions are always excited and delighted to encounter one another on their journeys, to see in the other the face of the Divine Presence (the *Shekhinah*), and to engage in conversations intended to illuminate and inspire each other. And these usually end with expressions of great emotion and powerful gratitude for having been fortunate enough to have had such a wondrous personal encounter, such intimate communion and connection.

What do we seek from a friend? Surely, among other things, it is to be *encouraged* when we are in need of encouragement. We instinctively know that we can turn to a friend whom we trust and in whom we have confidence, someone who genuinely sees us in our moment of need, perhaps in a state of fear or despair, someone who has our best interests at heart and who knows how much their attentiveness to us matters. Such a person gives us the strength to go forward, to seek a way. True friendships are, by nature of course, *reciprocal*. Today I need your encouragement, but tomorrow you will, without a doubt, need mine. R. Arele appears to recognize this when his language shifts from one person seeking out another who is "more awake" to the language of reciprocity and mutuality, that is, "to encourage one another."

The Hasidim, of course, are not the first to counsel the importance of one-on-one relationships. We need not look any further than an early Rabbinic text, *Avot de-Rabbi Natan* (The Fathers According to R. Nathan). Here is a passage commenting on the teaching of *Pirkei Avot* (The Ethics of the Fathers) 1:6 to "provide yourself with a teacher, and acquire a companion [*haver*]":

> This teaches that a person should get a companion for himself, to eat with him, drink with him, study Scripture with him, study Mishnah with him, sleep with him, and reveal to him all his secrets, the secrets of the Torah and the secrets of worldly things.[6]

This is one of the foundations of the Rabbinic tradition of *hevruta*, studying in pairs. From the point of view of *Avot de-Rabbi Natan*, studying Torah with another person is a great deal more than cerebral activity; this highly evocative, even disarming, teaching suggests that companionship around the study of Torah involves a fully committed personal engagement, involving trust and intimacy. A range of Hasidic traditions also provide us with a model of interpersonal trust and intimacy: "It is important for your spiritual life to arrange to find a close spiritual friend, so that you can always take counsel with him concerning how to carry out the service of God in the proper way."[7]

Rabbi Asher of Stolin goes much further by encouraging individuals to reveal "everything in your heart":

> See that you have a good friend, someone who can be depended upon and who is able to keep a secret. You should talk with this person half an hour every day about everything in your heart and your innermost thoughts that flow from the evil inclination.... And if you have worries, you should talk them out with a friend, and if something good happens to you, then you should share your happiness with your friend.[8]

It is clear here that when R. Asher speaks of "innermost thoughts" he includes *transgressive* thoughts, that is, those that "flow from the evil inclination." He tells us we should share our worries and our joys, but he does not stop there. Interpersonal intimacy permits us to share "troubling thoughts," what the Hasidim called *mahshavot zarot*. One of the important things about this is that the Hasidic rebbe often played the role of "confessor" for his disciples. The rebbe was a confidant, a person of infinite wisdom who could be trusted with a follower's most intimate thoughts and feelings. But here, as with a number of other Hasidic teachers, R. Asher insists that this practice can and should be carried out with a person's fellow, implying the reciprocity and mutuality about which I spoke earlier.

In contemporary culture it is the psychotherapist, of course, who often plays the roles described in these traditions. But, needless to say, the option of psychotherapy hardly obviates the need for deep, spiritual friendship. What, indeed, is *spiritual* about some friendships? Is it the special connection we may feel with friends within the context of a particular religious community? Is it the shared experience of a beautiful religious tradition and the shared values, sensibilities, and commitments that enrich friendship in distinctive ways? Surely, all these things are true. Yet, deep, meaningful friendship can also be forged in the absence of such commonalities. A spiritual friendship may be *any* friendship in which there are reciprocal feelings of trust, acceptance, and confidence, feelings that invite us, enable us, to be courageous and honest, to be vulnerable, to be ourselves.

In a world of social networking and digital friendship—where acquiring as many "friends" as possible seems to have such great value—kabbalistic and Hasidic practices of friendship serve to remind us that commitment, privacy and intimacy, depth of relationship, and face-to-face connection still deeply matter. Springsteen, our urban poet, got it right: "And a little of that human touch, just a little of that human touch."[9]

As with life itself, friendship is always a work in progress, always evolving. At times we stumble, and we need to do *tikkun*, the work of repair. And, of course, sometimes even substantial friendships come to an end. All genuine friendship is, in one way or another, loving friendship. Like love, such friendship has no need to announce itself, no need to impress anyone or satisfy anyone's ego. In the end, we cannot imagine human life without enduring, loving friendship. Jane Hirshfield expresses this with beauty in her poem "The Heart's Counting Knows Only One":

In Sung China,
two monk friends for sixty years
watched the geese pass.
Where are they going?
one tested the other, who couldn't say.
That moment's silence continues.

No one will study their friendship
in the *koan*-books of insight.
No one will remember their names.

I think of them sometimes,
Standing, perplexed by sadness,
Goose-down sewn into their quilted autumn robes.

Almost swallowed by the vastness of the mountains,
but not yet.

As the barely audible
geese are not yet swallowed;
as even we, my love, will not be entirely lost.[10]

Notes

1. Aaron Roth, *Hitragshut Ha-nefesh* [Agitation of the Soul], first published in 1934. Subsequently published as the first part of the "Tract on the Love of God" in the second volume of his collected writings, *Shomer Emunim* (1964), 372a–76a. The translation presented here is based on Louis Jacobs, *The Schocken Book of Jewish Mystical Testimonies* (New York: Schocken Books, 1997), pp. 308–9.

2. Arthur Green, *A Guide to the Zohar* (Stanford, Calif.: Stanford University Press, 2004), p. 72. With respect to the various circles of intentional kabbalistic fellowships in Safed in the sixteenth century, see Lawrence Fine, *Physician of the Soul, Healer of the Cosmos: Isaac Luria and His Kabbalistic Fellowship* (Stanford, Calif.: Stanford University Press, 2003). Concerning the intentional fellowship of Bet El in eighteenth-century Jerusalem, see Lawrence Fine, "A Mystical Fellowship in Jerusalem," in *Judaism in Practice: From the Middle Ages through the Early Modern Period*, ed. Lawrence Fine (Princeton, N.J.: Princeton University Press, 2001).

3. Roth was the founder of a Hasidic sect known today as Reb Arele's, which has thousands of followers in Israel. As a young person, Roth was recognized for being especially pious and ascetic in orientation. He devoted himself to spiritual development under leading Hasidic teachers in Galicia. Roth traveled several times between Eastern Europe and the Land of Israel. For more on his life, see the biographical entry by Adam S. Ferziger in *The Yivo Encyclopedia of Jews in Eastern Europe*, vol. 2, ed. Gershon David Hundert (New Haven: Yale University Press, 2008), p. 1597.

4. For a rich discussion of this theme in the *Zohar*, see Melila Hellner-Eshed, *A River Flows from Eden: The Language of Mystical Experience in the Zohar* (Stanford, Calif.: Stanford University Press, 2009), pp. 204–8.

5. *Zohar* 2:114a. Translation based on *The Zohar: Pritzker Edition*, vol. 5, trans. and ann. Daniel C. Matt (Stanford, Calif.: Stanford University Press, 2009), p. 137.

6. *Avot de-Rabbi Natan* 8. English translation, *The Fathers According to Rabbi Nathan*, trans. Judah Goldin (New Haven: Yale University Press, 1990), p. 50.

7. *Derekh Hayyim, Hanhagot Tzaddikim*, vol. 1 (Jerusalem, 1988), p. 872.

8. Asher of Stolin, *Hanhagot Tzaddikim*, vol. 2 (Jerusalem, 1988), p. 474.

9. Bruce Springsteen, "Human Touch," *Human Touch* (Columbia, 1992).

10. Jane Hirshfield, *The Lives of the Heart: Poems* (New York: HarperCollins, 1997), p. 7.

Rabbi Ebn Leader is director of the Bet Midrash and an instructor in Talmud, Jewish law, and Jewish mysticism at the Rabbinical School of Hebrew College. He is the coeditor of *God in All Moments: Mystical and Practical Wisdom from Hasidic Masters* (Jewish Lights). Prior to coming to Hebrew College, he served for several years as an educator at Jewish secondary schools in Jerusalem and Boston.

The Service of Love

EBN LEADER

"Jacob sent messengers before him to his brother Esau" (Genesis 32:4). We read this with the verse "A person wrestled with him" (Genesis 32:25) and with Rashi's explanation that the word *va-ye'avek* (wrestled) is related to raising dust (*avak*).

There is a debate regarding this verse in the Talmud (*Hullin* 91a). One opinion is that Jacob thought the person he wrestled with was a non-Jew, and another opinion is that he thought the person was a rabbinical scholar. This seems like a very strange argument....

To understand this we need to explain the verse "Your word is well refined, and your servant loves it" (Psalm 119:140).

It is known that a *tzaddik*'s prayer is answered when he prays for a sick person or for others in need. This seems as if the Holy Blessed One is subject to change, heaven forbid. But the root of the matter is as follows: The Blessed One created letters, which in their original state are pure potential. A *tzaddik* can reconfigure the letters so that they form whatever words he wants. These configurations are what a *tzaddik* does in prayer—he makes his own combinations. His prayer does not cause change in the Creator, as the letters he is using were always there. All he is doing is creating [new] combinations.

You could still ask: Why is a *tzaddik*'s prayer more effective than the prayer of any other person? Indeed the Sages wrote, "If there is a sick person in your home, approach a sage to pray" (Babylonian Talmud, *Bava Batra* 116a). Why couldn't any person pray and reconfigure the letters?

This is because the Torah was created with love, as we say "the One who chooses the people Israel with love." A *tzaddik* also loves both God and every person in the world. For example, Rabbi Yohanan said, "I greet every person in the marketplace before they have a chance to greet me, including non-Jews" (Babylonian Talmud, *Berakhot* 17a, where this is told of R. Yohanan).

Most people are not like this and therefore do not have the power to reconfigure the letters. Only a *tzaddik* who loves everyone has that power.

This is the meaning of the verse "Your word is well refined [*tzerufah*]"; it refers to the supernal letters that have one configuration in potential and are reconfigured (*metzurafim*) in actuality by the all-loving *tzaddik* through the "service of love" (reading the end of Psalm 119:140 as *avadecha ahavah*).

That is the meaning of the verse "Jacob sent messengers." This refers to letters and words, which are called "messengers."

"Before him" means that the letters were already there, the potential was there before Jacob, and he then made combinations of the letters through the power of his love for all. This is implied in the words "to his brother Esau," meaning that he totally accepted *even* Esau as a brother, like R. Yohanan, whose love included even non-Jews in the marketplace.

So also do we understand the phrase "a person wrestled with him": The word *va-ye'avek* refers to traces of something, like in the expression "traces of usury [*avak rebeet*]." In reality, a person may not love all equally—Jews and non-Jews. The love for a Jew could be complete while the love for a non-Jew might still be lacking, still retaining traces of foreignness. This is the Talmudic opinion that Jacob thought the person was not Jewish. That was the struggle: [to rid himself of] the traces [of foreignness] that remained.

Similarly, the Talmudic opinion that Jacob thought the person was a scholar implies that Jacob's love for this person was not complete. This was because Jacob realized that this scholar had not yet perfected his personality traits. Jacob did love him, but this love was still incomplete because of these deficiencies.

This is the meaning of the verse "A man wrestled with him until the rise of dawn [*alot hashahar*]." He struggled to remove the darkness (*shehorut*) within himself and to achieve perfect love.

So the Talmudic debate is not so strange after all. Each position highlights a different aspect of Jacob's ability to achieve perfect love for every person.

RABBI ELIMELEKH OF LIZHENSK, NOAM ELIMELEKH

Rabbi Elimilekh of Lizhensk, commonly referred to by the name of his book the *Noam Elimelekh*, is one of the leading figures of the formative generation of Hasidism, the disciples of the Maggid R. Dov Ber of Mezritch (d. 1772). The book is generally recognized as one of the important articulations of the new Hasidic model of leadership, the *tzaddik*. As such it was influential in the development of the figure and role of the Hasidic *tzaddik*. The relation between the spiritual leader and the community, which is a very minor topic in the writings of R. Dov Ber of Mezritch, is in many ways the main topic of the book *Noam Elimelekh*.

The term *tzaddik* functions throughout the book in two main ways. On one hand, it is a description of the spiritual status of an individual. In this sense the *tzaddik* is a righteous person, and in the Hasidic context a master of mystical achievement. On the other hand, the term *tzaddik* is also the description of the role a person fulfills as a spiritual leader serving the community of Hasidim. In this sense the Noam Elimelekh can refer to a "beginning *tzaddik*" (*tzaddikim hamathilim ba-avodah*) or one with a great deal of experience.[1] While the Noam Elimelekh does at times use the term with either one of these distinct meanings, the Hasidic *tzaddik* as addressed in the book generally merges the two.[2]

One of the unique characteristics of the Hasidic *tzaddik* is that his responsibility to the community is not limited to the spiritual realm.

The *tzaddik* functions as a conduit through which Torah and divinity flow to the community, but also as a conduit for "children, health, and sustenance" (Babylonian Talmud, *Moed Katan* 28a). Moshe Idel has contributed greatly to our understanding of this double-sided role by articulating what he calls the "mystico-magical model" of functioning and by showing the similarities between the function of the *tzaddik* and the function of the Renaissance magus and the shaman. As Idel has demonstrated, many Hasidic texts describe a process in which the *tzaddik* connects with God through mystical practice and then draws the power of the Divine into the world to impact human experience.[3]

There are many teachings in the *Noam Elimelekh* that seem to reflect this model. This is particularly true of some of the places that deal with the *tzaddik*'s power to annul divine decrees, to heal the sick, and in other ways to manipulate reality or perceived reality. Yet, in many cases, when describing the processes that lead to such manipulation of reality, the *Noam Elimelekh* uses terminology that we more often associate with interpersonal relationships and human leadership skills than with magical activity.[4] How then are we to understand the relationship between the magical and social dimensions of the *tzaddik*'s work?

In order to answer this question we must first address another issue. Who is the intended audience of the *Noam Elimelekh*? There is a common tendency to read the teachings on the topic of the *tzaddik* as if they were descriptive, meaning that the author is describing the powers of the *tzaddik* to a broad audience of Hasidim. It is indeed likely that the teachings were often understood this way by Hasidim. However, my impression is that these teachings are often more accurately read as prescriptions for the aspiring *tzaddik*, the student who will take on the role of leading a community. I read these teachings as the goals for a *tzaddik*-to-be, the process of working toward these goals, and the pitfalls along the way.[5]

The implications of this understanding for the topic at hand are that in these teachings the Noam Elimelekh is actually showing the aspiring *tzaddik* how to become a miracle worker. Yet as I hope to demonstrate regarding the teaching on *parashat Va-Yishlah*, very often the capacity to bring about change is framed in relational terms. The connections between the work the *tzaddik* does in the context of a relationship and the changes that occur are not always straightforward or logical, and often the practitioner does not have full control over the process. In this, they preserve something of a magical quality. Still, they are acted out in the interpersonal realm.

It is generally accepted that one of the important characteristics of Hasidism is its "psychologization" of the theosophy of Kabbalah. This means that while the Hasidic masters use the terminology and images of earlier Jewish mysticism, the divine processes described in these kabbalistic texts are now understood as occurring within the human soul.[6] I think that the Noam Elimelekh does something similar with the relationship between the *tzaddik* and the community. While preserving the language of miracles, divine decrees, and struggle for change within an unchanging divine will, these terms are now often used to describe the dynamics of the relationship between the spiritual leader and the community.

The teaching at hand offers us an interesting example of this phenomenon. As is often the case with Hasidic homilies, the sermon does not begin with an analysis of the biblical verses to be discussed. Rather, it poses a larger question to which the interpretation of these verses will be applied. The question posed is one that the Noam Elimelekh returns to again and again. How is it possible for the prayers of the *tzaddik* to change the divine will?[7] His answer in this case begins with a mystical model whose roots are to be found in classical Rabbinic literature.[8] Since God created the world by means of speech ("Let there be …" [Genesis 1]), letters are the building blocks of existence. It is through the myriad configurations of the letters that life comes to be. One who knows the secret art of letter configuration can reconstruct reality.[9]

But what kind of knowledge is this? In the opening of the homily, the Noam Elimelekh treats the process of reconfiguring the letters as a technical skill that anyone could learn. If that is the case, what need is there for a *tzaddik*? It is at this point that the Noam Elimelekh moves away from a purely mystical-magical model. The power to effect change does not depend on esoteric knowledge or practices alone, but rather on the way an individual relates to the people and the world surrounding him. The absolute love (*ahavah shlemah*) that the *tzaddik* has for every person is the force that changes (on its own—*mimeila*) reality.

Absolute love is a term that is defined elsewhere in the book, though most often it is used in relation to God.[10] The term refers to love that is totally altruistic, that has been purged of any personal interest, and as we see in this teaching, is nonjudgmental. However, as we see in this teaching, when applied to human beings, it is more accurate to speak of the absolute love as an aspiration. The *tzaddik* is described as engaging in an ongoing struggle to purify this love from the "traces of dust" that sully it—the remnants of self-interest and judgment.[11]

The two examples of people who challenge the *tzaddik* in his efforts are striking, to say the least. Given the historical context in which the Noam Elimelekh lived, it is not hard to imagine that it would be challenging for him and his disciples to feel love for *goyim* (non-Jews) or *Mitnagdim* (rabbinic and lay opponents of Hasidism)—each of which he could certainly have experienced as oppressors. In fact, one can find several references in the book to non-Jews and to Torah scholars that are less than absolutely loving.[12] Still, in this text the Master presents the patriarch Jacob as a role model for one who struggles to rid himself of dark, judgmental thoughts.

What then does it mean to say, as in the Noam Elimelekh's restatement of the verse from Psalms, that reconfiguring letters is the work of love? Why is unconditional love the key to reorganizing the building blocks of reality?

The story of the meeting of Jacob and Esau is a fascinating model for this process. What is the "miracle" Jacob performs to transform a potential clash with his brother into an embrace? Initially, Jacob can see the situation only through the prism of an old conflict with his brother (stemming from their contest for their father's blessing). From this perspective, the fact that his brother is coming to meet him with "four hundred men" (Genesis 32:7) can only be interpreted as a threat.

According to the Noam Elimelekh's reading of the story, Jacob spends the whole night attempting to change his perspective, to find within himself the capacity to move beyond fear and to love Esau fully as a brother. Jacob's success is evidenced in the fact that at the moment of the meeting with Esau, Jacob's whole family is present (after first dividing his camp in half as a tactical measure), and with his full household present, he can walk toward his brother and embrace him—miraculously, conflict is averted.

As mentioned previously, miracle working poses a theological challenge for the Noam Elimelekh. How is it possible for the *tzaddik* to assert his will over the unchanging will of the Creator? The idea of reconfiguring letters helps solve this difficulty by explaining that the *tzaddik* is not actually creating anything new, but rather is simply changing the relationship among existing elements. In other words, the *tzaddik* is reframing the situation so that the existing elements are seen in a new light, in which new realities are made possible.

The Noam Elimelekh makes a similar point when describing the role of Moses in relation to his brother Aaron after Aaron's two sons die (Leviticus 10:1–20 and 16:1–2). Moses is here seen as a model for the Hasidic *tzaddik*.

> The power of the *tzaddik* comes from the capacity to rise through prayer to higher worlds where there is only compassion and no judgment at all, where decrees do not exist.... The *tzaddikim* can conceive of higher worlds where joy and happiness dwell, as the verse states, "There is power and joy in [God's] place" (1 Chronicles 16:27). As a consequence, sorrow and trouble flee. Thus the verse states, "God brought out His people with joy, His chosen ones with song" (Psalm 105:43).[13]

As the Noam Elimelekh describes further in this teaching, this mystical journey can be one in which the *tzaddik* actually overturns a deathly decree. This, however, is not the case with Aaron, who has just experienced the loss of his two sons. The biblical narrative does not have Moses bring them back to life. The deaths of Nadav and Avihu are now among the building blocks of reality that no *tzaddik* can change. Seen in this light, the doctrine of reconfiguring letters is not only about the magical power of the *tzaddik*, it is also about the limitations of that power; it is about the humility of the spiritual leader, who must accept the "letters" he has to work with and recognize that which cannot be changed. Accepting this, the Noam Elimelekh tells the aspiring leader, will allow him to work other "miracles."

God created the world with love. This love is by definition unlimited by any personal interest and is nonjudgmental, as it leads to the creation of the entire universe—the good, the bad, and the ugly. The Noam Elimelekh teaches that if you aspire to re-create reality for others, you must have the capacity to integrate such love into your being. Through nonjudgmental love and compassion you can develop the capacity to see reality in a different light, not limited by your perspective or those of anyone else. Where there was once only anger and conflict, you can see love and care; where there was once only death and despair, you can see life and hope. Through your love for the people you are working with, this vision can be communicated to others, and reality can change without changing that which is given, the ultimate will of God.

A final comment on the story of Jacob and Esau: Even when Jacob achieves this great miracle and is able to meet his brother with love, the achievement is not long-lasting. It does not take much for the old patterns of thought and behavior to resurface and for Jacob to turn down his brother's offer to travel and live together (Genesis 33:12–17). The *tzaddik*, as the Noam Elimelekh teaches more than once, is not a person who has achieved perfection. Rather, he is a person who is always traveling along a path, always struggling for improvement, like a bush that is always burning but is never consumed.

It is with this vision in mind that we close with a brief teaching from the Noam Elimelekh on the meeting of Moses and God at the burning bush; a teaching about the *tzaddik*'s ongoing struggle to rid himself of his flaws, and the reality that this cannot be achieved with perfection:

"And God saw that he came [*sar*] to see" (Exodus 3:4–5). The Blessed One saw that our teacher Moses wanted to rid himself (*le-hasir*) of all his [negative] tendencies so that he could see great [divine] visions. But this is impossible until the time of the Messiah, when God will totally remove the spirit of impurity from the earth. "And [God] said: Do not come near"—it is impossible for you to attain this level. Rather, "remove your shoes from your feet." The word "remove" (*shal*) has the same letters as the word "borrow" (*she'elah*); meaning, take them [your moments of spiritual greatness] as a loan, for you cannot totally rid yourself of your tendencies until the coming of the Messiah, may it be speedily, in our days.[14]

Notes

1. *Noam Elimelekh, Shemot,* s.vv. *v'eleh shemot.*
2. For the development of this term in Hasidism, see Arthur Green, "The Zaddiq as Axis Mundi in Later Judaism," *Journal of the American Academy of Religion* 45, no. 3 (September 1977): 327–47. See also his chapter "Typologies of Leadership and the Hasidic Tzaddiq," in *Jewish Spirituality from the Sixteenth-Century Revival to the Present* (New York: Crossroad, 1987), pp. 127–56.
3. Moshe Idel, *Hasidism: Between Ecstasy and Magic* (Albany: State University of New York Press, 1995). See in particular chap. 3, pp. 103–46.
4. Rivka Shatz discusses this point in her essay "The Essence of the *Tzaddik* in Hasidism," *Molad* (August–September 1960): p. 372.
5. The interest of the Noam Elimelekh in training future *tzaddikim* is evident in many places throughout the book. This is expressed in a variety of ways, including the fact that he often refers to the *tzaddik*'s followers as *tzaddikim.* See, for example, *Shelah,* s.vv. *Oh yomar shlah.* See, also, *Va-yera,* s.vv. *v'ekcha pat lehem,* for an explicit description of the process through which followers become leaders.
6. See a description of this process in Arthur Green, *Menahem Nahum of Chernobyl: Upright Practices, The Light of the Eyes* (New York: Paulist Press, 1982), pp. 10–16. Idel has noted pre-Hasidic precedents for this in the history of Kabbalah (*Hasidism*, pp. 227–38). Idel also writes (ibid., p. 9) that while the theoretical literature of Hasidism addresses mainly the mystical relation of the mystic with God, the Hasidic stories reflect the relation of the mystic to the community. To the extent that this articulation is true, the *Noam Elimelekh* must be seen as an exception in that it is mainly concerned with the latter and applies the classic Hasidic hermeneutics to it.
7. See a discussion of this question and the various solutions proposed for it by the Noam Elimelekh in Gedaliah Nigal's edition of the *Noam Elimelekh* (Jerusalem: Mossad Ha'Rav Kook, 1978), pp. 45–48.
8. The most commonly referenced early sources being the Babylonian Talmud, *Berakhot* 55a, and the mysticism of *Sefer Yetzirah.*
9. For the use of this model elsewhere in the *Noam Elimelekh,* see Nigal's edition, pp. 53–54.
10. See, e.g., *Noah,* s.vv. *Va-yoled Noah.*
11. See examples of this later in our Torah portion, s.vv. *Va-yivater Ya'akov,* and in the portion of *Va-yera,* s.vv. *Ve-rahatzu ragleikhem.*
12. See, e.g., his expression regarding the oppression of exile at the beginning of this very portion, s.vv. *Koh tomerun.* The call for loving non-Jews, while rare in

Jewish mystical literature, is not unique to the Noam Elimelekh. His inspiration may well be the statement in Hayyim Vital's *Shaarei Kedushah* (1:5) that lists the love of all creatures, explicitly including non-Jewish people, as one of the prerequisites for mystical attainment. The idea also appears in the writings of a younger contemporary of the Noam Elimelekh, Rabbi Pinhas Eliyahu of Vilna, who devotes a chapter in the section on mysticism to the commandment of loving one's neighbor applying to non-Jews as well (*Sefer Habrit* 2:13:7). For the Noam Elimelekh's comments on clashes with "Torah scholars," see *Likutei Shoshanah*, s.vv. *Eizohi mahloket*.

13. *Aharei Mot*, s.vv. *Aharei mot*.
14. *Shemot*, s.vv. *Va-yare YHVH ki sar lirot*.

Barry W. Holtz is dean of the William Davidson Graduate School of Jewish Education at The Jewish Theological Seminary, where he is also the Theodore and Florence Baumritter Professor of Jewish Education. His books include, among others, *Back to the Sources: Reading the Classic Jewish Texts* and *Your Word Is Fire: The Hasidic Masters on Contemplative Prayer* (Jewish Lights), the latter co-authored with Arthur Green.

The Splendid Bird

Reflections on Prayer and Community

BARRY W. HOLTZ

Once in a tropical country, a certain splendid bird,
    more colorful than any that had ever been seen,
    was sighted at the top of the tallest tree.
The bird's plumage contained within it
    all the colors in the world.
But the bird was perched so high
    that no single person
    could ever hope to reach it.
When news of the bird reached the ears of the king,
    he ordered that a number of men
    try to bring the bird to him.
They were to stand on one another's shoulders
    until the highest man could reach the bird
    and bring it to the king.
The men assembled near the tree,
    but while they were standing
    balanced on one another's shoulders,
    some of those near the bottom
    decided to wander off.

As soon as the first man moved,
   the entire chain collapsed,
   injuring several of the men.
Still the bird remained uncaptured.

The men had doubly failed the king.
For even greater than his desire to see the bird
   was his wish to see his people
   so closely joined to one another.[1]
                RABBI URI FEIVEL OF KRYSTNOPOL, OR HAHOKHMAH

I've always wondered if the Hasidim who first heard this story saw the elements that might strike a modern reader as comic: I always picture this like a scene out of a circus with men balanced on one another's shoulders—and how even more absurd it seems if one pictures these men dressed in full Hasidic garb, their hats poking into the person's face above them.[2] And then of course some decide to wander off, and the whole act collapses! But comic or not, we might ask, what is this story about? What is being taught here?

The version above is the translation that Art Green and I did for a text found in *Or HaHokhmah* by Rabbi Uri Feivel of Krystynopol, Galicia (d. c. 1805). In its original context in *Or HaHokhmah*, the parable does not stand alone but appears as a story told by the Baal Shem Tov (the Besht), the founder of Hasidism, to explain an incident that he reports as having happened to him. But that incident itself is a kind of parable told by the Besht to elucidate a teaching of Rabbi Isaac Luria, the famed sixteenth-century Safed mystic.

The structure of these pages in the *Or HaHokhmah*, then, is (1) a comment by Isaac Luria; (2) an incident told by the Besht as an example of Luria's wisdom; (3) the parable of the bird; (4) a comment on the parable that brings it all back to Luria. In *Your Word Is Fire*, we told only the parable of the fabulous bird, interpreting it for the reader as a teaching about communal prayer.

Of course it turns out that the text *is* about communal prayer, though that may not be self-evident on a first reading. But the comment attributed to Isaac Luria is particularly fascinating and serves as the introduction to that which will follow: "The ARI [i.e., Isaac Luria] of blessed memory wrote that all people need to take upon themselves the *mitzvah* [precept] of 'Love your neighbor as yourself' before prayer." To begin with this is a rather remarkable statement. Don't we usually think of commandments like "Love your neighbor as yourself" as being part of the agenda of *mitzvot bein adam l'havero*, commandments that deal with *interpersonal* relationships, while prayer is the *mitzvah* sine qua non of *mitzvot bein adam l'makom*, commandments between human beings and God? Why should "Love your neighbor as yourself" be the *mitzvah* we are to think about before beginning to pray? It is clear that the ARI's statement is meant to refer to prayer in a *minyan*, not individual prayer by oneself. But even so, why does this particular *mitzvah* make sense in the context of prayer?

The ARI's answer, according to the *Or HaHokhmah*, is this: "The meaning of prayer," he says, "is *devekut*"—direct connection to God. And, he goes on to say, we can achieve that connection to God only by recognizing our need for the help of those on the "rung" above us. Each individual, the ARI says, is "a world unto itself," and we each have to "build a world of *hesed* [love]"—an individual world of love for ourselves. But the only way to do that, the ARI says, is to root ourselves in the world of *hesed* that is God. Without that connection to the ultimate source of love and meaning, we are unable to build that world for ourselves. But how can an individual directly connect to that powerful ultimate source? It is through the people above us, he answers, the people closer to ultimate meaning, more advanced in their connection to God. With their help we will be able to bring ourselves closer to God as well.

In this view the *mitzvah* of "Love your neighbor as yourself" is directly related to a mystical connection with God—the interpersonal and the transcendent are inevitably linked, in the ARI's presentation. The next part of the *Or HaHokhmah* passage elucidates this concept by telling a story that the author says he heard told by the Baal Shem Tov: Once the Besht was praying with his friends "with tremendous love" (*ahavah gedolah v'rabbah*), but his friends were not able to stay focused on prayer as long as he could. When the friends finished their prayers, they waited for the Besht to conclude, but after a while they began moving forward with their own business. When they came back to the Besht, he berated them: Because they had left, his friends had caused a disconnect (*peyrud*) between the Besht and the Divine. To explain what he meant, the Baal Shem Tov told them a parable. And it is at this point that the Besht tells the story of the wonderful bird quoted above.

What is this bird that the king desires so much? If the parable is an allegory, what might be the one-for-one correspondence for which the bird stands? Does it stand for prayer? If it *is* prayer, the meaning of the bird is not particularly obvious. Prayer is not an object to be acquired and handed to the king, the way wisdom might be. People *do* acquire wisdom or knowledge, and one could imagine that *that* might be the kind of analogy symbolized by a splendid bird. But prayer is an action, not an acquisition. Indeed, as I shall suggest below, prayer in this parable is a means and not an end.

This bird, it seems, can only be acquired by a group effort. By standing upon one another's shoulders, the men in the story can capture the bird. Thus the connection back to the ARI's teaching about "Love thy neighbor as thyself." Hasidism, with its powerful mystical and *personal* emphasis, might seem like an unlikely source for teachings that deemphasize the individual. After all, with its psychologizing of earlier Jewish concepts in which ideas like exile and redemption were reread so that they were "denoting no longer only what they actually mean, but standing for a personal state of mind"[3] and its focus on the "inner process of individual redemption,"[4] one would think that Hasidism would turn away from community to focus on the individual soul looking for connection to God. Yet, Hasidism, despite all that, was a religious movement about community. It was focused around a central leader, and it assumed a community of like-minded individuals. In the Hasidic consciousness, the search for connection to the Divine was always rooted in the fellowship of others. In the parable of the bird, we even see a kind of hierarchy of spirituality. It's not Isaac Newton's "We stand upon the shoulders of giants"; rather, it is we who stand below the giants who are above us!

The king desired the bird, but even more so "was his wish to see his people so closely joined to one another." So what, after all, does God want? Is it the fervor of prayer? Or is it the power of community? And which is the cause and which is the effect? When the Besht finishes with this parable, he explains it.[5] He tells the men in his *minyan* who had wandered off, "It appears that you do not really love one another and you went away ... and because of that everything collapsed and that which I wanted to achieve flew away from me." "Flew away" (*parah*)—the bird, it becomes clear, is not the act of praying but stands for the Besht's connection to God. He has been disappointed by them because their wandering away cost him his *devekut* (cleaving to God).

But for us, readers of this parable today, the meaning is wider. The world of spirituality, the parable teaches, is not at odds with the world of community. They are bound up with one another. Judaism is not about the individual mystic alone in his or her contemplative meditation. We build community by creating contexts for prayer with others. But community is not only an end in itself. It is both an end *and* a means. We care about community, true, but community also allows us to encounter the Divine in ways that may not be possible if we were only on our own. The matter is simple after all: if we are to rise up the ladder of connection to God, so this parable teaches, we are going to need one another.

Notes

1. Uri Feivel of Krystnopol, *Or HaHokhmah* 4:31b–32a. Translated by Arthur Green and Barry W. Holtz in *Your Word Is Fire: The Hasidic Masters on Contemplative Prayer* (Woodstock, Vt.: Jewish Lights, 1993), p. 25.

2. To be completely honest, the original text does not say "men" but "gentiles" (*goyim*). Is this perhaps a sly comment on the ways of the gentiles? Is that where the comedy may lie? Perhaps. But the parable is very closely related to communal prayer, so my fantasy of the Hasidic men in traditional garb is not entirely unrealistic.

3. Gershom Scholem, "The Neutralization of Messianism in Early Hasidism," in *The Messianic Idea in Judaism and Other Essays on Jewish Spirituality* (New York: Schocken Books, 1971), p. 200.

4. Moshe Idel, *Hasidism: Between Ecstasy and Magic* (Albany: State University of New York Press, 1995), p. 16.

5. We did not translate this "afterword" in *Your Word Is Fire*.

PART FIVE

Prayer, Repentance, Healing

Melila Hellner-Eshed is a professor of Jewish mysticism in the Department of Jewish Studies at Hebrew University in Jerusalem, as well as a senior research fellow at the Shalom Hartman Institute in Jerusalem. She is a member of the faculty of the Institute for Jewish Spirituality and is active in Sulha, an Israeli-Palestinian reconciliation project. She is the author of *A River Flows from Eden: The Language of Mystical Experience in the Zohar*.

Praying from the Depths

MELILA HELLNER-ESHED

Rabbi Hizkiyah opened: "A song of ascents. Out of the depths [*mi-ma'amakim*] I call You, O *YHVH*" (Psalm 130:1).

"A song of ascents"—anonymous, not specifying who said it.

However, "A song of ascents," to be chanted by all inhabitants of the world, for this song is intended for generation after generation.

What is the meaning of "Out of the depths [*mi-ma'amakim*] I call You, O *YHVH*"?

So it has been taught: Whoever offers his prayer before the blessed Holy One should convey his request and pray from the depth of his heart, so that his heart may be completely with the blessed Holy One and he may concentrate heart and aspiration.

Now, did David really say this? Look at what is written: "With my whole heart I seek You" (Psalm 119:10). This verse suffices; what need is there for "out of the depths"?

Well, so it has been taught: Every person who presents his request before the King should focus mind and will on the root of all roots, to draw blessings from the depth of the well, so that it will gush blessings from the spring of all.

And what is that?

The place from which the river issues and derives, as is written: "A river flows from Eden [to water the garden]" (Genesis 2:10), and similarly: "A river whose streams gladden the city of God" (Psalm 46:5).

This is called "out of the depths—*mi-ma'amakim*"—depth of all, depth of the well, springs issuing and flowing, blessing all.

This is the beginning of drawing blessings from above to below.

Rabbi Hizkiyah said: When the Ancient One, concealed of all concealed, desires to provide for the worlds, He pours all and includes all in this supernal depth, and from here the well draws and flows, gushing and feeding streams and springs.

Whoever offers his prayer should concentrate heart and will to draw blessings from that depth of all, so that his prayer may be accepted and his desire fulfilled.[1]

ZOHAR 2:63A–B

A song of ascents. Out of the depths I call You, O *YHVH*. (*YHVH*, hearken unto my voice; let Your ears be attentive to the voice of my supplications)" (Psalm 130:1–2). This psalm speaks of the desire for God to hear and answer our voice as we call from the depths of human sorrow and suffering. Rabbi Hizkiyah, a member of Rabbi Shimon bar Yohai's *hevrayya* (circle of companions) opens up this psalm for us with a surprising and magnificent *derashah* (homily).

The *derashah* begins by identifying that this psalm does not have an explicit heading: it is attributed to neither a specific author nor event, and it is not addressed to a specific audience. This is an unspecified psalm, anonymous. It is so, says Rabbi Hizkiyah, for this is the prayer-song that shall be sung by all people of the world, for all time. In a sense, it is the generic *tefillah*.

Maybe our *darshan* (preacher) hears the musical play between the words *ma'alot* (ascents) and *olamot* (worlds). Between the ascents and the depths, there are countless human situations from which people call on their God. The *derashah* has already opened the gate of surprise: we are now reading a psalm that is neither personal nor contingent upon time or place. This is the song of all humanity in all times.

Before our eyes, the *Zohar* now conjures up a timeless human image of a person praying before the Holy King. In this familiar image, we see the broken and lacking person standing in supplication, pleading that his or her request be fulfilled. This is the God as King that fills our liturgy: we may make requests of the King, but we know that our wishes are not always fulfilled. Man is small, and the King wields great authority and power. This King is both the Supreme Judge and the Source of Compassion. The depths, *ma'amakim*, are the depths of the heart, and from them do we humans pray to God the King.

And here comes a new Zoharic surprise. With the rhetoric of a Talmudic inquiry, the *darshan* asks whether the word "depths," *ma'amakim*, in our psalm actually relates to the depths of the heart. For there already exists another verse that calls on us to seek God with our whole heart: "With my whole heart I seek You" (Psalm 119:10). What, then, is the uniqueness of the word *ma'amakim* in this psalm, and what does it come to teach us? We now pass through the entrance gate to the depths; the secret of the verse emerges and opens in front of us.

We begin with our familiar elementary image: man standing in "prayer before the blessed Holy One." But suddenly, a grand image envelops this initial picture. The praying person is called to a new stance: to "focus mind and will on the root of all roots, to draw blessings from the depth of the well, so that it will gush blessings from the spring of all." The image of standing in supplication before the King makes way for a picture of a totally different order. The supplicant is called to release his hold on the imagery of standing before the King in His chamber. This royal chamber disappears, for a moment, and with it, the King; our consciousness is now directed to an image of divinity that is not personal, separate from the individual story that initially brought us to stand before God the King in supplication. The "mind and will" (*ha-da'at ve-ha-ratzon*) are directed to experience divinity that is the source, root, and primal pulse of all reality.

The depths have been inverted. The depths of the heart have become the depths of divinity, and we are invited to direct ourselves to these depths, to dive or take flight into them, and to connect our depths—the depths of our hearts—with the divine depths. The deep calls to the deep—*tehom el tehom korei*.

In another place in the *Zohar*, we also encounter this type of inversion, in a *derashah* on a verse from Song of Songs: "I am the lily of the Sharon, the rose of the valleys [*ha-amakim*]" (2:1). The *Zohar* reads "the rose of the valleys" as the *Shekhinah* when she is connected to her source in the deep recesses of divinity, the *amakim*. She is the rose of the depths.

The *kavanah* has expanded. No longer about the wish to fulfill our personal desires, it has now become the intention to draw forth the flow of all blessings from the Source of all. The outlines of the praying person have changed. The contracted ego of the suffering supplicant has now expanded, and with it the essence of the supplication. We no longer merely desire our own personal wishes, but seek to draw forth the flow of blessings from the Source of blessing—*mabua ha-kol*, the "spring of all."

But what is this depth called "the spring of all"? The *Zohar* does not answer in abstractions, but teaches with its unique genius of religious imagination. It invokes one of its favorite verses from the story of the dawn of creation: "And a river flows from Eden to water the garden" (Genesis 2:10). This verse is an ever-dynamic image encompassing the essence of the *Zohar*'s understanding of the Divine. Eden is divinity as source and being—sublime, subtle, pleasant, and blissful.

Eden is the depths of divinity as oneness, existing beyond language, beyond the discursive intellect, beyond time, and beyond all national or personal narratives. In the language of the *sefirot*, Eden is connected to the *sefirah Keter*; to the union of the three uppermost *sefirot*, *Keter*, *Hokhmah*, and *Binah*; or to *Binah*, mother of all reality, in union with *Hokhmah* and suckling from *Keter*. From this primordial Eden, a river flows forth. This river is the manifestation of the Divine as movement, power, creativity, and *eros*, sparkling with the infinite hues of divinity. In the language of *sefirot*, this ever-flowing river is connected to the *sefirot* that emerge from *Binah*: *Hesed*, *Gevurah*, *Tiferet*, *Netsah*, *Hod*, and *Yesod*. The river is connected to masculine *eros* and sexuality in the world of emanation. This river has a direction. It flows from the depths of Eden to the garden in order to water it.

The garden is the divine quality that receives the myriad qualities that flow in the river; from her union with this river, the garden nurtures and grows her saplings. This garden is a grand symbol of accentuated and multifaceted divine reality that we as humans can connect to and speak of. This divine reality is quintessentially feminine: in the language of *sefirot*, it is related to the *sefirah* of *Malkhut*, *Shekhinah*, divinity in its immanent manifestation, embodied and dwelling within reality. Symbolizing feminine *eros* and sexuality, the garden is also a symbol of the world and of human consciousness.

According to the *Zohar*, in a state of awakening and arousal, human consciousness can attune and connect itself to divine realms that are normally hidden from the eye. Itself a garden and a sapling, human consciousness can be watered and saturated with the abundance flowing into it. Thus are we invited to direct our mind and will to the depths of Eden. On the human awakening that rouses the flow of the divine world, the *Zohar* says elsewhere:

> "O God, do not be silent, do not be quiet or still, O God!" (Ps. 83:2)—so that the white light may never be torn from her. Similarly, "O invokers of *YHVH*, do not be silent!" (Isa. 62:2)— to arouse below that upon which may abide arousal above.[2]
>
> ZOHAR 1:77B

In this passage, the intention of prayer resonates with the poem of Hannah Senesh: that the abundance of the river flowing from Eden "shall never cease"—*she-lo yigamer le-olam*—and shall always reach its destination in the garden.[3]

From the great reservoir of images in human consciousness, the ones here are images of nature—fountainheads, springs, rivers, gardens, water and earth, flow and growth—and they are all divinity. And this religious language is neither hesitant nor apologetic. True, the *Tanakh* has already taught us that the voice of God appears on the waters and that in reaction to the presence of God, the rivers and trees applaud. Nature is filled with the Divine—but here, in the *Zohar*, Eden, the river, and the garden are experiential images of *divinity itself*.

How expansive has religious language become! How special would it be to invoke these images in our prayers or as a *kavanah* and meditation as a preparation for prayer!

The *darshan* brings another verse: "A river whose streams glad-den the city of God" (Psalm 46:5). This is that same river that flows from Eden, and its streams delight the *Shekhinah*, the *sefirah Malkhut*, here depicted as the city of God. To the images of flowing, abundant nature the *Zohar* adds the glorious image of the city of God, as well as the joy and gladness that arise from this union.

In the copy of the *Zohar* belonging to Gershom Scholem, we find his notes to this passage adding an articulation to the sefirotic scale.[4] Scholem reads the terms "spring of all" and "depth of the well" as sig-nifying, respectively, the *sefirot Hokhmah* and *Binah*. Scholem learns this from the language of Joseph Gikatilla, a thirteenth-century kab-balist connected to the Zoharic circle, and David ben Judah HeHasid.[5] In this understanding, the *kavanah* is to draw forth blessings from the "depth of the well" of *Binah*, creating a deeper drawing-forth of plenty from the "spring of all," the beginning of all existence, the *sefi-rah Hokhmah*. The *kavanah* to the spring of all attunes consciousness and actually creates the drawing-forth of plenty into our world. One needs to acknowledge the existence of the depth of the well in order to experience the flow of blessing.

Note that the *Zohar* invokes the images of the well, the spring, and the source without explicitly invoking the *sefirot*. On the one hand, using these sefirotic images can allow us to appreciate the com-plexity of kabbalistic understandings of divinity. However, it is pre-cisely the choice of the *Zohar* to refrain from technical language that allows us to experience the potency of its imagery.

Rabbi Hizkiyah continues his *derashah*, invoking yet other poet-ics through which we can contemplate the prayer from the depths. This language belongs to the Zoharic strata of the *Idrot*, essays that make up the mystical and dramatic apex of Zoharic literature. These essays relate the gatherings of all the members of the Zoharic circle with their teacher, Rabbi Shimon bar Yohai, in which profound secrets of divinity are revealed. "When the Ancient One, concealed of all con-cealed, desires to provide for the worlds, He pours all and includes all in this supernal depth." The Ancient One is the ancient and archaic face of God that is revealed and installed in the *Idra Rabba*, the Great Gathering. In a state of emergency, Rabbi Shimon calls all his disciples to establish a more vibrant and healing flow among the different aspects of the Divine—to create a renewed, deep connection with the face of divinity as oneness existing beyond duality and judgment. This is the face of the Holy Ancient One, *Atika Kadisha*, that overflows with unconditional compassion, the aspect of God that generally relates to the *sefirah* of *Keter*. Differing from the nature imagery of Eden, this quality of the Divine is personal, and the language here is active. This divinity "pours ... and includes" its abundance in the spring of all, allowing the deep well to draw this abundance and channel it into streams and rivers that flow forth and water all reality.

Our *derashah* here incorporates the *Idrot*'s language of divine faces, intertwining them with the images of nature and the city of God. And now, in a surprising move, the *derashah* reverts to its opening picture. In the closing sentence, we again face the image of a person praying. The final sentence is prescriptive for all prayer-sayers, wherever they are: "Whoever offers his prayer should concentrate heart and will to draw blessings from that depth of all, so that his prayer may be accepted and his desire fulfilled." We might have thought that the supplication and wishes of the individual would dissipate in the dive into the depths of the Source of all. But this is not so. The personal experience of the prayer of request has not disappeared; rather, it has now gained vast perspective. The images of the small individual praying for his own personal wishes and the grand *kavanah* to the depths of depth shimmer, reflecting each other. The small *ratzon* meets the great *ratzon*. The depths of the heart meet the depths of all. And the desire to be blessed unites with the Source of all blessings.

The meeting between the depths of the heart and the depths of divinity fulfills our desire. We are not who we were when we ventured on this journey. Our personal supplication is now bound up in all of reality's desire to be blessed. Suffering and lack are inherent to the human psychological-historical realms. Yet when we have connected our consciousness to the depths of all, our personal desires change. The expansion of our consciousness to include the cosmic and the divine allows us to let go of this suffering and relax into the river of plenty.

We call upon God the King, the Supreme Judge, *YHVH*, from the depths. We call upon God's connection to the ancient aspect of divinity as Source of all life, forgiveness, and compassion. All that we have opened has now come to a close. But how different is our standing now in front of the King! The King is now aglow with the light and plenty coming from the depths, and we are participants in this event. Our initial desire for a living and dynamic connection with the Source of all has been fulfilled.

Happy are we that the *Zohar* was written, inviting us to join this holy work, enriching our understanding and experience of *tefillah*!

Translated by Sara Meirowitz

Notes

1. Daniel Matt, trans., *The Zohar: Pritzker Edition*, vol. 4 (Stanford, Calif.: Stanford University Press, 2007), pp. 342–43.
2. Ibid., vol. 2 (2004), p. 7.
3. From the classic poem "Eli, Eli" ["My God, My God"] by the Hebrew poet and World War II resistance fighter Hannah Senesh.
4. In 1992, under the editorship of Yehuda Liebes, the Magnes Press of the Hebrew University of Jerusalem published a limited facsimile edition of the personal copy of the *Zohar* belonging to the eminent Gershom Scholem, in which the pages of his copious annotations in Hebrew and German were interlaced with the Zoharic text.
5. Joseph Gikatilla, "Sod Yod-Gimel Middot," in *Kitvei Yad Ba-Qabbalah*, ed. Gershom Scholem and Issachar B. Joel (Jerusalem, 1930), pp. 219–25; David ben Judah HeHasid, *The Book of Mirrors: Sefer Mar'ot ha-Zove'ot*, ed. Daniel Matt (Chico, Calif.: Scholars Press, 1982), p. 14. Also see editor's notes in *Zohar*, trans. Matt.

Rabbi Neal Rose is a family therapist and professor of theology at the University of Winnipeg and has studied and lived in the Bratslav community in Jerusalem. He has written about Martin Buber's presentation of Hasidism.

Carol Rose is a writer, educator, and counselor. She holds an MA in theology as well as degrees in religious studies and cross-cultural education. Her publications include *Behind the Blue Gate* and *Spider Women: A Tapestry of Creativity and Healing*, coedited with Joan Turner.

The Tainted Produce

A Parable of Possibilities

Neal Rose and Carol Rose

Once the king said to his beloved vizier: "Since I am a stargazer, I see that all the produce which grows this year will cause madness in anyone who eats of it. What advice do you have?" The vizier replied that enough food should be set aside so that the two of them would not have to eat of that produce. But the king answered: "If we alone, from among the whole world, are not mad, and everyone else is, we are the ones who will be considered madmen. We too must eat of that produce. But let us place signs on our foreheads, so that we shall at least know that we are mad. If I look at your forehead or you look at mine we shall see the signs—and know that we are madmen."[1]

Rabbi Nahman of Bratslav, *Sippurim Niflaim*

This brief parable is attributed to Rabbi Nahman of Bratslav (d. 1810), great-grandson of the spiritual founder of Hasidism, Rabbi Israel ben Eliezer, the Baal Shem Tov (d. 1760). Rebbe Nahman saw himself as a "renewer" of the innovative spirit of his illustrious ancestor, and he had little regard for rebbes (Hasidic masters) who simply imitated his great-grandfather's ways. Often outspoken, he antagonized several of his Hasidic peers. Yet to his followers he was (and continues to be) the one true spiritual master, and his presence continues to guide their lives. The Bratslavers have never chosen another leader and, hence, have been called "the Dead Hasidim." Rebbe Nahman's teachings have spread far beyond the Bratslav community, inspiring countless other spiritual seekers as well.

Toward the end of his life, Rebbe Nahman turned to storytelling as a new mode of expressing his religious worldview. Feeling that he had not adequately conveyed his teachings to his community through his preaching and theoretical writings, Rebbe Nahman sought to capture the imagination of his *hasidim* (disciples) through sacred fiction. As Arthur Green writes, the tales represent Rebbe Nahman's attempt to convey in mythological terms a vision of "the truth of the soul as well as the truth of the universe."[2] The truths this Hasidic master sought to convey are a complex blend of theology and psychology around issues of yearning, anguish, joy, and hope.

The tale of the "tainted produce" has fascinated us for years. In fact, we've used it in both teaching and counseling situations. One of the reasons that we continue to be drawn to it (and several of Rebbe Nahman's other stories) is that unlike many classical parables, this *mashal* does not have an obvious *nimshal* (an application or moral to the story). This is no scribal error or editorial omission, but a deliberate artistic and pedagogic technique. Rebbe Nahman invites the reader to explore the tale over and over again, discovering in it new insights with each encounter. As Howard Schwartz argues in *Imperial Messages*, parables need not have a clear-cut moral appended to them.[3] Rather, it is the parable's symbolism that is its true essence. Evocative images, phrases, and words create a rich symbolic field in which multiple meanings may be gleaned.

Below are a series of brief reflections based on our explorations of this dramatic tale. While our approach is primarily impressionistic and existential, it is also informed by a long involvement with Bratslaver literature and with time spent studying among Bratslaver Hasidim. We would especially like to acknowledge the gentle teaching and wise counsel of Rabbi Gedalia Koenig of Jerusalem. May his memory continue to serve as a blessing.

The Paradox

This tale is one that can be referred to as a "royal parable," since its characters are court personages—the king and his beloved vizier. In this case, the king, an astrologer, has discovered via the stars that the current grain crop is contaminated and that eating it will cause madness (the duration of these effects is not revealed). Even if one were to avoid consuming the tainted produce, he would still be considered mad because in an insane world the sane are regarded as madmen! As many of Rebbe Nahman's teachings do, this tale challenges the reader to confront the paradoxical nature of existence.

The only course of action left to the two royal companions is to consume the grain. The king, however, suggests that in the face of the inevitable, they retain awareness of their plight by placing a sign (*siman*) on their foreheads "so that we shall at least know that we are mad." The king continues, "If I look at your forehead or you look at mine we shall see the signs—and know that we are madmen." In parables, key words are often repeated in order to communicate leitmotifs. In this brief tale, the words "mad," "madness," and "madmen" are repeated five times in the space of just one paragraph.

The King

In many Jewish parables, "king" is code for God. If that is the case, then the tale becomes even stranger! It is the "King of all kings"—God—who recognizes that the world is going mad, and it is the Divine who willingly enters into a state of madness.

Is this a deity forced to accommodate to a world on the edge of madness? If so, this is also a relational God who refuses to be isolated from the rest of the world and so joins His creations in a life of insanity. Interestingly, the King also wants to look at the sign on his beloved companion's forehead in order to remember that they have gone mad. Why? Will it provide the Divine with enough awareness to maintain some measure of control over creation, so that this craziness does not lead to utter chaos? But will this strategy work? One can imagine that these experiences of restored consciousness might actually lead the King and his companion into a deeper state of madness.

The Vizier

Assuming that God is the king in our story, who is the beloved vizier? One textual association is with the figure of Abraham, who is identified in various biblical and postbiblical sources as "the friend of God" (see, for example, 2 Chronicles 20:7). In Rebbe Nahman's universe Abraham is one of the prototypes of the Hasidic *tzaddik*, the mystical adept and community leader who connects heaven and earth—a spiritual channel through which divine and human energies flow back and forth.[4]

According to this interpretation, God and the *tzaddik* serve as reminders for each other: "We too must eat of that produce. But let us place signs on our foreheads.... I will look at your forehead ... we shall see the signs—and know that we are madmen." Is Rebbe Nahman, the brilliant and embattled spiritual master, here articulating his profound loneliness in his fervent attempts to bring God's truth into the world? Several scholars have discussed the messianic strivings in Rebbe Nahman's thought, pointing to various personal statements and teachings in which the master describes himself as a redemptive figure.[5]

The Sign

What is the sign that the companions place on their foreheads? One possible answer is that this is an allusion to the *tefillin shel rosh* (the prayer box worn above the eyes). There are Rabbinic texts that envision both human beings *and* God wearing *tefillin* (see the Babylonian Talmud, *Berakhot* 6a, for example). In kabbalistic symbology, the head *tefillin* is connected to the mind—divine and human—and its condition.[6] Among the passages contained within the *tefillin* boxes—head and arm—is the *Shema* (Deuteronomy 6:4–9), which proclaims God's unity and speaks of the love between the Divine and the community of Israel. Two of the four biblical sources for the wearing of *tefillin* also link it to the redemption from Egypt (Exodus 13:9, 13:16). The parable, as we understand it, invites the reader to imagine a moment in which the two companions stand face-to-face and see the *tefillin shel rosh* on each other's brow. It is at this moment that they recall the madness of their world, their own madness, and their commitment to help sustain each other until the blight passes and redemption is possible.

The Source(s) of Madness

What is the cause of *shigga'on* (madness) in Rebbe Nahman's view? Is it the basic existential condition of the human being? Is it caused by the waywardness of the people of Israel or the sinfulness of the gentile nations (or both)? Perhaps it is the recalcitrance of the *Mitnagdim* (Jewish opponents of Hasidism) or the misguided leadership of lesser Hasidic masters? All of these are possibilities. In addition, Arthur Green has argued that Rebbe Nahman intuitively understood that a new social and ideological order was taking hold of Europe (moving west to east).[7] Green explains that one of Rebbe Nahman's great concerns was the fact that modernity was on the way and that traditional values and beliefs were beginning to lose ground. The master experienced this new reality as *shigga'on*. Might our parable be an imaginative way of talking about the struggle between a traditional and a modern worldview? Is Rebbe Nahman here wrestling with the pain of this emerging reality as he attempts to develop strategies for coping with the "tainted produce" of the new world?

Dreams, Nightmares, and Healing Imagery

What is the origin of this opaque parable? While there are no definitive answers, Howard Schwartz indicates that dreams are often the source of classic Jewish parables.[8] Interestingly, Rebbe Nahman is known to have utilized dreams as a source for his storytelling, in addition to his extensive use of classic Jewish textual sources and non-Jewish Eastern European folktales.[9] This parable may well have been one of many that came (in whole or in part) from Rebbe Nahman's dream life. In truth, it might be better characterized not as a dream, but as a *nightmare*—the master's own nightmare or his channeling of a divine nightmare. But is there a way out of this bleak situation? Does the story offer us the possibility of hope, healing, or redemption?

While there is much about this parable that is deeply painful, we have actually used it several times in therapeutic situations. We have found it to be particularly valuable in working with people struggling with change—internal, interpersonal, and communal. The story's powerful imagery has proved helpful to people in dealing both with the

inevitability of change and the disorientation—temporary or prolonged—that often accompanies significant life transitions. How can
we become more adept at "reading the signs" of change like the king?
How might the loving relationship between the monarch and the vizier
serve as a model for us in coping with the madness of life? What are
some of the objects, symbols, and markings that can help anchor or
restore us in moments of disorientation or dislocation? Are there relationships that, despite their maddening qualities, we refuse to walk
away from? Are there ways in which our elevated sense of self—as
royal personages—actually contributes to our alienation and loneliness? When is overidentification with the king or vizier harmful?

Further, as counselors we take seriously the healing powers of the
imagination, making extensive use of various visualization techniques
and reflection on dreams. As Zvi Mark comments, for Rebbe Nahman
"the dream acts as a bridge between a routine or normative state of
consciousness" and "exceptional states" of mind. Mark goes on to
suggest that Rebbe Nahman's homilies and stories are designed to
serve as pathways to exceptional states of consciousness, opening one
to "various mystical states of inspiration and revelation."[10] In our
experience, revisiting dreams and using imagery exercises to enter into
"waking dream" states (as our beloved teacher Colette Aboulker-
Muscat called them) can lead to moments of revelation and healing—
healing that includes the realization that God is present in the madness
that we call daily living.

Rebbe Nahman does not offer a clear and unambiguous interpretation of our tale, and for this we are most thankful. Rather, what he
does is send out a g'shry—a cry. And in that cry is the anguished realization that life is not yet as it should be, that much of what we consider "normal" or "routine" is actually madness. He also reminds us
that nothing will ever be as it once was—nothing but the desire to
continue the search, to discover traces of meaning, and to tell our
tales. These tales serve as markings of our pain and anguish and of
our joy and hope. In telling them, we affirm the fullness and complexity of life and our commitment to learn and grow as we continue our
journeys.

Notes

1. Translation by Arthur Green, *Tormented Master: A Life of Rabbi Nahman of Bratslav* (New York: Schocken, 1981), p. 173.

2. Ibid., p. 346.

3. Howard Schwartz, introduction to *Imperial Messages: One Hundred Modern Parables* (Woodstock, N.Y.: Overlook, 1991).

4. Moshe Idel, *Hasidism: Between Ecstasy and Magic* (Albany: State Univeristy of New York Press, 1995).

5. See, for example, Green, *Tormented Master*, pp. 182–220.

6. For a helpful discussion of the multiple meanings of *tefillin*—both mystical and nonmystical—see Aryeh Kaplan, *Tefillin* (New York: Union of Orthodox Jewish Congregations of America, 1993).

7. Green, *Tormented Master*, pp. 174–75.

8. Schwartz, *Imperial Messages*, p. xxiii.

9. Ora Wiskind-Elper, *Tradition and Fantasy in the Tales of Reb Nahman of Bratslav* (Albany: State University of New York Press, 1998), pp. 161–62.

10. Zvi Mark, *Mysticism and Madness: The Religious Thought of Rabbi Nachman of Bratslav* (London: Continuum, 2009), pp. 16–19.

Michael Fishbane is the Nathan Cummings Professor of Jewish Studies at the University of Chicago. He is the author of numerous works on biblical and Jewish thought, including *Biblical Myth and Rabbinic Mythmaking*. His most recent book is *Sacred Attunement: A Jewish Theology*.

Spiritual Wounds

Michael Fishbane

"The towns that you shall assign to the Levites shall comprise the six cities of refuge [designated for a manslayer to flee to] plus forty-two additional towns" (Numbers 35:7). In order to arouse the heart to truly comprehend [the import of this passage], one should first indicate that this commandment [*mitzvah*] is valid for all times, since the Torah is eternal; hence it is applicable even at this time as a rectification [*tikkun*] "for anyone who slays [*makkeh*] a person [*nefesh*] unintentionally" (Numbers 35:15). That is to say, anyone who unintentionally commits sins and transgressions and destroys their soul [*nafsho*] may perform this *tikkun* by accepting the yoke of the kingdom of Heaven in total love, and [by reciting] to God with exceeding great devotion [*mesirut nefesh*], truly and with all their heart, to God (be praised), the six words of the [proclamation] *Shema Yisrael HaShem Eloheinu HaShem Ehad* ["Hear, O Israel, the Lord our God, the Lord is One"]—for the six words of this recitation correspond to "the six cities of refuge." [And similarly, the scriptural reference to the] "forty-two additional towns" corresponds to the sum of words in the opening paragraph of the *Shema* recitation, this being [the section beginning with] "And you shall love (the Lord your God)"—for it, too, is comprised of forty-two words. Hence: by the acceptance of the love of God and His Torah with a complete heart and soul [*nefesh*] [viz., the second unit], and by a true and wholehearted devotion to accept the yoke of the kingdom of Heaven with a love of God and with all one's heart [viz., the first unit], one will have atoned for "having smitten [*makkeh*] their soul [*nefesh*] unintentionally."

Moreover, the Gemara in [the tractate of] *Makkot* [Stripes] adduces [the following teaching on the terminology used in Numbers 35:7]:[1] "Abaye said: The [original] six cities of refuge afford asylum both with and without cognizance [*bein la-da'at bein she-lo la-da'at*] [of the refugee; i.e., his awareness of finding safety there];[2] whereas the [additional] forty-two cities afford asylum only with cognizance, but not without [such awareness]." Now these [just noted conditions] may be interpreted in the same [spiritual] way [as above; namely, with respect to the recitation of the *Shema* prayer]. Thus, the first six words [of the *Shema*], whereby a person devotes their *nefesh*, spirit [*ruah*], and *neshamah* (supernal soul) to God in perfect truth, afford [spiritual] asylum [viz., *tikkun*, for the wounded soul]—whether this [recitation] is truly performed with cognizance and comprehension, or whether the act of devotion is so intense that the person nearly loses complete cognizance [in ecstasy]. Granted, the latter matter [viz., the recitation of the first verse] would seem to be more important and valuable than the former [involving recitation of the first paragraph], as the [traditional halakhic] Decisors [*Poskim*] have commented in several places.[3] And from [the gist of] their remarks one may conclude—whether or not the latter is more common than the former—that these six words [of the *Shema* proclamation] afford [spiritual] asylum both with and without [full mental] cognizance; whereas the forty-two words of the following paragraph [starting with] "And you shall love"—which enjoins the total loving acceptance of the love of God and His holy Torah and commandments—actually require great [knowing] cognizance and understanding. And [more] specifically, even were one to acquire a comprehension of the supernal Intellects [during this recitation], but achieved this while in a state of [ecstatic] incognizance, [these words of recitation] would not afford [any spiritual] asylum [for one's soul]. May God (be praised) grant us the merit of divine worship in love—performed in truth, in perfection, and in [complete] cognizance. Let this be God's will. Amen. Understand well the full [import of] this [instruction].[4]

RABBI AVRAHAM YEHOSHUA HESCHEL OF APT, OHEV YISRAEL[5]

This is a remarkable teaching, offering an insight into the mystery of the Torah and a spiritual practice for the wounded soul. What is the mystery of Torah? It is the belief that God's Torah is an eternal truth, applicable for all persons and times. It is thus, simultaneously, both a formative revelation of historical instruction *and* an ever-present teaching for the transformation of those who seek its deeper wisdom. To achieve this, one must first choose to stand in the circle of Sinai, and then its ancient words may speak anew. Indeed, for the Torah to be present to the heart, the receiver must first be present to it. Such is the mystery of spiritual presence. So: do not think that the laws of the cities of refuge were formulated for generations past alone. They are also addressed to you, too, when you hear them in your time and place as a holy instruction. And: do not say, I live in entirely different circumstances, and these old rules of accidental manslaughter have no bearing on my life. For who is the person who does not stray on the path of spiritual direction or wander without intent into situations that compromise their spiritual integrity? And so, if the Torah speaks about six cities of refuge for the initial stages of settlement in the Land of Israel and then adds forty-two more for times of expanded borders—all in order to provide asylum for someone who slays (*makkeh*) another person (*nefesh*) inadvertently—it also speaks to each and every person who falls within the spiritual circle of this law and smites (*makkeh*) their own soul (*nefesh*) mistakenly (*bishegagah* [Numbers 35:11]) and unknowingly (*beli da'at* [Deuteronomy 4:42, 19:4]). For it is one thing to hate or bear enmity toward another and quite another matter to have a weak will or unstable character. As an antidote, the Torah is not in heaven: it is at once addressed to the body and the social good, *but also* to the soul and its (inner) struggle for spiritual virtue. This is its twofold truth, its manifest and deeper dimensions. The Ohev Yisrael helps us to see the scriptural passage in this dual way; namely, as an ancient word directed to the body politic, and an ever-new teaching guiding the seeker—in our case one who is on and off the way, whose soul is wounded by inadvertence, but who has become cognizant of that wound and wants to make repair. From the depths of ancient contemplative practices, our master provides a *tikkun* for such a person: a healing practice for their spiritual wounds.

One aspect of unwitting sin is the unfocused and undirected heart. So, what can one offer in reparation? Precisely the renewal of theological focus and wholehearted spiritual devotion. And where and how might one do this, in the absence of the Temple service or the Sanhedrin and its various penances? Precisely in the temple of the soul and its service of the heart,[6] that is, in the course of one's verbal and mindful prayer, whose words derive from the Holy Torah itself. Repair thus involves a slowing down of one's religious life and renewing it word by word through focused intention and purity of heart. From this process, one may return to God and religious action with a healed will—purged of the dross of aimlessness.

Knowing all this, the Ohev Yisrael directs our attention to the *tikkun* potential of the *Shema* recitation. It has two aspects. The first of these is the initial six-word statement: *Shema Yisrael HaShem Eloheinu HaShem Ehad* ("Hear, O Israel, the Lord our God, the Lord is One"). Rather than unpack its language in terms of its theological specifics or consider the different divine Names as indicators of God's manifest or mystical reality (as do many masters in Jewish sources), he simply asserts that these words can provide the wounded soul with a series of verbal domains for spiritual refuge and repair. Indeed, the very articulation of the words in uttermost devotion help effect this healing—not least because they are the holy words of Torah and filled with divine powers of restoration. They may also effect healing and recuperation because of their particular content and focus. And what is that? Following a traditional interpretation, the opening (six) words of the *Shema* recitation are said to mark (or assert) one's commitment to "the kingdom of Heaven,"[7] that is, to the wholehearted devotion of one's entire soul to God's dominion over all existence. Hence, the soul begins its healing by being called to attend ("Hear") to the truth of Divine Unity. And for them to be effective, the reciters must hear these words as directed to their soul, even as they are expressed from within one's self. Thus, a person can put themselves in the position of receiving by first putting their entire being in the position of hearing (anew) the mystery of God's Lordship. Thus, the very articulation of this theological reality is a process that helps actualize its realization in the innermost heart of the speaker; indeed, it is a dynamic pronouncement that collects the broken fragments of one's natural consciousness and binds them into a new spiritual unity. The soul becomes one through a devoted enunciation of God's Oneness. This is the first level of repair.

The second stage involves the ensuing paragraph, beginning with "You shall love the Lord, your God, with all your heart, with all your soul, and with all your might." This forty-two-word recitation complements the first one insofar as it is traditionally said to mark one's commitment to "the divine commandments" in total love.[8] Thus, having accepted God's dominion in love, one must also accept this "yoke" of obligations and commitments in a full and most joyful love. Deftly, the Ohev Yisrael reinterprets the biblical phrase "all your soul" ("all your *nefesh*") as an act of "wholehearted devotion of the soul" (*mesirut nefesh*) to the love of God and the *mitzvot*—at all times of day and night, wherever and whenever one is alert, whether at home or in the world. Once again, as before, the soul may help effect its own repair—for without the human initiative of a devoted recitation the soul cannot begin its process of spiritual transformation and healing. An individual must first put themselves in the position of identifying with the words of this unit, and only then may their singular mystery enter the marrow of one's being. Now to be sure, this (second) act of repair is more worldly in its focus than the first. For if the opening recitation of the *Shema* directs the soul upward toward God and the divine dominion over all Being, the recitation of this paragraph redirects it earthward to the manifold of the world. And if the first part is a theological proclamation, formulated through the syntax of "is," the second one is a programmatic declaration, presented through the syntax of "shall" (or "ought"). The words of the *Shema* are thus addressed to the mind by a normative assertion; whereas those of the *Ve-ahavta* ("You shall love") are directed to the heart and hands and feet—to action and tradition (instruction) in this world. The transcendental Lordship of God thus imposes various obligations upon the creature below. And to understand and embody the connection between these realms is to be transformed by Torah, in body and soul. This is the second *tikkun*.

But the Ohev Yisrael goes further in his instruction, now adducing an ancient Talmudic discussion of our scriptural passage. In so doing, he adds yet another dimension to the (proper and permitted) recitation of the words of the *Shema* (the first verse and the opening paragraph) that they might enable a spiritual refuge and repair. Just what is involved? And how does this addition supplement the initial requirement to accept both the dominion and duties of God in love?

Faced with the distinction between six and forty-two cities of refuge, the Babylonian sage Abaye offers a practical difference: an individual could flee to any of the six cities and find safety, whether or not they knew that such locales were in fact cities of refuge (the terminology is *la-da'at* and *she-lo la-da'at*, "with cognizance" and "without cognizance"). But as for any of the other forty-two cities, the person would have to know their official status in order for them to afford refuge. This is puzzling. For what might such a distinction mean, insofar as the phrasing is not formulated as a pragmatic consideration for the refugee's own safety (so that this person should know which are the cities and just where they are located)? To the contrary, this sage's formulation stresses that these cities may only afford refuge (*qoltot*) if certain specific conditions of mind are fulfilled by the refugee. Hence a correlation is established between person and place, such that the viability of the latter is dependent upon the mentality of the former. Presumably, it was this particular feature that attracted the Ohev Yisrael and inspired him to interpret Abaye's distinction in light of his own spiritual concerns—now expanded to include the actual modes of mind of the reciter. Thus, in the Ohev Yisrael's hands, the ancient legal condition of mental "cognizance" is retained but spiritually transformed into matters of intention and consciousness. Interpreted in terms of one's mental awareness, the proper recitation of the (two above-noted parts of the) *Shema* may be fulfilled "with Mind-fulness" (or full consciousness) *and* "with No-Mind" (or an eclipse of thought through heightened or ecstatic meditation).

To be sure, as all *poskim* stress, a person must begin recitation of this verse with a clear intentional awareness of its meaning and import.[9] It is this that the text stresses by requiring the person who wants *tikkun* to recite the words with the fullness of their *nefesh*, *ruah*, and *neshamah*. Use of this triad now recasts the meaning and intensity of the recitation. Initially, Scripture had used the word *nefesh* to indicate a "person" of flesh and blood, whereas the Ohev Yisrael has gone further and interpreted the word in spiritual terms, to refer to one's "soul." But now, with the introduction of a common (threefold) mystical soul cluster,[10] our master indicates further spiritual dimensions. And since these three elements are not identical, but refer to levels of the soul, we may understand the triad to mark a graded spiritual sequence. Thus, a person may begin the recitation by first arousing the fullness of their psychosomatic being (*nefesh*); this may deepen so as to engage their intellectual and spiritual being (*ruah*); and finally, realization of these states may even evoke their higher super-soul (*neshamah*), that element that links the self to divine realities. Hence, if the first stage comprises one's bodily being in toto (as a center of spiritual gravity), the second includes one's mental and imaginative faculties (that orient the self upon a spiritual axis), and the third climactically points to one's most transcendental spiritual qualities (that bind one to God in metaphysical truth)—that is, revealing that one *is* an "image of God" in the deepest sense,[11] rather than God being merely some projection or figment (however purified and truthful) of one's human imagination. But having offered this heightened practice, the Ohev Yisrael now also allows for the possibility of a deeper mystical, or contemplative, intensification; for if the initial verse of the *Shema* is recited with a heightened concentration,[12] one may achieve a state of consciousness beyond "Mind." And just this spiritual result is validated by our teacher (who was himself reportedly transformed by such states). Thus, one may not only proclaim the divine reality during the *Shema* recitation with a focused intent, but may be momentarily transfigured as well. "No-Mind" is this state. And it was notably lauded by Maimonides himself when he stated that the ideal recitation of the *Shema* verse is when a person is able "to empty [their] mind of everything."[13] In fact, as he then goes on to say, this practice of spiritual focus has extended value, since it may serve as a paradigm for all other acts of focused mindfulness in the course of one's (ritual) life.

For the Ohev Yisrael, the second paragraph complements this initial recitation—though quite differently. In his teaching, our master now stresses that the forty-two words of this section *must* be enunciated with consummate cognizance and devotion, that is, with a fully conscious mindfulness. This assertion clearly distinguishes the second recitation from the first one, since he emphasizes that it is only valid to the extent that one is fully cognizant of what is being said. To underscore this point, he adds that even if one were to attain the most supernal insights about Being (i.e., the Highest Intellects) during such a mystical recitation, such an act would not benefit the soul but would, in fact, invalidate the *tikkun* involved. And why so? Presumably because the words of this paragraph refer to the practical consequences of the love of God and performance of the commandments. That is, the latter unit evokes the realm of *mitzvot* in this world, and such behaviors cannot and may not be properly realized in an altered state of mind. To the contrary: all worldly duties (religious and otherwise) require one's full and total cognizance, and training toward this focused mindfulness is part of the *tikkun* for the soul enacted during this type of recitation.

We are thus offered a spiritually inflected instruction. Starting from the ground of divine love, and accepting the comprehensive dominion of God, the soul can enact that love through worldly deeds and duties. These are divine duties in the deepest sense—not solely the *mitzvot* or commandments of Torah and tradition, but also the many tasks that our earthly reality calls us to heed. In just that hearing, the omnipresent voices of Sinai may still address us in our time and place and lay claim upon our lives.

As a great teacher, the Ohev Yisrael opens our minds—to God, to Torah, to Duty, and to Love. But their summons must be heard by each person. The *tikkun* of the soul is not automatic and is not generalized. It offers a space within prayer for the most profound personal work. For starters, the master calls our hearts to account. We can only begin the healing of the soul through honest awareness of its specific wounds and lack. This awareness is the beginning of *teshuvah*. The task of repair must be undertaken with unswerving dedication. But the final healing belongs to God, through the words of Torah and the spiritual realities it communicates. The Ohev Yisrael wants you to understand this very well. One must not abuse spiritual gifts. Hear and do his great teaching—but with a humble heart. And then the eternal Torah will transform your soul.

Notes

1. Babylonian Talmud, *Makkot* 10a.
2. Interpreting this locution with Rashi's Talmudic comment. It is not the only possibility, but certainly the one the Ohev Yisrael would have noted and absorbed.
3. See the discussion of intention in reciting the opening verse of the *Shema* in the *Shulhan Arukh, Hilkhot Keri'at Shema* 60:5 (following the earlier formulation of Maimonides, *Mishneh Torah, Hilkhot Keri'at Shema*, 2:1; and cf. *Kesef Mishneh*, ad loc.) and also 61:1 (regarding the special spiritual state to be engendered). On both features, see the subsequent discussion of the Magen Avraham. These are the legal decisors the Ohev Yisrael might have had in mind. These matters are based on the discussion in the Babylonian Talmud, *Berakhot* 13b, especially, where the opening verse has to be recited with a special *kavanat ha-lev* (intention of the heart). This is the opinion of R. Meir, and the *halakhah* follows his ruling. See further below.
4. *Sefer Ohev Yisrael, Parashat Mase'ei.* Following the original Zhitomer edition of 1863; the teaching occurs at the end of the *parashah*. The collection was gathered and brought to publication by the Rebbe's grandson, R. Meshullem Zusia of Zinkov.
5. A disciple of the Rebbe Elimelekh of Lizhensk, the Apter died in 1825.
6. Cf. Babylonian Talmud, *Ta'anit* 2a.
7. This is known as acceptance of the *ol malkhut shamayim*, the "yoke of the kingdom of Heaven" ("Heaven" being a Rabbinic name for God). Note already the ancient formulation of R. Yehoshua ben Korha, in response to the query why the *Shema* recitation precedes the paragraph specifying the commandments ("If you obey My commandments"—the second full paragraph): "So that one would first accept on oneself the yoke of the kingdom of Heaven, and subsequently the yoke of the commandments" (*Mishnah Berakhot* 2:2). The Ohev Yisrael treats the first full paragraph (beginning "And you shall love") as evoking the duty of the commandment (see below). He does so, for present purposes, because the word count of this paragraph has the proper tally. See the ensuing discussion.
8. This is the complementary category of acceptance of the *ol ha-mitzvot*, the "yoke of the commandments." See note 7.
9. The basis for this is a teaching of R. Meir in the Babylonian Talmud; see above, note 3.
10. This triad was known by the acronym *NaRaN*. Several soul types were isolated (based on Scripture) by the ancient Rabbinic sages; medieval philosophers and mystics developed each of them in light of their particular spiritual psychology.

The three listed here were common in early Hasidism and often invoked by the masters in their *torahs* (teachings).

11. See the comment of Nahmanides at Genesis 2:7 ("And He [the Lord God] breathed into his nostrils [viz., of 'the *Adam*'] the *neshamah* of life"): Scripture hints to us here the exaltation of the *nefesh*, both its (heavenly) foundation and mystery, for it mentions here the full (twofold) Name (Lord God) and states that "He breathed into his nostrils the *neshamah* of life," to inform us that it does not derive (either) from the (earthly) elements ... nor is it concatenated from the separate (heavenly) Intelligences, but that it is the Spirit (*ruah*) of the Great Name...."

12. See note 6 (and 9), where the term for deeper concentration is *ha-lev*, "the Mind-Heart"—i.e., the deeper, affective Mind; the alert, intensive Heart.

13. See his *Moreh Nevukhim* 3:51.

Rabbi Or N. Rose is an associate dean at the Rabbinical School of Hebrew College and codirector of CIRCLE: The Center for Inter-Religious and Communal Leadership Education of Hebrew College and Andover Newton Theological School. He is the coeditor of *Righteous Indignation: A Jewish Call for Justice* and *God in All Moments: Mystical & Practical Spiritual Wisdom from Hasidic Masters* and contributed to *Jewish Theology in Our Time: A New Generation Explores the Foundations and Future of Jewish Belief* (all Jewish Lights).

Sarah and Moses

God's Teachers of Compassion

OR N. ROSE

"Sarah lived to be one hundred years and twenty years and seven years old. These were the years of Sarah's life" (Genesis 23:1).

Rashi explains, "The numbers of years are written separately—one hundred years and twenty years and seven years—to tell us that just as at age twenty she was without sin, so too at one hundred. The verse ends with the words 'These were the years of Sarah's life' because she was equally virtuous at all of these ages."

What else is alluded to in this verse? Of all the righteous women mentioned in the Torah, none are spoken of as highly as Sarah. This is even more striking when considered in light of what is written of Abraham upon his death. When Abraham our father dies, the Torah also says, "He lived one hundred years and seventy years and five years" (Genesis 25:7), and Rashi there explains that this was because Abraham also lived without sin. And yet, at the end of the verse we do not find the words "These were the years of the life of Abraham," which might tell us, as with Sarah, that all of these years were considered equally virtuous.

In the holy book *Ma'or V'Shemesh*, we find a comment from R. Menahem Mendel of Rymanov[1] ... concerning a teaching found in the Talmud (Babylonian Talmud, *Berakhot* 5a). R. Shimon ben Lakish says, "The Torah uses the word 'covenant' in its description of salt (Leviticus 2:13) and in its description of suffering (Deuteronomy 28:69). This teaches us that just as salt purges meat, so does suffering purify a person." R. Menahem Mendel of Rymanov adds the following: "Just as meat must not be oversalted for one to enjoy it, so too must suffering be properly combined with mercy and carefully measured in accordance with a person's capacity to tolerate it."

Rashi asks, "Why does the Torah recount the death of Sarah directly after the Binding of Isaac?" He answers: "When Sarah was told of the binding of Isaac—of how he was prepared for slaughter, and how the knife was laid at his throat—her soul fled from her and she died."

So Moses our teacher, the faithful shepherd, placed the death of Sarah and the Binding of Isaac side by side in order to advocate on our behalf. Moses is demonstrating what happens when a person's suffering is too severe, as was the case with Sarah—"her soul fled from her." And if this happened to Sarah the great *tzaddeket* [righteous woman] ... if she could not bear such pain, how can we be expected to do so?

Further, even though our mother Sarah took the Binding of Isaac so much to heart that her soul fled from her, she died for the good of the Jewish people. She gave up her life in order to show God that Israel cannot bear too much suffering. Even though a person, with the mercy of God, may survive his suffering, nevertheless, elements of his strength, his mind, and his spirit are broken and lost to him—"What difference does it make whether all of me or part of me is killed?" (Babylonian Talmud, *Bava Kama* 65a).

This explains the meaning of the words "These were the years of the life of Sarah." For it might appear that Sarah sinned by shortening her life span; had she not taken the binding of Isaac so much to heart, she would have lived longer. However, since she acted for the good of the Jewish people, the Torah alludes [to Sarah's righteousness with the words], "These were the years of the life of Sarah." Meaning, all of the years of Sarah's life were equally good, including the years [that she would have lived] beyond 127. For even with the years [she surrendered] she did not sin.

Therefore, may God grant mercy to us and to all of Israel, and swiftly redeem us—spiritually and physically—with revealed kindness.[2]

RABBI KALONYMUS KALMAN SHAPIRA, *ESH KODESH*

Shortly after the end of the Second World War, a laborer working on the site of the destroyed Warsaw Ghetto discovered a container buried in the ground. Inside the container were several manuscripts written by the famed Hasidic master Rabbi Kalonymus Kalman Shapira, the Rebbe of Piaseczno. Among the manuscripts was a collection of sermons referred to by the author as "Torah insights from the years of wrath 5700–5702 [1939–1942]." This was the last text R. Shapira wrote before the Nazis murdered him in 1943 and the last work of Hasidism written in Poland during the Holocaust. The book was later published in Israel under the title *Esh Kodesh* (Holy Fire).[3]

As Nehemia Polen has noted, while there has emerged a significant body of religious writings attempting to deal with the horrors of the Shoah, most were written *after* the war. *Esh Kodesh* is one of the few extended religious responses to the Holocaust penned from "within the heart of darkness itself."[4]

The sermon before us was delivered on November 22, 1939, several weeks after Germany's brutal invasion of Poland. Like the rest of the book, it demonstrates the Piaseczner's determined effort to continue to engage in Jewish religious life and leadership in the face of mounting oppression and great communal and personal loss. R. Shapira suffered the deaths of his son, his mother, and two extended family members between mid-September and early November of that year.[5] This sermon (the first recorded after these tragic losses) is at once an expression of spiritual resilience and a piercing cry to God. Using the classical rabbinic *derashah* (homily) as his medium, the Piaseczner issues an anguished call to God for compassionate intervention: "Therefore, may God grant mercy to us and to all of Israel, and swiftly redeem us—spiritually and physically—with revealed kindness." We hear in this cry echoes of the voices of the biblical figure of Abraham and the early Hasidic master R. Levi Yitzhak of Berditchev calling on God to deal justly and mercifully with His human subjects.[6]

R. Shapira's plea takes the form of a carefully crafted and poignant reflection on Sarah's death and Moses's role in the placement of the written record of this event immediately after the Binding of Isaac in the book of Genesis. The homily opens with Rashi's comment (based on earlier Rabbinic teachings) that the reason the Torah records the years of Sarah's life in three discrete units is to underscore her virtuousness from childhood through old age. The Piaseczner strengthens this teaching by pointing out that when one compares the language used in the Bible to describe Abraham's death, it does *not* include a second mention of his life span. This, the Rebbe argues, is indicative of Sarah's exalted status; not only is she the greatest *tzaddeket* in the Torah, but she even surpasses Abraham in her virtue.

At this point in the sermon, the Piaseczner turns his attention from the Bible to early Hasidism. He leaves aside for the moment the story of Sarah's death and quotes a brief teaching from R. Menahem Mendel of Rymanov on the nature of suffering. The Rymanover begins by affirming the Talmudic teaching that suffering, like salt, purifies the soul. However, he adds an important caveat: like salt, suffering must be dispensed with great care; it must be combined with mercy and administered in direct proportion to one's ability to tolerate the pain. In quoting this teaching, the Piaseczner seems to be saying that, while the Jews of modern Europe may be in need of purification for sinful behavior and/or spiritual growth, the suffering is just too much for them to tolerate; it must be alleviated, or they will be ruined by it.[7]

It is the Rymanover's teaching that serves as the bridge back to the biblical world and to the previous discussion about Sarah's death. Utilizing Rashi's commentary once again, R. Shapira explores the age-old Rabbinic question of why the report of Sarah's death comes immediately after the narrative of the Binding of Isaac (*Akedat Yitzhak*, or simply the *Akedah*). Rashi's answer is that upon hearing about this agonizing test of faith, Sarah's soul "fled from her" and she died.[8]

Having set the necessary exegetical elements in place—Sarah's unparalleled righteousness, the precarious nature of suffering, and the matriarch's dramatic demise—R. Shapira intensifies the discussion with a bold assertion about Moses. According to the Piaseczner, it was Moses who was responsible for placing the text about Sarah's death immediately after the story of the *Akedah*. The prophet's action, says R. Shapira, was a form of literary advocacy: Moses juxtaposed these texts to summon God's attention, to demonstrate to the Almighty that the people of Israel cannot bear extreme suffering. After all, if Sarah—arguably the most righteous figure in the entire Bible—could not tolerate such pain, how can the rest of us be expected to cope with comparable experiences of suffering?[9]

Needless to say, these are powerful claims that sound particularly daring coming from a traditional Torah commentator. However, it should be remembered that, as a Hasidic rebbe—a *tzaddik*—the Piaseczner understood it as his duty to serve as an intermediary between heaven and earth. As James Diamond has noted, the Rebbe presents Moses's "scribal activism" as an example of courageous and compassionate leadership. The prophet juxtaposes the texts in Genesis to urge God to see things from a human perspective. While from the heavens it might appear that Israel's suffering is appropriate, from earth it feels unbearable.[10]

The sermon continues to build in its intensity with the Rebbe's final comment about Sarah. Some might be inclined to think that the matriarch responded too strongly to the news about the *Akedah*. Had she been able to better control her emotions she would have lived a longer life, and the preservation of life is among the highest values in Jewish tradition.[11] The Piaseczner refutes this charge by stating that Sarah did not die because of her own sorrow, rather she martyred herself for the sake of her people. In the wake of God's terrifying test of Abraham and his family, Sarah decided that she urgently needed to show God the destructive consequences of causing people too much pain. While she may have been able to persevere, her descendants would not be able to do so. This is why Sarah intentionally surrendered the remaining years of her life. The Piaseczner here depicts the matriarch as a deeply compassionate and steadfast defender of her people, who took decisive action (through surrender, paradoxically) at a crucial moment in the unfolding relationship of the Divine and the nascent community of Israel. In his defense of Sarah, R. Shapira teaches that the phrase "the years of Sarah's life" alludes to the fact that not only were the 127 years Sarah lived all equally virtuous (as Rashi and others taught), but so were the years she relinquished.[12] In an ironic twist of events, while Abraham did not ultimately sacrifice Isaac on Mount Moriah, Sarah sacrificed herself for the sake of her offspring.

R. Shapira ends this impassioned commentary with a heartrending appeal: he asks that God remember Sarah's heroism and bring spiritual and physical redemption to the Jews of Europe. He adds that his request is for *hasadim nig'lim*, "revealed kindness." As a teacher of a mystical tradition in which there is much discussion of God's hidden and manifest presence and action, he states unambiguously that what he is calling for is revealed kindness—nothing less will do.

I first encountered this text a few years ago as I was preparing a *derashah* (sermon) on the Torah portion of *Hayyei Sarah*. Fascinated, but overwhelmed by the pain emanating from the teaching, I quickly turned to other textual resources. However, I have since returned to this homily several times, studying it more carefully and discussing it with others. I have been drawn back to it for a number of interrelated reasons.

As a person deeply committed to Jewish thought and practice but who struggles with core questions of belief, I find the Piaseczner's honest and searching exploration of suffering very moving. The fact that he wrote this highly original and daring sermon under such painful circumstances makes it even more inspiring. This is a stunning example of the work of a brave spiritual leader trying desperately to protect and comfort his community while dealing with tremendous personal loss.

Among the several intriguing elements of this sermon is the Piaseczner's portrayal of Sarah. It is not often that one reads in Hasidic Torah commentaries a description of a "righteous woman" who takes such bold initiative. Even Abraham—the father of monotheism—does not receive the same level of praise from R. Shapira. Nehemia Polen has suggested that this sermon was inspired, in part, by the death of the Rebbe's mother less than a month before her son delivered this sermon. Apparently, Mrs. Shapira succumbed to a heart attack brought on by the tragic news of the death of her grandson and other relatives in the German bombardment of Warsaw. I wonder to what extent the Piaseczner himself identified with the figure of Sarah as he was mourning his mother, his *only* son, his daughter-in-law, and a relative visiting from the Land of Israel. With this knowledge in mind, the citation from the Talmud "What difference does it make whether all of me or part of me is killed?" (Babylonian Talmud, *Bava Kama* 65a) takes on even greater poignancy.[13] It is not surprising that this Hasidic *tzaddik* viewed Sarah as a model *tzaddeket* who attempted to use her own experience of suffering to protect her community from future *Akedot* (plural of *Akedah*).[14]

As was mentioned above, the Piaseczner presents not one but two models of leadership in this sermon. Moses follows Sarah as another great advocate of the people of Israel. While the matriarch surrenders her life for her offspring, Moses lives on to remind God of her story and to continue to agitate on behalf of his community. Like Moses, the Piaseczner continues to lead his flock, using his exegetical creativity and moral standing to try and convince the Divine to intervene on behalf of the Jews of Europe.

While the focus of the sermon is on the courageous efforts of Sarah and Moses to arouse God's mercy, I believe this presentation of the loving and noble deeds of these biblical figures also calls us to reflect on our own behavior. Why do we not show more "revealed kindness" to others? Will our experiences of suffering—whether we view them as divinely ordained or not[15]—lead us to greater empathy or embitterment? What are we willing to sacrifice for others? How widely can we draw our circles of compassion?

Finally, part of what drew me to this text is the fact that like so many other Jews of European descent, I lost many relatives in the Shoah. My mother's pain in particular, as the child of refugees, was part of my consciousness from a very young age. It was in this context that many of my early and lasting theological questions first emerged. Reading the writings of the Piaseczner provides me with a meaningful framework in which to explore these difficult issues and to feel a greater sense of connection to lost family and community members. It also serves as a powerful reminder of the great privilege I have of living in a society in which I can practice my Judaism freely, drawing on the wisdom of my ancestors as I seek to carry forth my religious tradition into the future.

May the memory of the Rebbe of Piaseczno continue to be a source of courage and compassion.

Notes

1. R. Menahem Mendel of Rymanov (d. 1815), a prominent fourth-generation Hasidic master, was a disciple of R. Dov Ber, the Maggid of Mezritch (d. 1772), and R. Elimelekh of Lizhensk (d. 1778). *Sefer Ma'or V'Shemesh* is a collection of sermons on the weekly Torah portions and Jewish calendar cycle by R. Kalonymus Kalman Epstein (d. 1825), a younger colleague of R. Menahem Mendel of Rymanov and an ancestor of our author R. Shapira.

2. Kalonymus Kalman Shapira, *Sefer Esh Kodesh, Hayyei Sarah*, 5700 (1939). In preparing this translation, I consulted and adapted J. Hershy Worch's rendering of this text in his book *Sacred Fire: Torah from the Years of Fury, 1939–1942*, ed. Deborah Miller (Northvale, N.J.: Jason Aronson, 2002), pp. 12–14. This is, to the best of my knowledge, the only complete translation of the *Esh Kodesh* in English. I also made use of Nehemia Polen's translation of the latter portion of this homily from his study *The Holy Fire: The Teachings of Rabbi Kalonymus Kalman Shapira, the Rebbe of the Warsaw Ghetto* (Northvale, N.J.: Jason Aronson, 1987), pp. 96–97.

3. See Polen, *Holy Fire*, p. xv. Rabbi Polen's book was an invaluable resource to me in writing this brief essay. I also wish to thank him for his ongoing mentorship and collegiality.

4. Ibid., p. xvii.

5. Polen notes that R. Shapira, like earlier Hasidic preachers, avoids explicit reference to the political events of his day—"Nowhere in *Esh Kodesh* do the words German or Nazi appear" (ibid., p. 17). Unlike most Hasidic writers, however, the Piaseczner dates his homilies, thus allowing us to reflect on possible connections between the contents of his writing and events in his life. Occasionally, the Rebbe will make a brief comment about his personal situation or that of his community.

6. On the subject of protest within faith in Judaism, see Anson Laytner, *Arguing with God: A Jewish Tradition* (Northvale, N.J.: Jason Aronson, 1998). It is important to note that while in this sermon the Rebbe assumes an activist posture, in other cases he preaches about the need for an unquestioning acceptance of the divine will in the face of suffering. See Polen's explanation of this dialectical stance in *Holy Fire*, pp. 70–105.

7. See Polen's treatment of the Rebbe's various attempts to grapple with the question of why the Jews of modern Europe were being subjected to such great suffering in *Holy Fire*, pp. 106–15.

8. This teaching from Rashi, like the previous one, is based on earlier Rabbinic legend. See Tamar Kadari, "Sarah: Midrash and Aggadah," in *Jewish Women: A Comprehensive Historical Encyclopedia*, ed. Paula E. Hyman and Dalia Ofer, Jewish Women's Archive, http://jwa.org/encyclopedia/article/sarah-midrash-and-aggadah.

9. As the Rebbe goes on to say quite dramatically, the issue is not only about survival, but also what is lost to the survivor in the course of his or her suffering.

10. James A. Diamond, "The Warsaw Ghetto Rebbe: Diverting God's Gaze from a Utopian End to an Anguished Now," *Modern Judaism* 30, no. 3 (2010): 311–15. See Diamond's discussion of earlier Rabbinic and mystical sources that may have influenced the Rebbe's understanding of Moses's role in the composition of the Torah and his own role as an interpreter of Torah.

11. See Elliot N. Dorff, *Matters of Life and Death: A Jewish Approach to Modern Medical Ethics* (Philadelphia: Jewish Publication Society, 1998), pp. 14–33.

12. See Don Seeman, "Ritual Efficacy, Hasidic Mysticism and 'Useful Suffering' in the Warsaw Ghetto," *Harvard Theological Review* 101, no. 3–4 (2008): 484. See also Seeman's brief comments on the presentation of martyrdom in this text in comparison with the Piasczner's prewar teachings and those of earlier Hasidic preachers (p. 485).

13. I want to thank Erin Leib Smokler for sharing this insight (and others) with me in our discussion of this homily.

14. See Mimi Feigelson's discussion of the Piasczner's teachings on the biblical figure of Miriam and his relationship with his wife and daughter in "Rechtche's Sabbath Candles," *Eretz Acheret: About Israel and Judaism*, September 24, 2009.

15. The issue of the spiritual significance of human suffering is, obviously, one that has challenged religious writers for centuries. For an introduction to the subject in Jewish thought, see Neil Gillman, *The Way Into Encountering God in Judaism* (Woodstock, Vt.: Jewish Lights, 2000), pp. 71–108; and David Hartman, "Suffering," in *Contemporary Jewish Religious Thought*, ed. Arthur A. Cohen and Paul Mendes-Flohr (New York: Scribner, 1987), pp. 939–45.

Prof. Haviva Pedaya teaches Judaism and culture in the Department of Jewish
History at Ben-Gurion University of the Negev. She is the author of *Vision and
Speech: Models of Prophecy in Jewish Mysticism* (Hebrew), *Within the Eye of the
Cat* (Hebrew), and other works. Prof. Pedaya is also an award-winning Hebrew
poet and musical director of the Yonah Ensemble, a project devoted to the revital-
ization of the liturgical and mystical music of the Near East.

Crisis and Repair, Trauma and Recovery

Haviva Pedaya

And when the blessed One wanted to create the world, He had
no place to create it, because everything was infinite; therefore
he contracted [*tzimtzem*] the light to the sides, and by that contraction [*tzimtzum*] vacant space was created.... The vacant
space had to exist for the creation of the world, because without
that vacant space there would have been no place for the creation of the world. This *tzimtzum* of the available space cannot
be understood or grasped until future times, because two opposite things must be said about it: existence and nothingness. The
vacant space is made by *tzimtzum*, which is ostensibly the
tzimtzum of the divinity, because there is, as it were, no divinity
there. For otherwise it would not be vacant, and [since] everything is infinite there would be no place for the creation of the
world at all. But in absolute truth, there is divinity there nevertheless, because certainly there is no thing without it, and therefore it is impossible to grasp the existence of a vacant space at all
until the future.

And you must know that there are two kinds of *apikorsut*
[heresy, disbelief]: there is *apikorsut* that comes from external

sciences—which come from permissible things, from the aspect of the breaking of the vessels. For due to the abundance of light, the vessels were broken, and from there the *kelipot* [shells] came into existence, as it is known.... And therefore whoever falls into that *apikorsut*, he is able to find rescue and leave that place. For since they come from the breaking of the vessels there are some sparks of sanctity there and some letters were broken and fell into there, as it is known—the person can therefore find divinity there and the wisdom to resolve the difficulties of that *apikorsut*....

However, there is another kind of *apikorsut*, and these are the wisdoms that are not wisdom. But because they are deep and people do not grasp them, they seem to be wisdom.... And in truth it is impossible to resolve those difficulties, because the difficulties of that *apikorsut* come from the vacant space—and there in the vacant space there is no divinity, as it were. Therefore those difficulties that come from there, since they possess the aspect called "vacant space," it is impossible in any way to find an answer for them—that is to say, to find the blessed One there—because if the blessed One were found there as well, then it would not be vacant, and everything would be Infinity, as mentioned above.

For the blessed One fills all the worlds and surrounds all the worlds, so we find that He is, as it were, within all the worlds and around all the worlds. And there must be a difference, as it were, between the filling and the surrounding. For if that were not so, then everything would be one. But through the aspect of the vacant space—from which He contracted His divinity, as it were—within it He created all creation, and therefore it is fitting to say that He fills all the worlds. That is, all creation was created within the vacant space, and He also surrounds all the worlds—that is, He also surrounds the vacant space. And in the middle the vacant space separates, for as it were He contracted His divinity from there....

These are the complexities and difficulties of that *apikorsut*, which comes from the vacant space. They are the aspect of silence, since there is no wisdom or letters to resolve them, as noted; for creation was by means of speech ... but the vacant space, which surrounds all the worlds, as noted, is vacant of everything, as it were. Nothing is there—not even wisdom, nor are there letters. And therefore the complexities that come from there are in the aspect of silence ... and every *tzaddik* who is in the aspect of Moses, in the aspect of silence, can examine these complexities, which are in the aspect of silence, as noted. And one must particularly examine this, in order to raise the souls that fell into there ... and know that by means of the melody of the *tzaddik*, who is in the aspect of Moses, he raises the souls from that *apikorsut* of the vacant space, which had fallen there.

RABBI NAHMAN OF BRATSLAV, *LIKUTEI MOHARAN* 1:64

What is the vacant space? The Kabbalah of Isaac Luria speaks of the origin of the world in two stages of occurrences within the total divine light. The first stage is *tzimtzum*: the divine light had to withdraw in order to leave space for what was separate from it—for the world, for the cosmos, which is its *Other*. However, always in order to leave space for the *Other*, one must leave his or her space. One must step aside. This is a kind of *Other*-self scheme, which was separated out from within the infinite light into the vacant space. And the second thing is the act of disintegration, breakdown, which is a kind of collapse that takes place during the process in which the infinite light seeks to individualize itself and "flow" in a structured form and as a hierarchical system, which, in the end, will be communicative to humanity and make possible the existence of this world. That collapse shattered the system of the infinite light. The break took place while the infinite light sought, as it were, to descend, and when it split into the contained light and the vessels (which are a kind of containing light), the break caused the scattering of the lights, the departure of some of them upward, and the descent of some of them as remnants downward. Hence it requires the rebuilding of this process in measured fashion. The rebuilding of the system will be called "repair."

Rabbi Hayyim Vital, the greatest disciple of the ARI, who recorded his teachings in *Etz Hayyim* (The Tree of Life), describes the vacant space in the image of the empty point in the center of a circle, a circle that the lights fill and is pressed to the sides, leaving an empty point in the center. However, Rabbi Nahman—extending Rabbi Yisrael Saruk's interpretation of the ARI—describes the empty space more as a kind of interval between the light that fills the whole world and the light that surrounds it.

That interval, existing as it were between two circles, is one of Rabbi Nahman's concepts. It is therefore a kind of narrow band; in parallel with that description there is also an extremely different conception of the divinity, as well as two different conceptions of mind and memory.[1]

As an extension to Rabbi Nahman's conception, which I wish to develop here, I will describe the *tzimtzum* as it takes place in the mind. It is like a manner of traveling and of the separation of one area of contact from another area of contact, and the placement of an impassable distance between them. Thus the vacant space is created as an empty ring that separates between two of the divinity's manners of being present.

The vacant space as a kind of vacuum can be conceptualized—already in connection with the ARI's procedure—in various ways that are connected to the relation between the conscious and the unconscious. However, in relation to Rabbi Nahman's exegetical procedure about difficulties in the teaching above, I will try to suggest another conceptualization relating to the issue of trauma and to the source of language. In my exegetical and creative step, I will suggest another reading of this teaching, not like the one that struggles with *apikorsut*—with the question of belief and intellect—as it is discussed in the model studies by Yosef Weiss and Arthur Green,[2] but as a struggle with the question of tragedy and trauma. I will carry on from the place where Rabbi Nahman takes the two sequential stages of *tzimtzum* and breakdown from the ARI and makes them into two structural paradigms; I will read them as two paradigms for coping with situations of tragedy and crisis, which are inherent in human existence, as a situation of suffering and as a tool for conceptualizing the tension between structural trauma and acute trauma. The justification for such a reading derives from several places: on the one hand, the struggle with the dead-end road of silence, and on the other hand, the fact that on the biographical level Rabbi Nahman experienced great suffering. Hence it is quite likely that part of the conceptualization that he suggested at that time can be read simultaneously as a conceptualization of the struggle with trauma following a tragedy or crisis.

Following that, with the inspiration of Rabbi Nahman, I will propose that in fact we have two different paradigms for coping with suffering. The first paradigm is that of breakdown. It is connected to the struggle with a crisis that can be the basis for change, enabling the discovery of an advantage or solution—a situation in which, within a certain collapse that took place in life, there is still open contact with the remnants of the "explosion" of the crisis. Language remains, even if it is broken. In contrast, the second paradigm is that of *tzimtzum*. It is connected to trauma and terrible tragedies in which a separation is produced. On the one hand, in its isolation of the tragic event, it preserves the possibility of existence; and on the other hand, it contracts the forms of the continuation of existence.

In the paradigm of breakdown, the remains of the collapse are within reach—perhaps they scratch, hurt, and wound, but they are still present within the range of the extended arm of the falling person. And concurrently, all that flows from the break, from that disintegration, from that collapse are things that can be understood. They are things that can be repaired. They can be grasped; there is a chance that the mind can attain and conceptualize them.

In the paradigm of *tzimtzum*, the traumatic event forms a ring of emptiness and absence—the lacuna is connected to the experience of the absolute absence of the Divine as a type of experience of absence and not as an intellectual controversy. The emptiness that is created at the moment when God takes a step back, any tragedy that comes from that place, is in principle impossible to understand. It is connected to the Hasidic riddle of the existence of a place devoid of God, and there is no possibility of understanding it: congenital disability, death at a young age, collective disasters, unbounded evil of one person to another. This type of disaster and horror causes, as many studies of trauma have shown, the opening of a kind of hole in the system, the emergence of a lacuna inaccessible to the mind.

Rabbi Nahman speaks about *apikorsut* and not about disaster, but it is possible to suggest that if we understand the basic difficulty of the question of heresy and faith, the absence or existence of God, and if we allow ourselves to read this harsh existential difficulty from within the world of a believing, religious man—who, in a moment of disaster and tragedy, calls out for the presence of God at his side—we can estimate that this teaching is a brilliant and striking theological theory, and that the impulse to create it probably cannot be detached from the various disasters that Rabbi Nahman underwent in his life,[3] and from his existential call for help.

Therefore, without denying other possible readings (for is that not the power of homily, and especially of Rabbi Nahman's homilies, that it is possible to read them in multiple ways?), I locate the reading of this homily in the context of trauma. If we read the homily as a testimony to and conceptualization of traumatic experience, indeed Rabbi Nahman is speaking about a kind of suffering about which one can only keep silent. He even uses the deep symbol of the vacant space in a manner that reads it as a place void of God. From this point of view, the "vacant space" is grasped as a lacuna that cannot be represented. If the "breakdown" is a catastrophe or trauma, it is an accessible trauma, which can be treated and approached and conceptualized to put the break back together. If so, it is also possible to apply speech to it. However, the "vacant space" is a lacuna that dwells in the heart of the traumatic event. It is absolute emptiness. From the viewpoint of the traumatized person, there are no words in her mouth and there is no capacity to testify to a horror beyond words. Specifically, the excess of dread, or the terror, the shock, and the evil to which the traumatized person is exposed, is grasped and experienced as lack, absolute emptiness that is beyond words and with which words have no contact; here the sufferer is doomed to silence.

However, the kernel of the traumatic reading is located deeper. The teaching of the ARI is essentially, as I understand it, a theology of crisis; hence it can also be read as a brilliant conceptualization of trauma.[4] Rabbi Nahman takes this further. *Tzimtzum* is the act by which the fullness becomes emptiness, and therefore it is a paradigm of the extreme traumatic crisis of what is beyond words. One can point out the existence of the lacuna, but it cannot be represented in words:

> And in truth it is impossible to resolve those difficulties, because the difficulties of that *apikorsut* come from the vacant space—and there in the vacant space there is no divinity, as it

were. Therefore those difficulties that come from there, since they possess the aspect called "vacant space," it is impossible in any way to find an answer for them—that is to say, to find the blessed One there—because if the blessed One were found there as well, then it would not be vacant.

It is impossible to construct a language and it is impossible to put together fragments in a place where ab initio there are no materials. Repair by means of speech, by means of language, can only correct what has left behind remains and fragments. Fragments can be gathered and put together, a new organization can be proposed, but what cannot be expressed, what hovers beyond the bounds of attainment, what remains in the area of the unconscious, is distanced to the place where there is no time—it cannot be reorganized; it is beyond the realm of speech.

The theological-metaphysical paradigm of *tzimtzum* is the absence of God as infinite light, which was necessitated to make being possible for existence itself. In the psychological paradigm, the structural traumatic experience leaves behind a lacuna that cannot be represented—but at the same time it is also an absence of the sense of the Divine Presence in grave situations of disaster and trauma, in situations of a loss of existential potency. This absence is pure horror, an experience of dread divorced as it were from words: "There is no divinity, as it were." This does not refer to the intellectual difficulty of skepticism as to whether or not there is a God. This is the loss of an inner grip on the minimal sense of presence (whether we call it divine or not) that holds a person from within and enables him to continue to live and act. Regarding that situation, there is only silence.

Any effort to "understand" such levels of suffering or blows of fate is also foolish. On the conscious level, and this parallel is exact, the space or gap can be an expression of cognitive dissonance, which, in this instance, is identical with the absence upon which being is based, or with the emptiness that is located in the center of the circle and defines the circle although it cannot be grasped at all in itself.

Any effort to approach a person who is tormented by suffering of this kind and to console him with a theological explanation, with a kind of bookkeeping logic that finds a reason and purpose in such sufferings, is to be dismissed like the counselors of Job. God will appear to them among the hairs of their heads to say that in the tempest of that trauma there is a confrontation with the unknown.[5] There is no answer. God's revelation to Job from the tempest and his exaltation of nature above his disaster is in fact also a kind of absence of a divine explanation for the evil that strikes a person like a blow from nature.

In this place, pens are broken and words are halted. There is such suffering that the effort to explain and explicate it with theological terms itself shatters theology. Religion often earns contempt for itself when it tries to explain things that by definition are impossible to explain or touch. We can only be silent or conceptualize the pain and the abyss itself. To speak about the gap. Sometimes the gap can be as narrow as a hair, and sometimes it can seem like the ocean.

In the original theory of the ARI, we may say that *tzimtzum* is a voluntary act, which is defined as an act of mercy and grace that makes the existence of the world possible, or it is even possible to formulate it as the existence of the *Other*, whereas the breaking is an involuntary, catastrophic act, a breakdown of the system. In contrast, in Rabbi Nahman's structural theory, there is a change of relations and an entirely different emphasis in the definitions: *tzimtzum* is experienced as far more catastrophic because the means for coping with it are more *restricted* by nature, whereas the breakdown is less catastrophic because the means to cope with it are richer and more extensive. *Tzimtzum* is a kind of blockage: "Come to here and no farther," whereas the breakdown pushes forward, and sometimes the breakdown is the only impetus to development. Without a breakdown, the personality undergoes fewer metamorphoses, and it will push less for a process of perfection and integration.

At the same time, the process of conceptualizing trauma in connection with language is powerful. In the framework of understanding silence as a wall that we have encountered and against which the possibility of understanding smashes, it permits Rabbi Nahman to propose a practice of coping for the person who suffers or those who wish to comfort her.

Acknowledgment of the tragedy or trauma of this grave kind contains solace first of all in the language that conceptualizes and describes the structure. For it is an articulation that connects individual suffering to the basic structural breakdown of the cosmos, to the tension between God's being and not-being, to the fate of the human being as a conscious creature who is vulnerable like any other thing or object to disaster and inexplicable destruction.

There is an area of silence within the injured person, which we must bypass cautiously and on tiptoe. Rabbi Nahman suggests that we should not endeavor to make silence into speech, that we should recognize the refusal or the nonsusceptibility to verbalization and transmute the nonverbal force into music; both music and silence are wordless situations, but music touches upon the emptiness, it brings with it metaphysical solace. Only music can enter the realm of the *Other*'s horrible pain, the place of the breakdown that is not capable of simple consolation, to the distortion that cannot be set right or the lack that cannot be reckoned; the one who as a teacher or physician can bring with her the healing melody is also the one who knows how to be silent with the sufferer, to bring silence that is like a kind of music: "And I found nothing good for the body except silence, for there in the vacant space there is nothing better than silence, because it is forbidden to enter there except if one is in the aspect of silence."[6]

In the place where language and words break down, in the place where silence has swallowed language—in that empty lacuna, in that black hole, which sucks everything in and dissolves everything that draws near to it, there is one thing that can approach that black hole not only without being damaged and without being sucked into it but that also can help, and that is music, melody.

The healer identifies the hole in existence that was opened (the lacuna of trauma that can be called a "hole" in Lacanian terms), with which he struggles, and his task is to soothe the suffering of *tzimtzum*, to help as much as possible in sorting out the subjective from the objective, to help in processing and transforming the hole into nothingness, and to make it possible to give means for conceptualizing the emptiness, to point out the vacant space.

The other paradigm of trauma is that of breakdown. Here we have material to deal with: there are remnants, things left over. There is the breaking into parts—here a person can deal with the collapse of an existential structure that perhaps appears to him to be the foundation of his life, but he must go beyond the stage of denial and anger, within which he continued this crisis, and define it as a natural disaster. The pain, the fighting, the disagreement, the suffering all point to an unprocessed and undigested remnant, to a place where these fragments of the breakdown are stuck in the personality, and the existential insult and suffering burst out. They are painful and pressing, and therefore they enable those who do not deny that pain to touch it and process it and break out and move forward.

Sometimes with correct guidance we discover that, in being human, we have attributed too much of our suffering to situations of absolute blockage. But if we expand our relation toward them, we will discover that they can be seen as a breakdown and not as *tzimtzum*; we expand the demand that pain and suffering require of us: to develop, to process the remains; our cry of "despite everything" against the emptiness will grow stronger, and we will be aware of growth.

The Impassable Gap and the Story of the Seven Beggars

We suggest that the subject of the vacant space is not only discussed directly and theoretically in Rabbi Nahman's Teaching 64 but that it also flows in the deep foundations of the story of "The Spring and the Heart," which is a section of "The Seven Beggars." In another deep reading, which I cannot present in full in this framework, I would suggest that Rabbi Nahman's story complements his conception of melody. Both are events in language that circumvent it and also circumvent certain conditions of consciousness in an effort to offer constructive memory, to heal pain (the pain of remembering and forgetting as a kind of constant lack of healing), and at the same time to arouse the mechanical consciousness (forgetting as a kind of automatic existence and memory as a kind of awakening). Here we must be content with seeing a passage from the story (which is, from the start, an arousing linguistic reality) as an expression of the idea of melody. In the story within this story, we are told about "the heart of the world," which is a sort of body that is all heart, from its toes to its head, and it always longs for the spring, which it cannot reach. The distance between them cannot be crossed, because in every single moment the heart must draw the vitality of its existence from the well, and if the heart starts to walk toward it, a great mountain that stands in the middle of the spring will hide it from his eyes. In these concepts, the heart is the *ego*, and the spring is the *self*. The heart is immanent, and the spring is transcendent. The distance between them is the gap of the vacant space that cannot be crossed. Since what separates them is absolute nothingness, the distance between them cannot be traversed. That is to say, Rabbi Nahman's story expresses in narrative fashion an unmistakable situation of existence as an unanswered question. The antinomy is the essence of life. Rabbi Nahman, who often dealt with questions of voice and language and the tension between the verbal and the semiotic, joined two fundamental phenomena together here, consciously or unconsciously—phenomena in which a leap above language takes place: trauma as a psychic situation on the one hand, and stammering as a not fully explained physiological phenomenon on the other. Research and much firsthand evidence show that some marvelous singers stammer when they speak. That which marks their speech does not mark their singing.[7] On the metaphorical level, then, it is impossible to resolve dreadful suffering; it is possible only to try to cope with it. Language remains and will remain broken, and both existence and language are henceforth experienced as the remains of something that once existed but no longer is. In this situation, life is an existential stammer that will sometimes burst into song, but when it does, those moments will be moments of metaphysical consolation and perhaps of vocation.

In the place where the vacant space stands in the way as a ring of absence and absolute nothingness, the pain of the heart's silence leaps, and it is no coincidence that the teller of this story is the beggar with a speech impediment. The stammering and broken voice bursts forth toward the spring in song and music (in *lider*). That which stands between the spring and the heart is an impenetrable barrier of fullness that is emptiness, and the melody makes the leap, the transition. Thus, together, the possibility is created of grasping again (grasping and raising and bearing and suffering) the world and life.

Translated by Jeffrey Green

Notes

1. On this see my book *Constructions of the Self in Jewish Mysticism* (Tel Aviv: Yediot Ahronot, forthcoming).
2. Arthur Green, *Tormented Master: The Life and Spiritual Quest of Rabbi Nahman of Bratslav* (reprint, Woodstock, Vt.: Jewish Lights, 1992), pp. 285ff.; Yosef

Weiss, "The Difficulty," in *Studies in Braslav Hasidism* [Hebrew] (Jerusalem, 1975).

3. The date of the sermon is not indicated in the sources, but Green is also of the opinion (*Tormented Master*, p. 305), that it is probably connected with the years 5565–66 (1805–6). I lean toward dating it to the end of 5566, after the death of R. Nahman's son, which led to the collapse of his messianic hopes and the awakening of many doubts, both his own doubts in himself and the doubts of his *hasidim* in him. It cannot be earlier than that, because I also see in it, with respect to its contents, a harbinger of a change of direction in the stories, a change of direction that is expressed in *Likutei Moharan* 1:60, which was delivered on Rosh Hashanah, 5567.

4. I discuss this at length in my book *Constructions of the Self in Jewish Mysticism*.

5. *Editor's note:* This is an allusion to an interpretive play found in *Midrash Bereshit Rabbah*, section 4, correlating the phrase *min ha-se'arah* ("from out of the whirlwind") in Job 38:1 to the encounter with God in the hairs (*mi-bein se'arot*) of a person's head. The encounter with God takes place in the very physical pain of suffering and trauma.

6. These lines are drawn from the continuation of Rebbe Nahman's homily in Teaching 64, though it should be noted that the phrase "And I found nothing good for the body except silence" is taken from *Mishnah Avot* 1.

7. See Haviva Pedaya, "Both and Both—an Essay on Stammering" [Hebrew], *Daka* 1 (2007): 32–38.

PART SIX

Torah, *Halakhah, Mitzvot*

Dr. Eitan Fishbane is assistant professor of Jewish thought at The Jewish Theological Seminary. He is the author of *As Light Before Dawn: The Inner World of a Medieval Kabbalist* as well as numerous scholarly articles. Fishbane is currently researching a new book, tentatively titled *The Poetics of the Zohar*, for which he was awarded a fellowship from the American Council of Learned Societies. He is coeditor of *Jewish Renaissance and Revival in America* and contributed to *Jewish Theology in Our Time: A New Generation Explores the Foundations and Future of Jewish Belief* (Jewish Lights).

Shabbat Candle Lighting

EITAN FISHBANE

In the midrash it is taught[1]
that the light of a person's face during *hol* [the weekdays]
is different from the light of his face on Shabbat.
This means that on Shabbat
the inwardness [*penimiyut*] is revealed,[2]
as it is written:
"A man's wisdom lights up his face."[3]

This is the revelation of the extra soul.[4]
And so too at large in the world,
the inwardness is revealed on the holy Shabbat.[5]
As it is written:
"Let there be light [*va-yehi or*]."[6]

And our Sages of blessed memory taught
that God hid that light
for the righteous in the time to come.[7]
The utterance "Let there be light"
is to be found in every detail of creation—
for all the work of creation
holds a portion of that light.[8]

It has just been hidden,
and on Shabbat
light is revealed
from that concealed source.
During the six days of the week
that light exists in the sense of
the *aspeklaria* that does not shine [a darkened lens],
and on Shabbat it is like
the *aspeklaria* that does shine [a clear lens].[9]

And thus
the lighting of the Shabbat candles
is a *mitzvah* that hints to the revelation
of the hidden light on the holy Shabbat.

The children of Israel anticipate
the disclosure of the hidden light
as they feel the darkness of this world—
as it is written:
"Though I sit in darkness, the Lord is my light."[10]
For on the holy Shabbat,
God be He blessed
reveals to us a semblance of the light
of the world to come.
As it is written:
"God called the light Day ..."[11]

The essence of characterizing "Day" and "Light" as "good"
is the Torah—
as it is written in the midrash:[12]
the Torah preceded the creation
of the world by two thousand years ...
which is to say: two days of creation.
"For in Your sight a thousand years
are like yesterday that has passed."[13]

And on Shabbat
there is a revelation
from those two "Days";
Shabbat bestows *Hokhmah* [Wisdom]
and *Binah* [Understanding] upon the children of Israel
for all the days of the week.[14]

For this reason
there is a reading of the Torah on Shabbat,
as the light of Torah is revealed in that moment.
And thus did our Sages interpret
the verse:
"if you would but heed His Voice this day"[15]
as referring to the holy Shabbat
through which [the Jews]
can hear the voice of Torah.[16]

RABBI YEHUDAH LEIB ALTER OF GER, *SEFAT EMET*

How sweet and full of light are those first moments of Shabbat, when the aches and weights of the workweek fade away, when the world feels as though it has been created once again. They hold the sublime silence of a world at rest, the tranquility of a soul sated in the calm of Divine Presence.

Our work and frenzy are set aside; the pressures and to-do piles are released from their everyday urgency. We are freshly bathed and dressed; the house has been transformed into a sacred space. The air is filled with the warmth of the coming meal, the smells we associate with peace and family. The candles shine with an otherworldly glow— a reminder of the radiant Presence that has begun to envelop us, transforming our ordinary space into a small sanctuary, a place made ready for God's Dwelling.

God is the pure light that pulses at the core of creation, the force of all that is; we yearn for that radiance in every unaware moment of our daily lives, crying out from the narrowness of superficial obsession. Slowly finding our way to the bright gleam of divinity, and like the lover and beloved of the Song of Songs, we leap over mountains in quest of the Heart of all hearts.

Most of the week we dwell in darkness—hovering over the face of the deep, unconnected to our spiritual Source. In that time, the time of the ordinary, the light of the divine face remains hidden in the innermost chambers of our selves—it is unrevealed, and so often inaccessible.

Such is the light that was hidden in the Torah at the dawn of time.

As the ancient Rabbis tell us, when God first created the world, there emerged a light through which one could see from one end of the earth to the other. But God feared that this pristine light would be abused by the wicked, and so He hid the light away for the righteous in the time to come.

And where did He hide that light?

In the Torah—to be retrieved by great students of Torah in each generation.

In this passage from the *Sefat Emet*, Shabbat is presented as that time when the primal light of creation is once again revealed. For, according to ancient tradition, Shabbat is a semblance of the world to come (*me-ein olam ha-ba*) that can be accessed while one is still in this world (*olam ha-zeh*). It is a time when the transcendent wonder of all things is disclosed to the human eye, a time when the timeless sparkles with the shimmer of heaven, a moment when a portal to the immortal divine mystery is opened wide to our limited and mortal vision.

It is on Shabbat that the first light of creation shines through to us; each week we return to Shabbat as a source of warmth and illumination. And this is the Hasidic reading of the midrash: a person's face glows in a fundamentally different way on Shabbat; on that day the full brilliance of divinity is made manifest, that which is inward becomes revealed, and we are restored to the peace of primordial perfection.

As the Sefat Emet says, "This is the revelation of the extra soul" (*ha-neshamah ha-yeteirah*). First mentioned in the late ancient Rabbinic literature, this idea was developed at length by the medieval kabbalists. They believed that, on Shabbat, each Jew receives the influx of an extra measure of soul, an overflow of divine blessing from the realm above. In the text we have before us, the extra soul force that descends upon the Jew is experienced as a moment of illumination, a radiance of heavenly purity in the face of the one enveloped by the holiness of Shabbat.

Our Hasidic author teaches that the primordial divine light is present in the whole of creation; it is a glow that dwells hidden beneath the surface of reality, and it is the same light that was concealed in the Torah.

The letters of Torah form the structure of the natural world—all of Being is nothing but the great speech of God. And so Shabbat is the time when the hidden light of Torah is revealed, when the garments of concealment are lifted, and we stand in the presence of Divinity.

This, the Sefat Emet says, is the significance of reading the Torah portion on Shabbat: the reading and hearing of the sacred words releases divine light into our midst—the first glow of creation is sent into our hearts and souls on that day that is *zekher le-ma'aseh bereshit* (a remembrance of the work of creation).

What is more, we are given a beautiful *kavanah* (intention) for the lighting of the Shabbat candles (*hadlakat ha-neirot*) on Friday night. Though we may feel that we wander in darkness during the week, Shabbat comes to light up our homes and our inner lives. Such is the way that the Sefat Emet reads the words of the prophet (Micah 7:8): "Though I sit in darkness, the Lord is my light" (*Ki eshev ba-hoshekh YHVH or li*). During the week of ordinary time, we struggle to make a living and to accomplish our seemingly endless tasks. Sometimes this world can be a place of pain and great suffering; sometimes we can become mired in narrow and superficial thoughts. But Shabbat has been given to us as a precious gift of restoration and healing. As sunset arrives on Friday evening—as we breathe deeply and ignite the sacred flames of the Shabbat candles, the light of the world to come shines bright, and the radiance of the divine face eclipses all of our weekly worries. In this moment we are made whole again, and we are reminded of all that is good and sublime in this world.

Notes

1. *Bereshit Rabbah* 11:2.
2. The inner force is always present, pulsing at the center of Being. For the Sefat Emet, the *penimiyut* is the very presence of God—the life-breath of divinity that dwells within. But during the six days of the week, we experience that life force as through a veil of concealment, and only on Shabbat is it fully revealed to us.
3. Ecclesiastes 8:1.

4. Building upon earlier ideas, the medieval kabbalists articulated the notion that the Jew receives an "extra soul" on the Sabbath—a spiritual force that dwells within them from Friday evening until *Havdalah* on Saturday night. Here the Sefat Emet attributes the glowing countenance of the Jew on Shabbat to the presence of that extra soul within. An influx of divinity, the Sabbath soul is an entity of pure light descended from the celestial realm above.

5. The *penimiyut*—the divine force of inwardness—is not only found in the heart and soul of the person. It is also the life force that dwells at the center of the world at large, at the core of Being itself. This is the primary way in which the Sefat Emet expresses his theology of radical immanence—a view that accords with the broader Hasidic conception. God is not relegated to the transcendent heavens above; divinity is to be found in the world below, in the realm of earthly and ordinary things. But just as the presence of God in the person is often concealed during the six days of the week, so too is that divine light revealed in the world on the holy Sabbath. God's presence is a force of light, and the sacred time of Shabbat opens our spiritual perception so that we may see that which is otherwise hidden from us.

6. Genesis 1:3.

7. This is an allusion to a highly influential passage in the Babylonian Talmud, *Hagigah* 12b, wherein the Rabbis assert that God first created a light so powerful and majestic that one could see through it from one end of the world to the other. But God became concerned that this pure light would be abused by the wicked, and so He hid that light away for the righteous in the time to come. And where did God hide that light? In the Torah, to be discovered anew in each generation by those who study the Torah with pure hearts.

8. In this statement the Sefat Emet has transformed the Talmudic idea into the seed for an immanentist theology. The first light of creation—the *va-yehi or*—was cloaked within the world at the dawn of time, and it remains there as the radiance of Divine Presence, waiting to be discovered by the spiritual seeker. Shabbat is that time of pure discovery, the moment when the veils of darkness recede and the light of divinity emerges to full glow. The light *is* the Divine Presence; "all the work of creation holds a portion of that light"—God is present in all the details of creation.

9. Here the Sefat Emet is alluding to the kabbalistic resonance of these phrases. Already in Rabbinic literature a distinction is made between those prophets who see God through the *aspeklaria she-einah me'irah* (a darkened or cloudy lens) and the prophet Moshe, who alone saw God through the *aspeklaria ha-me'irah* (the clear lens, the shining lens). In medieval kabbalistic symbolism, the *aspeklaria she-einah me'irah* refers to *Shekhinah*, the tenth *sefirah*, the feminine dimension of divinity, and the *aspeklaria ha-me'irah* refers to *Tiferet*, the masculine dimension of divinity. On the kabbalistic understanding of prophetic visualization of God,

see Elliot R. Wolfson, *Through a Speculum That Shines: Vision and Imagination in Medieval Jewish Mysticism* (Princeton, N.J.: Princeton University Press, 1994).

10. Micah 7:8.

11. Genesis 1:5.

12. See *Midrash Tehillim* 90.

13. Psalm 90:4.

14. Already in the midrash, the two thousand years before creation, when the Torah was created, are characterized as two great cosmic days. In the kabbalistic system, these two "days" refer to the *sefirot Hokhmah* and *Binah*. These two upper *sefirot* bestow the primal energy of Torah on the six "days of the week"—the six *sefirot* between *Binah* and *Shekhinah* (*Hesed, Gevurah, Tiferet, Netzah, Hod, Yesod*). *Binah* and *Shekhinah* are both understood to represent Shabbat within the divine realm, and the six sefirotic days between them are like the six days of the week sandwiched between two Sabbaths—the Sabbath that precedes the new week, and the Sabbath that follows the workweek. The primordial Torah is contained within *Hokhmah* (for what is wisdom, both the ancient Rabbis and the medieval kabbalists ask, other than Torah?), and that force of Torah—that primal hidden light—is sent down into the lower *sefirot* to be revealed on Shabbat.

15. Psalm 95:7.

16. *Sefer Sefat Emet, Parashat Bereshit*, teachings delivered in 1888.

Ron Margolin is associate professor of religious studies and modern Jewish thought at Tel Aviv University and a senior researcher at the Shalom Hartman Institute in Jerusalem. He is author of *The Human Temple: Religious Interiorization and the Structuring of Inner Life in Early Hasidism;* and *The Inner Religion: Phenomenology of Inner Religious Life and Its Manifestation in Jewish Sources* (both in Hebrew).

Why Do We Need the *Mitzvot?*

RON MARGOLIN

What our Sages of blessed memory said (in Babylonian Talmud, *Yoma* 28a on Genesis 26:5), "Our father Abraham of blessed memory kept even the *eruvei tavshilin,*"[1] may appear to be baffling, for whence came his knowledge of this? If we say that he arrived at the *mitzvot* and laws through a process of reasoning, we would still be left with the problem of how he arrived at the [unexplained and unexplainable] *hukim*, like the law of the red heifer and the other *hukim*. But as stated, what the Sages of blessed memory asserted was that "He said to Moses, to you will I reveal the sense of the heifer and unto others it will be *huka*"[2] [unexplained and unexplainable law], for all the *hukim* have their root and sense above in the order of creation, since creation took place in accordance with the Torah. Not every mind is capable of grasping this, and therefore unto the others it is *huka.* But the Torah does not address exalted figures like Moses and Abraham our father of blessed memory, for whom there was no impediment to *huka*, because for them, all *hukim* were *mitzvot* to know and grasp fully in their sense and root: it would not have been possible for the *hukim* to become *mitzvot* unless the *mitzvot* had been annulled for them. For example, the prohibitions "You shall not murder," "You shall not commit adultery," and "You shall not steal" were no longer appropriate because they had broken themselves of all lusting through the corporeal *middot* [attributes] and did not function in the physical realm at all except in the service of God. And the gratification of their passions became as disgusting to them as the filth of slime and excrement about which no one needs cautioning because it is naturally disgusting. And in the same vein that King David of blessed memory said in Psalm 109:22, "My heart is wounded within me," we see that for a person [like King David] to whom the *mitzvot* do not apply, the reasons and sense of the *hukim* are revealed and become like *mitzvot*. And this is what our Sages of blessed memory said in Babylonian Talmud, *Nidah* 51b, "The *mitzvot* will be nullified in the time of the Messiah," "for the world will be filled with knowledge of the Lord" (Isaiah 11:9), and they will have a different Torah and the *hukim* will become *mitzvot*, and as one goes from strength to strength and higher and higher to the root of all the Torah and *mitzvot*, which is *Anokhi*, "I am the Lord your God"—in other words, pure unity and *Ein Sof* [Infinity]—all the wings of *mitzvot* and *hukim* will fold, and all *mitzvot* and *hukim* will be nullified, as this itself is the eradication of the *yetzer ha-ra*, the evil inclination, so that we will stand in the exalted place as it was before creation when there was no *yetzer ha-ra*.[3]

RABBI MENAHEM MENDEL OF VITEBSK, *PRI HA'ARETZ*

In *Devotion and Commandment,* Arthur Green explores various approaches to the Talmudic dictum "Our father Abraham of blessed memory kept even the *eruvei tavshilin*" and discusses in depth what the early Hasidic masters taught concerning this dictum. As he writes in his introduction to the book:

The disciples of the Maggid knew full well that they were not about to set aside the halakhic system in practice.... While there is a good deal of variety within the school, such prominent members of the circles as Levi Yitzhak of Berdichev (1740–1810) and Menahem Mendel of Vitebsk (1730–1788) record in their homilies traces of significant inner turmoil on the

question of the place of law and commandments in the face of
the single all-embracing commandment to strive without compromise for intimate union with God.[4]

This reference to Menahem Mendel of Vitebsk clearly alludes to the
passage quoted above from *Pri Ha'aretz*, and in what follows I shall
concern myself with Menahem Mendel's teaching from a contemporary Jewish perspective.

For modern Jews with a tendency to value behavior based on
autonomous morality and freedom of choice more highly than obedience to extraneous law, the concept of *mitzvah* as heteronomic commandment is particularly confusing. The dictum of R. Hanina, "One
who performs a precept having been commanded to do so is greater
than one who performs a precept without having been commanded to
do so" (Babylonian Talmud, *Kiddushin* 31a), utterly negates what to
most is the obvious view of things. Is someone who acts through obligation rather than free will truly greater? Is R. Hanina really implying
that it is preferable to adhere blindly to law than to obey it with an
understanding of what it means?

To people in the modern age, the state's imposition of a legal system on its citizenry seems reasonable and necessary. It is clearly justifi-
able for the elected representatives of a democratic state to enact a
code of civil law, without which society would become anarchic. But
for many Jews who achieved citizenship with equal rights and obligations in the countries they inhabited or in their national homeland, the
State of Israel, the halakhic system of heteronomic law seemed dupli-
cated in the legal framework of the state.

Those who willingly accepted the civil code were troubled by its
similarity with the code of *halakhah*, particularly with respect to the
laws of society. What is the spiritual significance of accepting the yoke
of heaven if it is only a mirror image of legislative law expanded to
more private concerns and rituals? Little wonder, then, that a consider-
able number of Jews regard those components of *halakhah* that have
no parallel in the legal system, i.e., ritual laws observed today, as the
very essence of Judaism. Hence, to them, the vast corpus of *halakhah*
dealing with social issues is either of small concern or a matter of theoretical scholarship; otherwise, where is the spiritual advantage of

divine law over civil law? What they seek is the added value neither government nor society can provide in order to give meaning to their religious life.

The words of Menahem Mendel of Vitebsk offer a key to understanding the recondite concept of *mitzvah* as distinct from law.[5] The interpretation he offers recaptures the concept of *mitzvah* as a means of communicating with God in fulfillment of the magnificent Talmudic idea that is reflected in the expression "the joy of *mitzvah.*" Observance of the Torah commandments becomes a way of working on oneself in order to draw closer to the Divine, to that which lies beyond the technical, structural, and peripheral aspects of life.

The words of R. Yohanan ben Zakai concerning the *mitzvah* of the red heifer stress the outward obligation of performing a *mitzvah*: "The Holy One said, I have set it down as a statute. I have issued it as a decree. You are not permitted to disobey My decree. 'This is the statute of the Torah' [Numbers 19:2]."[6] According to this view, the unintelligibility of a *mitzvah* actually increases its importance, since the presence or absence of an intelligible reason behind its observance has no bearing on its value as such. Commandments given for no apparent reason like the *mitzvah* of the red heifer reaffirm the heteronomic basis of the Torah.

In contrast to this view, R. Menaham Mendel of Vitebsk says explicitly that "all the *hukim* have their root and sense above in the order of creation." He bases his claim that there is no law without a humanly intelligible reason on his reflections concerning the negative commandments. The long list of negative commandments is relevant only to those who may be tempted to violate prohibitions. R. Menaham Mendel of Vitebsk interprets the words of Psalm 109:22, "My heart is wounded within me," as referring to a person whose heart, having been emptied of all temptation, no longer feels the lure of sin. The negative commandments for such a person become insignificant, null and void. They remain necessary only for those who are still caught up in their passions, as a means of warding off temptation. There is a direct correlation between an individual's state of being and that person's rationale for observing the commandments. To those whose inner world is free of temptation, seemingly unintelligible laws become an intelligible way of communicating with God. The commandments, according to

R. Menahem Mendel of Vitebsk, form a spiritual ladder of ascent; yet
once a person reaches the top rung and cleaves to the root of the
mitzvot in the infinite oneness of divinity, all laws and commandments
are annulled. The *mitzvot* that derive from the root become superfluous for those who already adhere to this root. This in effect is what is
implied concerning Abraham. Because he ascended to the top of the
spiritual ladder and remained there in permanent communion with the
root of the Torah commandments, cleaving to God, the Sages could
say that he observed all the laws that derive from it.

R. Menahem Mendel prefaces his discussion of the Talmudic dictum that Abraham observed all the Torah commandments with the
Lurianic idea introduced in *Sefer Etz Hayyim*: before the creation
nothing existed save the infinite and inconceivable oneness of the
Creator, who contracted Himself out of a desire to create. As to what
follows the dictum of the Sages that "the Lord looked at the Torah and
created the world,"[7] R. Menahem Mendel explains that the division of
the Torah into positive and negative *mitzvot* is reflected in the two elements of the first verse of the Ten Commandments. The first, beginning with the word *Anokhi*, "I am," and the second, with "You shall
not make for yourself," attest to the two stages of creation. The
Anokhi and the positive commandments deriving from it preceded the
contraction, and "You shalt not make for yourself" and all the negative commandments deriving from it followed the contraction.

On the matter of the creation of the world, it is known that in the
beginning He and His Name were One, were a simple unity utterly
inconceivable, unimaginable, and limitless, that is, *Ein Sof*. When the
will to create manifested in Him, He contracted Himself as is known
and described in the opening of the *Sefer Etz Hayyim* (Book of the Tree
of Life). And here the matter of simple unity and *Ein Sof* pertains to the
commandment of *Anokhi*, "I am" (the first commandment in Exodus
20:2), and the positive *mitzvot,* while *tzimtzum* (contraction), which is
Gevurah, pertains to the negative *mitzvot*. And the commandment "You
shall not make for yourself" (the second of the Ten Commandments)
and all the different permutations of the negative commandments in the
whole Torah are derived thereof in their minute details.[8]

Anokhi, the word through which God reveals Himself to His people, proclaims the infinite unity of the Divine that compels *devekut*

(cleaving). As a result, all the positive commandments are in fact different ways of attaining intimate union with God, represented by the word *Anokhi.* The negative commandments deriving from the contraction of the light of *Ein Sof*, which permitted creation, prohibit anything that might lead one astray from union with the *Ein Sof.*

The word *Anokhi* is declared as the root and purpose of all *mitzvot.* The Hasidic view of this is that the purpose of religious worship is to release humankind from the illusions of a separate ego, the "I am" that cuts one off from the Godhead. This is what enables a person to conceive of his wholeness as a creature of God, absorbed in the Divine. R. Menahem Mendel further elucidates the spiritual purpose of Torah commandments as union with the Divine through the well-known story of Hillel's answer to the gentile who asked to be converted while standing on one foot.[9] There he states explicitly:

> To understand the *mitzvot* we must begin from the end. Depart from evil in the beginning and later do good, for at first man is "a wild ass's colt" [Job 11:12] and on a very low rung, and it is from here that he must cause the profane to rise higher and higher to the sacred, the "I am the Lord your God." Therefore the meaning of the gentile who came to convert and wanted to learn the entire Torah standing on one foot, is like standing upon the One. And he taught him thus in truth that the source of everything is *Anokhi*, "I am the Lord your God," but the gentile was only able to grasp *Anokhi* at first through the negative "You shall not make" because he was at such a low rung. And this is what Hillel said: "The rest is but an elaboration of this one central point. Now go and learn it." Because the commandment of "You shall love" and the negation "That which is hateful to you do not do to your fellow" are the same as the commandments *Anokhi* and "You shall not make."[10]

Hillel's answer, "That which is hateful to you do not do to your fellow," according to Rashi, is the same as "You shall love your friend as yourself, I am the Lord" (Leviticus 19:18). R. Menahem Mendel associates Hillel's answer with what he says above. If the root of all Torah commandments is the commandment *Anokhi*, then the other verse,

"You shall love your friend as yourself, I am the Lord," defined by
Hillel as the root of Torah, is identical with what was previously stated
about the word *Anokhi*. A further look at the passage will reinforce
this claim, for "I am the Lord" and *Anokhi* are identical statements—
hence the meaning of "You shall love your friend as yourself" is the
same as *devekut* with the divine *Ein Sof*. One who cleaves to God
loves the other, and one who loves the other ultimately cleaves to God.
This teaching was the theoretical background of *ahavat haverim*, the
principle of loving fellowship at the heart of the community R. Menahem Mendel of Vitebsk established with a group of his disciples in
Tiberias by the Sea of Galilee after reaching Palestine in 1777.

The picture becomes clearer: Abraham, who is identified with the
quality of *hesed*, or loving-kindness, in kabbalistic literature, spent his
entire life in *devekut* with God, and therefore the Sages could say that
he fulfilled all the commandments of the Torah. Thus the *mitzvot* are
not comparable to the upturned vat with which God covered the people of Israel when they stood near Mount Sinai, as Rav Avdimi bar
Hama bar Hasa says in the Babylonian Talmud, *Shabbat* 88a. The
commandments were transmitted to the people of Israel as a means of
approaching divinity and cleaving to God. It is the unintelligibility of
the commandments that makes them seem coercive, as though
imposed from without, but this understanding is indicative not of the
commandments themselves but of the human beings who are commanded. The person who is ruled by passion is compelled to face evil
and its temptations by means of the negative commandments. Such a
person has difficulty understanding the greater portion of the positive
commandments intended to draw him directly to God. As a result he
finds some of these *mitzvot* unexplained and unexplainable. The person who reaches the higher rungs of the ladder and is no longer domi-
nated by his passions is exempt in effect from the negative
commandments and obligated only by the positive commandments.
For such a person, even *hukot* become intelligible, though for the person at this level there is an even higher ideal of cleaving to the root of
the *mitzvot* and divinity through love.

In a previous exegesis on *Noah* in *Pri Ha'aretz*, R. Menahem
Mendel explicitly states that the word *mitzvah* means the language of
communication, and stems not from *le-tzaveh*, "to command," but

from *le-tzevot*, "to accompany" (Babylonian Talmud, *Berakhot* 6b), and therefore signifies not commandment but accompaniment and communication. The *mitzvot* induce us to work on ourselves in order to break ego limits and connect with God. At the first stage, we must overcome the passions that emanate from divine contraction and prevent us from connecting to God. Then it becomes possible to focus on the various *mitzvot* as a means of attaining *devekut*, especially through joy and loving fellowship.

The Neoplatonic image of the ladder of ascent, which had such a pervasive influence on Jewish thought during the Middle Ages, is likewise manifest in R. Menaḥem Mendel's teaching that only Abraham and Moses were able to reach the highest rung, where they could grasp the root of the *mitzvot*. It would seem that such an achievement lies beyond the capability of most human beings; how many of us can realize the ideal of "My heart is wounded within me" and claim to overcome all passion? Yet R. Menaḥem Mendel's words were addressed to his followers, ordinary human beings, and modern Jews too may find in them a life teaching. Although he retained a medieval kabbalistic asceticism in his aspiration to this highest of ideals, the fact that he reiterates so many times in his teachings that the highest fulfillment of *devekut* in God is loving fellowship shows that his criterion for spiritual attainment is inward relatedness rather than outward fasting and self-mortification.

The dualism implied by R. Menaḥem Mendel's words about overcoming the passions is certainly foreign to the modern mind, as is the concept that the purpose of the soul is to ascend from this world into intimate union with the Divine. The ascetic practices of the medieval kabbalists that Hasidism tried to diminish are likewise alien to most contemporary Jews. But the idea that ultimately the *mitzvot* are ordinary deeds performed with the intention of connecting to divinity and guidelines for loving God through loving fellowship offers modern Jews the hope of redemption from enslavement to alienating, technical, and superficial life. And therein lies a key for those who would aspire to find meaning in the commandments of the Torah.

Notes

1. The Rabbinic ordinance that allows cooking and making preparations for Shabbat on *Yom Tov* (in a situation where Shabbat immediately follows the *Yom Tov*) by setting aside a special dish for the Sabbath before *Yom Tov*, and thus symbolically beginning the cooking intended for Shabbat before *Yom Tov*.
2. *Bemidbar Rabbah* 19:4.
3. Menahem Mendel of Vitebsk, *Sefer Pri Ha'aretz, Parashat Toldot*.
4. Arthur Green, *Devotion and Commandment: The Faith of Abraham in the Hasidic Imagination* (Cincinnati: Hebrew Union College Press, 1989), p. 8.
5. Franz Rosenzweig deals extensively with this distinction in *The Star of Redemption*; see Franz Rosenzweig, *The Star of Redemption*, trans. Barbara E. Galli (Madison, Wisc.: University of Wisconsin Press, 2005), p. 191.
6. *Pesikta de-Rab Kahana*, trans. William G. Braude and Israel J. Kapstein (Philadelphia: Jewish Publication Society, 1975), 4:7.
7. *Bereshit Rabbah* 1b.
8. Menahem Mendel of Vitebsk, *Sefer Pri Ha'aretz, Parashat Toldot*.
9. Babylonian Talmud, *Shabbat* 31a.
10. Menahem Mendel of Vitebsk, *Sefer Pri Ha'aretz, Parashat Toldot*.

Rabbi Nehemia Polen is professor of Jewish thought at Hebrew College. He is the author of *The Holy Fire: The Teachings of Rabbi Kalonymus Kalman Shapira, the Rebbe of the Warsaw Ghetto* and *The Rebbe's Daughter*, recipient of a National Jewish Book Award. He is also a contributor to the award-winning *My People's Prayer Book: Traditional Prayers, Modern Commentaries* (Jewish Lights).

Jacob's Remedy

A Prayer for the Dislocated

NEHEMIA POLEN

Our Sages of blessed memory taught that [Jacob] instituted [*tikken*] the evening prayer service, *Arvit* (Babylonian Talmud, *Berakhot* 26b).

Now the Torah portion *Va-yetzei* (Genesis 28:10–32:3) presents our patriarch Jacob's provision of a remedy [*tikkun*] and pathway even for such people who are not privileged to be within, such as our own generations—we who have been expelled from our home, our life source.

In fact, there is a remedy [*tikkun*] to be found everywhere, by the power of Torah. The biblical emblem of this power is our patriarch Jacob, of blessed memory, as Scripture says, "Give truth to Jacob" (Micah 7:20); and truth is equivalent to Torah [thus setting up the equation Jacob = truth = Torah].

The Torah gives location and stability to everything. This is what our Sages intended when they taught, "There is nothing that does not have its place" (*Pirkei Avot* 4:3).

This is the meaning of the words "And he alighted upon the place ... [and he took] from the stones of the place ..." (Genesis 28:11).

My teacher, my grandfather, [Rabbi Isaac Meir Alter] of blessed memory, explained that the letters [of the Hebrew alphabet] are called stones. Those letters—the signifying traces of Torah—are to be found everywhere.

But note: there are some places where those traces are more manifest, such as the Land of Israel and the Holy Temple—where God's sacred name is invoked; and there are other places where the signifiers are disarranged [be-irbuv], out of sight. In such places only the holiest individuals can discover the letters and arrange them appropriately.

We find this with the text of the Torah itself: there are some passages that can be understood readily according to their plain sense, while others require interpretation. This is also similar to [the Rabbinic interpretive practice] of "removing a letter, adding a letter, and explicating [a phrase or verse based on this rearrangement]" (Babylonian Talmud, Yoma 26b) and [of cases where there is] a lacuna, a clause omitted in a mishnah which is restored by the Talmud.

This is the meaning of the continuation of the verse in Genesis, "... and [Jacob] took from the stones of the place and positioned [them] under his head (Genesis 28:11)."

"Positioning" [simah] is synonymous with "arranging" [siddur], as in the verse "And they shall arrange [ve-samu] the staves" [of the Ark of the Covenant; the priests carefully positioned or arranged the poles of the Ark in preparation for travel] (Numbers 4:6).

Therefore Scripture gives us Jacob's statement: "And this stone that I have placed [samti] as a monument will be a house of God" (Genesis 28:22). This means that Jacob arranged and built a structure and a home from the letters.

And this is the meaning of the Talmudic statement (cited above) that Jacob "instituted [tikken] the evening prayer service, Arvit."[1]

RABBI YEHUDAH LEIB ALTER OF GER, SEFAT EMET

The scriptural reading that prompts this teaching[2] is Parashat Va-yetzei (Genesis 28:10–32:3), the story of Jacob's flight from home in Beer-sheba, his arrival in Haran, and the subsequent events. Before Sefat Emet begins his discussion of this parashah (Torah portion), he cites a Talmudic passage from Tractate *Berakhot* on the origin of fixed prayer. Rabbi Yose son of Rabbi Hanina is quoted as saying that Abraham, Isaac, and Jacob instituted the thrice-daily prayers. The ensuing discussion specifies that Jacob instituted the evening prayer (*Arvit*), based on Genesis 28:11—"And he alighted [*va-yifga*] upon the place," with another proof-text demonstrating the linkage between *pegiyah* and prayer.

Sefat Emet's introduction of a Talmudic passage before even mentioning the biblical text is rather unusual and demonstrates the centrality of this "evening prayer" in this piece, whose central concern is, what precisely is the meaning of evening prayer, *tefillat Arvit*?

To understand Sefat Emet's method, we first examine some key terms in the piece. Perhaps the most salient word is *tikkun*, which we have translated as "remedy." The word is fraught with significance in the mystical tradition. In Lurianic Kabbalah, *tikkun* is a technical term signifying a process of cosmic restoration and reintegration, the work of reorganizing "the disorderly confusion that resulted from the breaking of the vessels."[3] As Gershom Scholem notes, the details of this process are enormously complex, essentially comprising the "restoration of the universe to its original design in the mind of its Creator." As Lawrence Fine has explained, Luria and his disciples also used the word *tikkun* in a more individualized sense, to describe regimens of penitential rites such as fasting to reverse the negative effects of specific sins.[4]

Sefat Emet is well aware of *tikkun*'s rich semantic associations in the Kabbalah. But his first move is to remind us of the lexical connection between the kabbalistic *tikkun* and the Rabbinic *tikken*—"instituted," "established." The famous Talmudic passage in *Berakhot* cited above presents two alternate contexts for the three daily statutory prayer services. One view, attributed to Rabbi Yehoshua ben Levi, is that the prayers were designed to correspond to the sacrifices offered in the Temple. The other view has them precede the Temple by many centuries, setting them back in the biblical period and associating them with the three Patriarchs. What is at issue in this dispute? For Rabbi Yehoshua ben Levi, *tefillah* (verbal prayer) is a ritual offering, responsible for maintenance of creation like the Temple service; while for Rabbi Yose son of Rabbi Hanina, the statutory prayers are linked to personal narrative, to the dramatic events in the lives of the Patriarchs and by implication our own. Sefat Emet's exposition develops the existential implications of Rabbi Yose's view.

As Nahum Sarna observes, at this point in the Genesis narrative, Jacob "is now an exile, utterly alone and friendless, embarking on a long perilous journey."[5] He "alights" upon a certain place. We should understand that the place does not appear to be special to Jacob in any way. Spiritual power and proximity to heaven are the last things on Jacob's mind. He is a young man in perplexity, confused and troubled by the family dynamics that have been revealed and intensified by recent events. The only thing he knows for sure is that his brother is quite understandably furious and may indeed be in hot pursuit right now. Jacob hopes for nothing more than a safe, quiet, uneventful respite from his troubles, a pause in his breathless decamping. It is for this reason that the dream and the vision of God are so astonishing, so unexpected, so transformative.

All of this is brought forward by Sefat Emet to his own time (the piece was written in 1885) by the phrase "we who have been expelled from our home, our life source" (*nitgarashnu mi-bet hayyenu*), which refers at once to the loss of Jewish independence after the defeat at the hands of the Romans two thousand years ago, but also to the nineteenth-century Jewish migration from the shtetl to big cities like Warsaw and Lodz, with the fragmentation of the secure, insulated world that had nurtured Hasidism from its early years. Sefat Emet creates a lattice-work of correspondences: between the biblical Jacob finding unexpected divine presence, promise, and protection; the Talmudic Jacob's institution of *ma'ariv* (evening) prayer; and the Hasidic master's own efforts to construct religious meaning and spiritual power in the face of ideological and social instabilities of urban modernity.

At issue here is the meaning of sacred place, which in Genesis 28:10–22 is a specific geographical location. As a result of his dream encounter with God, Jacob knows that the place where he has slept—which he calls Bethel—is "the house of God, and that is the gateway to heaven" (Genesis 28:17). This locative sense is consistent with the use of *makom* throughout Genesis, where the word typically means "cultic center," a location of sacred power attracting worshippers in search of supernatural guidance and assistance. For the Talmudic Rabbis, however, sacred place comes to include synagogues and study halls, *batei kenesiyot u'batei midrashot*. While retaining the locative notion of sacred place—the Temple Mount, Jerusalem, and the Land retain holiness in Mishnah and Talmud—sacred place for the Sages includes the four walls of the *bet midrash* and the four *amot* of the *halakhah* (Babylonian Talmud, *Berakhot* 8a). For the Rabbis, holiness is found in the word and the heart as much as in geography. Sefat Emet continues and extends this process, making explicit what in the Talmud is largely implicit: that Torah study is not just the learning of eternal truth or interpreting divine will, but the active creation of meaning, of sacred domains limned by mind and spirit.

In this reading, what saves Jacob is his ability to "assemble the stones of the place" around his head. According to Sefat Emet, this means that out of the shambles of his fugitive life Jacob arranged an edifice of meaning, a coherent conceptual structure, a "Torah of the place." In like manner, each generation is bidden to take the particularities of its own place and time, its own existential circumstance, and shape them into Torah.

Sefat Emet draws on an old tradition from *Sefer Yetzirah* that speaks of the primary elements of language, the letters of the alphabet, as stones; and the permutation of letters—a fundamental mystical praxis—as rearranging stones. The Rabbinic linkage of Jacob and Genesis 28:11 with the evening prayer now emerges as deep *peshat* (plain sense or contextual meaning). There is much more than a linguistic play at stake here; with one stroke, Sefat Emet convincingly shows why Jacob is assigned the evening prayer specifically. We are reminded that he is leaving his family, the land of his birth, not like his grandfather Abraham to find the Promised Land, but to escape it. It is dark; Jacob's fortunes seem in decline; the sun is setting for him! He is lost, confounded. He is, to use a word from our text, *be-irbub*, in a state of confusion, all mixed up. To the extent that he can assemble the stones of his place into a structure of meaning, he has indeed prayed the first *ma'ariv* (evening/mixture of day and night) prayer. He has instituted the prayer against perplexity, the prayer that sets order against chaos.

In the process, we see an expansion of the possibilities of sacred space. Since the sacred letters of Torah are everywhere, they can be found, accessed, unscrambled, deployed to inscribe a sacred locus any-where. While *Eretz Yisrael*, Jerusalem, Zion, the Temple Mount retain their original geographical referent and sanctity, now Warsaw too, that place of urban confusion, of the jostling of competing ideologies, polit-ical affiliations and social mores, where all that was solid seems to melt into air, can be reconstituted as sacred place.

The variations of geography parallel the variations in the Torah itself. There are some passages—and places—whose meaning is clear, direct, that speak to us with transparent power; and there are other passages and places that need much mindful attention. As the Talmud frankly acknowledges, in order to make a *derashah* (interpretation) work, elements of the text may need to be rearranged. And in order to make sense of a mishnah, the Talmud sometimes posits that there is a gap in the received text that must be filled in. This is an activist con-struction of meaning.

In our *Sefat Emet* teaching, all the levels are set into precise corre-spondence and dialogic relation. It is hard to identify one element at the center of gravity to the exclusion of others. Is this text about the biblical Jacob? Yes, but it's also about Talmudic exegesis. Is it about the power of prayer, the evening prayer? Yes, but it's equally about the power of Torah. Is it about the power of the person embodying exact-ing, meticulous holiness—"Only the holiest individuals can discover the letters and arrange them appropriately"? Yes, but it is also about the power of vital, fresh, creative reading—with at least a touch of what we might today call deconstruction, reading against the grain, for the purpose of construction to be sure.

Finally, the piece is manifestly about sacred space—which, as we've said, is no longer limited to special, chosen locations such as the Holy Land and the Temple (although it is certainly there in a particu-larly manifest way), but is anywhere we create a perimeter of the sacred by arranging the stones about us meaningfully.

So while this teaching is about our relationship to place, it is also about our relationship to time: how Jacob's time and our own time speak to each other, mutually inform each other—*ke-doroteinu*—"like our generations."

Our past informs our present, but just as important, our present speaks to our past. The generations communicate with each other, and one of the tasks of today's telling the story of the Exodus is to articulate the order hidden in the chaotic events of long ago. We try to discern divinely imposed order where the original protagonists were confused and bewildered by their oppression. Here the hermeneutic enterprise becomes an instrument of liberation, reforming our understanding of past events and in a sense, the events themselves.

Once the *Sefat Emet* has selected and arranged the stones of his own exegetical construction, they come into precise correspondence. Each layer of text, each stratum of historical experience informs and enriches all the others. No single stratum, layer, or idea is the sole meaning or message of the piece. What Sefat Emet has constructed for us is an ordered yet expansive relational latticework, but perhaps rather than a lattice we might simply speak of a ladder—Jacob's ladder, where we are observing the angels ascending and descending. Perhaps we *are* the angels. The goal is not necessarily to reach the top, to get to heaven, but to continually ascend and descend, exploring the view from each step on the ladder. Meaning emerges in the contemplation of the correspondences and the constructed meaning that we call Torah. We might say that rather than climbing the ladder, we become the ladder. Our epiphany bursts forth when we realize that there is no single privileged position from which to observe truth; all rungs of the ladder must be honored, must be inhabited, must be invited patiently to tell their story. In contemplating this ever more deeply, we unite ever more richly and securely with all stages, all historical periods, all perspectives.

And here we come to his exegetical coda just before the end of the piece: "'Positioning' [*simah*] is synonymous with 'arranging' [*siddur*], as in the verse 'And they shall arrange [*ve-samu*] the staves' [of the Ark of the Covenant] (Numbers 4:6)." By "positioning the staves" we understand slipping them into their rings straight and true, aligning them properly. This is "true" in the structural, architectural sense: true as rectilinear, at right angles to the Ark and the Tablets. This is the truth that Jacob represents and that Sefat Emet demonstrates for us on every page of his commentary. This is truth that cannot be captured in simple propositions or creedal affirmations. We feel this truth in our bodies, in the gentle pressure of the staves on our shoulders, knowing only that we have arranged the words of the covenant with all the integrity we can bring to the task at this time and this place, so that, like Jacob, our feet move lightly as we step forward, greeting the future with faith and hope.

Notes

1. Thanks to the research of Rabbi Arthur Green and others, we have a better understanding of the teachings of Rabbi Yehudah Leib Alter of Ger (d. 1905), known by the title of his work *Sefat Emet*. This includes the Gerer Rebbe's teachings on the *nekudah ha-penimi* (the inner point) and the phenomenological categories of *Olam/Shanah/Nefesh* (Space/Time/Spirit) and their confluence in the experience of Shabbat. We owe a debt of gratitude to Rabbi Green for being among the first in the academic community to draw attention to Sefat Emet and to highlight this master's power as a spiritual teacher and guide for our contemporary world. See Arthur Green, *The Language of Truth: The Torah Commentary of the Sefat Emet* (Philadelphia: Jewish Publication Society, 1998).

2. *Sefat Emet, Parashat Va-yetzei*, s.vv. *Ya'akov tikken tefilat Arvit*. I consulted and adapted the translation of my colleague Rabbi Or N. Rose, prepared for the evening of study in celebration of the one hundredth anniversary of the publication of *Sefat Emet*, March 26, 2005.

3. Gershom Scholem, *Kabbalah* (Jerusalem: Keter, 1974; New York: Meridian, 1978), p. 140.

4. Lawrence Fine, *Physician of the Soul, Healer of the Cosmos: Isaac Luria and His Kabbalistic Fellowship* (Stanford, Calif.: Stanford University Press, 2003), pp. 167–86.

5. Nahum M. Sarna, *The JPS Torah Commentary: Genesis* (Philadelphia: Jewish Publication Society, 1989), p. 197.

Rabbi Shai Held is cofounder, *rosh ha-yeshiva*, and chair in Jewish thought at Mechon Hadar in New York City. He is completing a doctoral dissertation on the religious thought of Abraham Joshua Heschel at Harvard University. He contributed to *Jewish Theology in Our Time: A New Generation Explores the Foundations and Future of Jewish Belief* (Jewish Lights).

On Faith Beyond Perception

The Slonimer Rebbe

SHAI HELD

Just as the holy Torah speaks to every single Jew, and to his every spiritual and physical situation, similarly prayer is independent of all spiritual situations and emotions of the heart. Rather, it is an all-encompassing teaching that applies to every time and situation.

This can be explained by reference to a passage found in *Tanna Debe Eliyahu Rabbah* 17: "Four billion nine hundred and sixty million[1] ministering angels stand from sunrise to sunset and declare: 'Holy, holy, holy is the Lord of hosts; the whole world is filled with His glory.' And four billion nine hundred and sixty million ministering angels stand from sunset to sunrise and declare: 'Blessed is the Lord's glory from His place.'"

The commentators were troubled: what relevance do sunrise and sunset have above, in the angelic realm? After all, the sun is only part of this, the corporeal world! And further: why do they say "Holy, holy, etc. ..." from sunrise to sunset, and "Blessed is the Lord from His place" specifically from sunset to sunrise? And even beyond what they raised, there is another difficulty, in that we say, "As the sweet words of the assembly of the holy Seraphim who thrice repeat 'holy' unto You, as it is written by Your prophet: And they call one to another and say, 'Holy, holy, holy is the Lord of hosts; the whole earth is filled with His glory.'" Those facing them offer praise and say, "Blessed be the Lord's glory from His place"—from which it is clear that the two groups of angels make their respective declarations all at once, at the very same time!

The explanation of this is that there are four billion nine hundred and sixty million ministering angels whose service above has the aspect of transparency (behirut)[2]—that is, the aspect of sunrise. They see that the whole world is filled with God's glory. And there are four billion nine hundred and sixty million ministering angels whose service is from a place of divine hiddenness, according to the aspect of sunset—in that they do not see transparently that God's glory fills the whole world. They say, "Blessed is the Lord's glory from His place"— that is, even though they do not perceive that God's glory fills the world, they nevertheless know that He is in His holy abode, and they proclaim, "Blessed is the Lord's glory from His place."

Each of these groups makes its respective declaration, each one according to its root and essence. The first group [which sees God's glory clearly] is not greater than the second [which does not see it], nor does one group speak with greater or lesser enthusiasm than the other, but rather each turns to the other [and they make their declarations together, simultaneously]....

Through this teaching, our Sages of blessed memory instruct us in the path of prayer: sometimes a Jew prays to God from the aspect of sunrise and sometimes from the aspect of sunset.... It shouldn't make any difference to one whether he feels with the entirety of his heart and flesh that God's glory fills the world, and he sees the Creator, may He be blessed, every-where in creation, or whether, in contrast, right now he only believes that "Blessed is the Lord's glory from His place"— because, ultimately, they are one and the same. The same delight that God derives from one group, God also derives from the other. And so we also revere and sanctify according to the aspect of each of these groups, whether at a time of divine hid-denness or of divine manifestation, "our God is one God," and

the prayer we utter is pure and accepted like the sweet words of
the assembly of the holy Seraphim.[3]

RABBI SHALOM NOAH BEREZOVSKY, *NETIVOT SHALOM*

The *Musaf* liturgy for Shabbat contains a fascinating anomaly:
"God's glory fills the world," the angels reportedly proclaim. And
yet, we are told, they proceed to ask one another, "Where is the place
of God's glory?" On the face of it, the order of these phrases in the
Kedushah prayer is rather curious: the liturgy would make more obvious sense were it to begin with a question, "Where is the place of
God's glory?" and conclude with the answer, "God's glory fills the
world." But instead we find an answer followed by a question, a declaration of God's all-pervasive presence followed by an almost plain-
tive query, "Yes, but where?"[4]

I would suggest that there is something at once courageous and
compassionate about this liturgical unit: beginning with a question and
ending with an answer may represent a logical progression, but it may
equally falsify the dynamic ebb and flow of human experience and perception. Beginning with an answer and ending with a question, in contrast, at once articulates a destination for the human search—the
confident perception that God's glory fills the world—and yet makes
space for the ongoing journey of those who are still on the path
toward this perception and hence need to ask, again and again, "Yes,
but where?" More radically, the text implicitly admits that none of us
is permanently and unshakably at the destination, that none of us
owns the perception of God's presence as an eternal possession. We
are, all of us, vulnerable to the vicissitudes of faith and prone to flashes
of light followed by periods—sometimes prolonged periods—of relative (or even total) darkness. Put differently, we might say that there is
no "once and for all" in the religious life, no perception that cannot
dissipate as surely as it appears. By projecting the dynamics of human
faith upwards—that is, by suggesting that angels, too, are susceptible
to the fluctuations of religious perception—the liturgy subtly comforts
those of us still, always, on the path: even the angels share in the var-
iegated complexity of faith.

In the remarkable passage from the *Netivot Shalom* translated
above, a similar idea is at play. Twice every day (and three times on

Shabbat and holidays), during the *Kedushah* prayer, Jews describe—
and seek to imitate—the process by which the angels sanctify God in
the highest heavens. Two groups of angels are pictured as engaging in
a kind of call-and-response: invoking the prophet Isaiah, the first
declares, "Holy, holy, holy is the Lord of hosts, the whole world is
filled with His glory" (Isaiah 6:3). In response, following the prophet
Ezekiel, the second proclaims, "Blessed is the Lord from His place"
(Ezekiel 3:12). The careful reader (or attentive worshipper) cannot but
note the subtle contrast between the two formulae: while the first con-
fidently asserts God's omnipresence ("the whole world is filled with
His glory"), the second merely blesses God wherever He might be
("from His place"). A striking passage from the midrashic collection
Tanna Debe Eliyahu, cited by R. Berezovsky, picks up on just this contrast and paints an arresting image of the two angelic choirs: the first,
more confident group makes its proclamation during the light of day,
while the second, somewhat more modest group speaks its words during the darkness of night. R. Berezovsky perceptively develops the
insight implicit in the midrash, insisting that night and day here are
not times of day (for what relevance do sunrise and sunset have in the
highest angelic realms?), but rather polar states of perception. In other
words, one group sees God's presence in the world "transparently"
(*be-vehirut*), hence its bold formulation of God's omnipresence. The
second sees more dimly—or perhaps not at all; and yet it "knows that
God is in His holy abode" and blesses Him appropriately.

The central thrust of the *Netivot Shalom* is to insist that neither
group is greater than the other, nor does greater vividness of perception necessarily imbue one with a higher spiritual status. On the contrary, R. Berezovsky tells us, each group prays with equal passion and
enthusiasm (*hitlahavut*), and each one turns to and beckons the
other—as if in recognition of its respective greatness—and prays simultaneously with it. It is here that R. Berezovsky subtly shifts the meaning of the midrash: whereas the earlier text pictured the two groups
praying separately, at different times, the Hasidic master imagines
them praying simultaneously and together (an image, it should be
noted, more congruous with the *Kedushah* liturgy itself than that of
the midrash). The message to the Rebbe's listeners could not be clearer:
some of us are blessed with fine spiritual antennae and may perceive

the presence of God everywhere and at all times, while others of us may perceive less clearly, or less often, or both. But let us avoid the temptation to rank ourselves based on degree of perception: those who see "transparently" ought not to conclude that they are spiritually superior, and those who see dimly (or again, not at all) ought not to decide that they are therefore somehow inferior. No, both groups are equal. In fact, the Netivot Shalom subtly points out, the depth of your perception may well be entirely beyond your control and hence reflect no achievement or failure on your part; after all, he reminds us, each group sees "according to its root and essence."[5]

Rabbi Berezovsky here offers a stunning piece of consolation to those not able to perceive God's presence everywhere—and, for that matter, to those not able to perceive it anywhere: true religious heroism is found in faith rather than perception, in "knowing" God whether or not one sees Him.

But if the Slonimer's words are a source of comfort, they also represent a profound challenge. We are called to recognize that faith is not primarily a subjective experience (which would render it fleeting and momentary at best) but rather a life commitment, an existential posture. In other words, the Slonimer suggests, mature faith does not wax and wane based on the vicissitudes of the moment, but instead persists and endures through whatever the moment brings.

To be indifferent to religious experience is to run the risk of reducing faith to rote, of cultivating obedience to the exclusion of living relationship. But to overprivilege religious experience, in turn, is to overvalue subjective perception, which is inherently ephemeral and thus unreliable. This is, of course, precisely the shortcoming of religion as a form of mere "feel-goodism": in keeping me focused exclusively on myself and my inner life, it demands no sacrifices, makes no demands, and thus elicits no self-transcendence. I pray when, and only when, I am moved to do so (whether by gratitude, joy, or despair); I observe only those commandments that speak to me, and only when they speak to me. *I* remain, in other words, firmly entrenched at the center of my spiritual universe. But what the Slonimer points to is something very different: religion as a form of self-dedication, a commitment to serving God even in moments when I am less than inspired, when God's presence eludes my perception. It is this fundamental lesson that R. Berezovsky seeks to teach us: far more important than my subjective awareness (or lack thereof) in this particular moment is the overarching commitment of my life. To be sure, *mohin de-gadlut* (expansive consciousness) is a good thing, but just as the value of my worship does not decrease during *mohin de-katnut* (limited consciousness), so neither does my obligation. This is what it means to place God rather than self at the center, to live in covenantal relationship instead of celebrating the merely subjective.

What we have before us, then, is a Hasidic text that runs against the grain of certain popular perceptions of Hasidism. The Slonimer does not denigrate the perception of God's presence, of course, but neither does he valorize it without qualification. It is, simply, what it is: a perception, here one moment and gone the next. As the Hasidim never tire of reminding us, *ha-hayot ratzo va-shov* (Ezekiel 1:14)—our perceptions are forever "dashing to and fro." But our commitments, the Slonimer hastens to add, need not follow suit.

The Slonimer's lesson about a mature faith can be easily translated to other crucial domains of our life as well. When we say that we love our spouses, what do we mean? At bottom, of course, the love of another is not—or certainly not just—a fleeting feeling, a passing fancy, a merely subjective experience. Again, what we declare is an existential commitment to act lovingly even in those moments when the depth of emotion and the intensity of passion somehow elude us. To be sure, a relationship from which passion has permanently faded is a tragedy, but so, equally, is a relationship that threatens to dissipate with every diminution of passion. As every meditator knows, we can witness the ebbs and flows of consciousness without being slaves to them.

This core human truth applies to the life of *hesed* as well. On the one hand, Torah ideally prods us to cultivate an integrated personality, in which the inner experience—love—matches the outer behavior—kindness. But what do I do when I just don't "feel it"? Am I exempt from "walking in God's ways" because love happens to escape me at the moment? Of course not. A life of true *hesed* means that I perform acts of *hesed* even when the inner state of love eludes me. I visit the sick, for example, regardless of what I happen to feel at a particular moment—whether compassion or fear, connection or repulsion. Once again: the ideal toward which we strive is the integration of the inner and the outer, but our commitment to action remains even when my emotions or perceptions just won't seem to cooperate.

So, in other words, implicit in the Slonimer's words is an argument for *halakhah*—if not necessarily for *the halakhah*, then surely, at least, for *a halakhah*—or, perhaps more accurately, for the importance of *keva*, fixity of practice and commitment. In a movement that so emphasizes the importance of *kavanah* (intention),[6] the Slonimer offers a crucial counterweight: if an exclusive focus on norms can be stultifying and even deadening, an unmitigated obsession with subjective states, in turn, can engender a dangerous descent into narcissistic self-preoccupation. As Abraham Joshua Heschel, Thomas Merton, and countless other spiritual masters have taught us, there can be no authentic self-realization without self-transcendence.

With these words, the Slonimer thus embodies a deep truth about what it means to function as an authentic spiritual teacher: he challenges his listener-readers even as he comforts them. A lack of *mohin de-gadlut* in this moment is not a sign of failure or of spiritual poverty, but neither is it an excuse to give up and turn away from God (or, as I have emphasized, from the human other). These words are a balm even as they are a goad: praise God, whatever your mood. And know that delight is caused above when we praise God *ba-asher anahnu sham*, from wherever we find ourselves.

Notes

1. It is worth noting that the number 496 is the numerical equivalent of the word *Malkhut* (Kingdom). The kabbalistic significance of this term (as a symbol of God's indwelling presence on earth) may well come later than this midrashic image, but the numerical value is nevertheless significant, as both angelic groups are engaged in a powerful affirmation of God's sovereignty and presence.

2. Lit., "effulgence."

3. R. Shalom Noah Berezovsky (Slonimer Rebbe, d. 2000), *Netivot Shalom, Tefillah* 3:6.

4. I am aware, of course, that this is not the only possible interpretation of the liturgical passage at hand. One might suggest, for example, that what we have in this text is a declaration that God's glory fills the world (*malei olam*), followed by a question about the primary locus or abode of that glory (*mekom kevodo*). Be that as it may, the reading I have presented is at very least plausible and, I would insist, more in line with R. Berezovsky's teachings. In the context of writing about a

216 TORAH, HALAKHAH, MITZVOT

Hasidic text, at any rate, it hardly seems necessary to add that the surface meaning of the canonical text is hardly of the utmost importance.

5. We might put this in even stronger terms: if each group can be said to be praying in accordance with its "root and essence," then praying from and with the aspect of darkness may well be precisely what God wants from me. The state of my perception is not the result of my own failing, but rather a manifestation of the way God created me.

6. It might be useful to note that in the Slonimer's own community, presumably all of his students pray three times a day. The shift he is enacting, therefore, is primarily one of consciousness—decentering perception or experience and emphasizing constancy and commitment. Read in more liberal environments, however, where commitment to regular prayer may be lax or even absent, his words obviously have an added force.

Rabbi Zalman Schachter-Shalomi, known as Reb Zalman, is the father of the neo-Hasidic Jewish Renewal movement. He is professor emeritus of psychology of religion and Jewish mysticism at Temple University, as well as world wisdom chair emeritus at Naropa University. He is the author of many articles and books, including *First Steps to a New Jewish Spirit: Reb Zalman's Guide to Recapturing the Intimacy & Ecstasy in Your Relationship with God* (Jewish Lights); *Spiritual Intimacy*; and with Nataniel Miles-Yepez, *Wrapped in a Holy Flame: Teachings and Tales of the Hasidic Masters*.

Teyku—Because Elijah Lives On!

ZALMAN SCHACHTER-SHALOMI

Why do the Rabbis promise that all questions will be answered by Elijah the Prophet when he comes to announce the Messiah and not by Moses, who will then be resurrected? The answer is that Moses died, and we cannot hope to be helped with our current problems by Moses, who completed his life, peace be upon him. Since the days of Moses, the Torah has been placed in our hands. If a person's soul is from the side of grace [*hesed*], everything is pure, permitted, and kosher, but if a person's soul is from the side of rigor [*gevurah*], the opposite is true. Yet, each person according to his rung is a vehicle for the word of the living God. This is why the Sages, realizing the need for *hesed* in this world, set the *halakhah* [law] down according to the teachings of Hillel. Now, a person who is alive and participating in this world knows well what the needs of the times are and the attributes we need to live by. A person who does not live on this plane of existence does not know the attributes we need to live by in this world. Since Elijah is alive, having never tasted the taste of death, and has remained all the time on this plane, he, and no other, is capable of resolving our questions.[1]

RABBI LEVI YITZHAK OF BERDITCHEV, KEDUSHAT LEVI

What is the meaning of *teyku*, which is Aramaic for "let it stand"? There are times in the Talmud when the Rabbis delve deeply into an issue, question and debate, but come to a standstill, unable to reach a firm conclusion. In such cases, they proclaim, "*Teyku!*" Now, some say that in addition to its literal meaning, *teyku* is also an acronym for *Tishby Yitaretz Kushiyot U'ba'ayot* (the Hebrew letters *taf, yud, kuf, vav*), meaning "Elijah the Prophet will resolve difficulties and questions."

So Reb Levi Yitzhak asks the question, "Why don't we ask Moses?" After all, he is our most direct source of Torah; shouldn't we turn to him for help? Why go to Elijah? The answer is that Moses lived and died while Elijah lives on. According to the Bible, Elijah was taken up to heaven in a whirlwind while still alive (2 Kings 2:11). It is also said that there will come a day when Elijah will return: "Behold, I will send unto you My messenger, Elijah. And he will reconcile the hearts of parents unto the children, and the hearts of the children unto the parents" (Malachi 3:24).

Over the centuries, there have also developed many legends about the prophet's surprise visits to people in need. In Jewish folklore Elijah is regarded as something like the figure of Hermes in Greek mythology. If you have a conundrum and you seek a way out of it, he will manifest and reveal the answer. It is for this reason that on occasions like the Passover Seder or a circumcision, when we need intergenerational connection, we invite Elijah to join us. On Saturday night, as we bid farewell to the Sabbath, we sing the song *Eliyahu Ha'Navi* as we attempt to connect *Shabbos* to the rest of the week. Elijah is uniquely suited to see us through moments of change or transition—both in the here and now and in the future—drawing on the wisdom of the ages, providing us with insight appropriate for this particular moment in time.

A brief Hasidic story illustrates the difference between Moses and Elijah: A man comes to Reb Elimelekh of Lizhensk and asks if he should go forward with a certain business deal. The Rebbe says yes: "It is going to be good; God will help." The man then goes to the

Rebbe's disciple, Reb Ya'akov Yitzhak of Lublin, and asks him the same question. And Reb Ya'akov Yitzhak says, "You're going to get wiped out." So the man says to himself, "I asked the teacher, and he said I'm going to do well, and then I asked the disciple, and he said I'm not going to make it. Which one should I listen to, the teacher or the disciple?" The man decides to go with the teacher and makes the deal. At first, it goes exceedingly well, but in the end he loses his shirt. The man returns to Reb Ya'akov Yitzhak and asks him, "Why did things turn out this way?" Reb Ya'akov Yitzhak answers, "Because my master, my teacher, Reb Elimelekh, saw only until his dying day. And to his dying day, you were successful. But he didn't see any further. I can't see past my dying day either, but I saw further because your failure was within my lifetime." Moses, as great as he was, could only see until the end of his lifetime, while Elijah can see far beyond.

Reb Levi Yitzhak continues his teaching by saying that every soul comes into the world with a kind of imprint from a particular branch of the Tree of Life. Some people come from the branch of grace (*Hesed*), while others come from the branch of rigor (*Gevurah*). Sometimes, when two souls like this meet they feel as if they are banging their heads against a wall. "Why don't you see things the way I do?" Hillel and Shammai are perhaps our most famous examples of two such souls. Hillel saw everything through the lens of *hesed*, and Shammai through the lens of *gevurah*. Both are necessary, and each is a vehicle for the word of the living God. However, realizing the need for more grace than rigor in this world, the Rabbis tipped the scales of *halakhah* in Hillel's direction.

It is said that when God created the world, He began with the attribute of justice, *ra'ah sh'ayn ha-olam mitkayem*, but seeing that the world would not be able to exist that way, *shitef bo middat ha-rahamim*, He added the attribute of mercy (*Bereshit Rabbah* 12:15). This is what allows us a "second chance," the opportunity to learn and grow without being beaten down by our mistakes. Therefore, in premessianic times the world needs more Hillel than Shammai, because we haven't yet reached the kind of righteousness that Shammai demanded. God willing, we will one day reach that level of consciousness and then be able to go with Shammai's rulings. But now it is the grace and mercy of Hillel that are necessary. And it is only the person who is alive and present to the needs of the world who understands the attributes we need to live by.

Very often people will refer you to this authority or that holy text, saying, "You have got it all wrong; that is not the way to do it." But you must ask from what time period did this text come or out of what paradigm did it emerge? Yes, it may have been true in that time, but is it true in our time? The answer may be yes, but it may be *no*. Since Elijah is ever alive, having never "tasted the taste of death," he is uniquely suited to resolve our questions. In his vital, living presence, he can assess the needs of the hour and offer guidance for our time.

It is no surprise that this teaching comes to us from Rabbi Levi Yitzhak of Berditchev, for he is known as a rebbe (Hasidic master) of great kindness and compassion, whose loving spirit was felt throughout the Hasidic world. He would often travel to surrounding communities to acquaint himself with the village Jews, to better understand their challenges and help support them. And like Abraham, he was known for debating with God on behalf of other people. For no one knew better the aches and pains of the Jewish community and how hard his community tried to remain faithful to the Master of the universe. Once, along with a group of others, Reb Levi Yitzhak watched as a wagon driver greased the wheels of his wagon while wearing his tallit and tefillin. The others laughed and scolded the filthy man, but Reb Levi Yitzhak was amazed. "Look," he said to God, "how your servant praises and honors you, even while greasing his wagon wheels!"

Like Elijah the Prophet, the Berditchever was keenly aware of the need to provide his community with a vision of Judaism that was in deep dialogue with the past and responsive to life in the present. And like Hillel, he was a brilliant sage who understood that in his generation the world needed a Torah of *hesed*. May the memory of Rabbi Levi Yitzhak continue to serve as a blessing.[2]

Notes

1. R. Levi Yitzhak of Berditchev (d. 1810), *Sefer Kedushat Levi, Likkutim* 108b, edited translation.

2. For further reading on this topic, see Zalman Schachter-Shalomi, *Wrapped in a Holy Flame: Teachings and Tales of the Hasidic Masters*, ed. Nataniel M. Miles-Yepez (San Francisco: Jossey-Bass, 2003).

Suggestions for Further Reading

Buber, Martin. *Hasidism and Modern Man*. New York: Horizon Press, 1958.

Elior, Rachel. *The Mystical Origins of Hasidism*. Oxford: Littman Library of Jewish Civilization, 2005.

Fine, Lawrence. *Physician of the Soul, Healer of the Cosmos: Isaac Luria and His Kabbalistic Fellowship*. Stanford, Calif.: Stanford University Press, 2003.

Firestone, Tirzah. *The Receiving: Reclaiming Jewish Women's Wisdom*. New York: HarperCollins, 2003.

Fishbane, Eitan. *As Light Before Dawn: The Inner World of a Medieval Kabbalist*. Stanford, Calif.: Stanford University Press, 2009.

Fishbane, Michael. *Sacred Attunement: A Jewish Theology*. Chicago: University of Chicago Press, 2008.

Ginsburg, Elliot K. *The Sabbath in the Classical Kabbalah*. 2nd ed. Oxford: Littman Library of Jewish Civilization, 2008.

Green, Arthur. *Ehyeh: A Kabbalah for Tomorrow*. Woodstock, Vt.: Jewish Lights, 2003.

———. *A Guide to the Zohar*. Stanford, Calif.: Stanford University Press, 2003.

———, trans., ann. *The Language of Truth: The Torah Commentary of the Sefat Emet, Rabbi Yehudah Leib Alter of Ger*. Philadelphia: Jewish Publication Society, 1998.

———. *Radical Judaism: Rethinking God and Tradition*. New Haven: Yale University Press, 2010.

———. *Seek My Face: A Jewish Mystical Theology*. Rev. ed. Woodstock, Vt.: Jewish Lights, 2003.

———. *These Are the Words: A Vocabulary of Jewish Spiritual Life*. Woodstock, Vt.: Jewish Lights, 1999.

———. *Tormented Master: The Life and Spiritual Quest of Rabbi Nahman of Bratslav*. Reprint, Woodstock, Vt.: Jewish Lights, 1992.

Green, Arthur, and Barry W. Holtz, eds., trans. *Your Word Is Fire: The Hasidic Masters on Contemplative Prayer*. Reprint, Woodstock, Vt.: Jewish Lights, 1993.

Hecker, Joel. *Mystical Bodies, Mystical Meals: Eating and Embodiment in Medieval Kabbalah*. Detroit: Wayne State University Press, 2005.

221

Hellner-Eshed, Melila. *A River Flows from Eden: The Language of Mystical Experience in the Zohar*. Translated by Nathan Wolski. Stanford, Calif.: Stanford University Press, 2009.

Heschel, Abraham Joshua. *The Earth Is the Lord's: The Inner World of the Jew in Eastern Europe*. Reprint, Woodstock, Vt.: Jewish Lights, 1995.

———. *A Passion for Truth*. Reprint, Woodstock, Vt.: Jewish Lights, 1995.

Idel, Moshe. *Hasidism: Between Ecstasy and Magic*. Albany: State University of New York Press, 1995.

Jacobs, Louis. *Hasidic Prayer*. Oxford: Littman Library of Jewish Civilization, 2006.

Krassen, Miles. *Uniter of Heaven and Earth: Rabbi Meshullam Feibush Heller of Zbarazh and the Rise of Hasidism in Eastern Galicia*. Albany: State University of New York Press, 1999.

Kushner, Lawrence. *The Way Into Jewish Mystical Tradition*. Woodstock, Vt.: Jewish Lights, 2001.

Kushner, Lawrence, and Nehemia Polen. *Filling Words with Light: Hasidic and Mystical Reflections on Jewish Prayer*. Woodstock, Vt.: Jewish Lights, 2004.

Lamm, Norman, ed. *The Religious Thought of Hasidism: Text and Commentary*. New York: Michael Scharf Publication Trust of Yeshiva University Press / Hoboken, N.J.: KTAV, 1999.

Langer, Jiří. *Nine Gates to the Chasidic Mysteries*. Translated by Stephen Jolly. Northvale, N.J.: Jason Aronson, 1993.

Magid, Shaul, ed. *God's Voice from the Void: Old and New Studies in Bratslav Hasidism*. Albany: State University of New York Press, 2002.

Matt, Daniel. *The Essential Kabbalah: The Heart of Jewish Mysticism*. New York: HarperCollins, 1995.

———, trans., ann. *Zohar: Annotated & Explained*. Woodstock, Vt.: SkyLight Paths, 2002.

———. *The Zohar: Pritzker Edition*. Multiple vols. Stanford: Stanford University Press, 2003–.

Michaelson, Jay. *Everything Is God: The Radical Path of Nondual Judaism*. Boston: Trumpeter Books, 2009.

Polen, Nehemia. *The Holy Fire: The Teachings of Rabbi Kalonymus Kalman Shapira, the Rebbe of the Warsaw Ghetto*. Northvale, N.J.: Jason Aronson, 1977.

Rose, Or N., ed., trans. *God in All Moments: Mystical & Practical Spiritual Wisdom from Hasidic Masters*. With Ebn D. Leader. Woodstock, Vt.: Jewish Lights, 2004.

Schachter-Shalomi, Zalman. *Paradigm Shift: From the Jewish Renewal Teachings of Reb Zalman Schachter-Shalomi*. Northvale, N.J.: Jason Aronson, 2000.

Schachter-Shalomi, Zalman, and Netanel Miles-Yepez. *A Heart Afire: Stories and Teachings of the Early Hasidic Masters*. Philadelphia: Jewish Publication Society, 2009.

Shapiro, Rami, trans., ann. *Tanya, the Masterpiece of Hasidic Wisdom: Selections Annotated & Explained*. Woodstock, Vt.: SkyLight Paths, 2010.

Slater, Jonathan P. *Mindful Jewish Living: Compassionate Practice*. New York: Aviv Press, 2004.

Wiesel, Elie. *Souls on Fire: Portraits and Legends of Hasidic Masters*. Reprint, New York: Summit Books, 1982.

Wolfson, Elliot R. *Through a Speculum That Shines: Vision and Imagination in Medieval Jewish Mysticism*. Princeton, N.J.: Princeton University Press, 1994.

JEWISH LIGHTS BOOKS ARE AVAILABLE FROM BETTER BOOKSTORES. TRY YOUR BOOKSTORE FIRST.

About Jewish Lights

People of all faiths and backgrounds yearn for books that attract, engage, educate, and spiritually inspire.

Our principal goal is to stimulate thought and help all people learn about who the Jewish People are, where they come from, and what the future can be made to hold. While people of our diverse Jewish heritage are the primary audience, our books speak to people in the Christian world as well and will broaden their understanding of Judaism and the roots of their own faith.

We bring to you authors who are at the forefront of spiritual thought and experience. While each has something different to say, they all say it in a voice that you can hear.

Our books are designed to welcome you and then to engage, stimulate, and inspire. We judge our success not only by whether or not our books are beautiful and commercially successful, but by whether or not they make a difference in your life.

For your information and convenience, at the back of this book we have provided a list of other Jewish Lights books you might find interesting and useful. They cover all the categories of your life:

Bar/Bat Mitzvah	Life Cycle
Bible Study / Midrash	Meditation
Children's Books	Men's Interest
Congregation Resources	Parenting
Current Events / History	Prayer / Ritual / Sacred Practice
Ecology / Environment	Social Justice
Fiction: Mystery, Science Fiction	Spirituality
Grief / Healing	Theology / Philosophy
Holidays / Holy Days	Travel
Inspiration	Twelve Steps
Kabbalah / Mysticism / Enneagram	Women's Interest

For more information about each book, visit our website at www.jewishlights.com

Printed in the USA
CPSIA information can be obtained
at www.ICGtesting.com
JSHW022321140824
68134JS00019B/1225